ARIZONA
RAMBLIN'

Helen,

we are so blessed
to Have This PATH
to Journey upon.

" Do Good Feel Good "

Regards

Steve Zivan

ARIZONA
RAMBLIN'
A Recovery, Love & Adventure Novel
Some Historical ... Some Hysterical

Steve L'van

SYCAMORE SOUL PUBLISHING

ARIZONA RAMBLIN'
A recovery, love & adventure novel
some historical...some hysterical

Published by Sycamore Soul Publishing, Sedona, AZ

Printed in the United States.
Cover design: Wendy L'van
Interior book design: Jane Perini,
www.thundermountaindesign.com
Photography, pages 9, 18, 42, 49, 378:
© Fredric Shore Photography, www.frshore.com

ISBN: 978-0-615-98061-4

SERENITY PRAYER

God grant me the serenity

to accept the things I cannot change;

courage to change the things I can;

and wisdom to know the difference.

This book is dedicated to all that strive to
help themselves and others along the trail of life.

FOREWORD

E ven though I have not yet met Steve L'van face-to-face, I know him. I know him because we both belong to "a fellowship of men and women who share their experience, strength and hope with each other in order to solve a common problem." This group is known as Alcoholics Anonymous. I, myself, have been a member for 32 years.

In that time, I have met and made close friends with others who have recovered from a seemingly hopeless state of mind and body. Although it was actually pure coincidence that Steve happens to be in the same fellowship, once I found out he was, an instant bond was established between us. This bond is an unspoken, intuitive understanding between alcoholics. It's a wonderful and rare appreciation of our common outlook on life.

Steve and I were introduced to each other through the publisher of this book. She recommended me to him for the job of editing and proofreading his manuscript. *Arizona Ramblin'* is a tale of what is possible once an alcoholic decides to stay sober, then turns his life over to caring about others more than himself. Alcoholism is a disease of crippling selfishness, what alcoholics term "the bondage of self." The irony of the disease is that even though we are thoroughly self-absorbed, we hate ourselves. "Egomaniacs with inferiority complexes" is one way to put it. To turn this type of mindset around is nothing short of a miracle.

The antidote to negative self-absorption is intensive work with others. Steve describes this in his book: how a man had a spiritual awakening with the help of a spirit guide. Listening to this guide and taking her advice seriously, his life took on a whole new meaning when he began to help others. Unseen forces magnetized all the material and financial help he needed to bring his good works to fruition.

As the adventure of Salvadore Dusi's new-found mission begins to unfold, what began as a solo journey becomes a community effort. Because Sal's altruistic intent and joyful effort in carrying out his mission is noticed by others, these townsfolk now want to join in on what is making him feel so good, which, of course, is his generosity of spirit.

Reading about Sal's lively pursuits, especially for the young, can be a wake-up call to action. Anyone who has the power of introspection may pick up on the subtext of Mr. L'van's tale: reaching out to and caring about others benefits the giver much more than the receiver. It can actually be fun to be of service to others. Now, if I were to go any further, I'd be giving the story line away. So read on, reader. It'll be time well spent. You will be inspired.

MAP OF
ARIZONA
Population ——— 40,440
Area sq. miles __ 113,929

PREFACE

T his tale is an unwinding thread from a spool of many stories, based on the people, places and situations that are the backbone of Arizona. Sal Dusi travels over the state from one exciting experience to another. His is a grand state of life in the Grand Canyon State. The characters encountered on his ramblings all have a story; some wanting and willing to share their tales, others never realizing that they had a tale to share. Many of these stories are like the fabric of our lives, partly truth and partly fiction, some happening so long ago, others in the present. The author, like the reader, is never sure which is which. I have taken many liberties with the dates, places and names so as to better fit the storyline. Although the story is partially born in truth its mainly "FICTION."

As Sal travels this path across Arizona, his strong commitment to sobriety through A.A. is intensely fortified. The reader may or may not identify with the trials and tribulations of following this road to sobriety and serenity that Sal finds himself on, but will hopefully find in the telling some peace and knowledge to deal with similar situations that may occur in one's own life. This story of Sal's ramblings is an eclectic mix: some Arizona-history lore, some lies, some metaphysical occurrences, but mostly the attainment of self-respect through sobriety and the joy of helping others.

Hopefully the reader can enjoy Sal's adventures without having to endure the discomfort of 115 degrees in the shade or the dangerous encounters he experiences. This work was not meant to be authentic historically, but hopefully the reader will find it occasionally hysterical. An adventure in sobriety: finding oneself, developing a passion, discovering a soul mate, accepting the existence of "non-normal" reality. This is a "Fun" book that contains many lessons and ideas for the young or, perhaps, not so young.

The greatest reward this writer could achieve from this virgin undertaking would be if someone, somewhere were to take one or two of these "Spirit-Inspired" ideas presented by "Sal" and turn them into his own reality, thereby helping others who are in need. I hope that readers of any age—I did strive to ensure a G or PG rating—may find the inspiration and courage in the lives of the characters of this book to attempt to better their own circumstances, perhaps by utilizing one or two of the lessons this writer has found to be beneficial in his life.

If only one reader's life is improved, I will consider this work a success. I would encourage anyone struggling with ANY issue to put their thoughts down on paper; I truly believe that the act of writing alone will bring clarity to the situation, hopefully guiding them to a solution.

In compiling the adventures herein, whether inspired by others or by my own imagination, I have found my attitude improved, coming to realize that all creatures sharing this planet deserve Love and Consideration. WE ARE ALL IN THIS TOGETHER...

CHAPTER 1

FREEDOM

As Sal Dusi had always said, happiness would be Fort Huachuca in the rearview mirror. On this fateful day in July, the weekend of the Fourth during the hectic Vietnam era, if his grin were any wider his ears might split. He was driving out of the base onto the main drag of Sierra Vista, Arizona, a town that was originally named Fry, Arizona. His good buddy, Sergeant Kyle Kinney, was with him. He thought how they must have named the town "Fry" back then. Could it have been named while celebrating the original pioneers' first Independence Day on a day when it was 115-degrees? Sal laughed out loud. He was celebrating his own Independence Day. It was just 110 degrees. Even though they always say, "it's a dry heat," so is an oven. The name "Fry" certainly was fitting.

Sal was dressed in civies. The realization was sinking in fast that he may never have to wear a uniform again, having just been honorably discharged that very morning from the Army. He was looking over his shoulder expecting First Sgt. Daniel Washington to be running after him with court martial papers in his hand. Since he never forgave him the insults yelled into the barracks intercom, or for embarrassing him by being the first soldier in the U.S. Army to "early out" by 87 days to bartend at his parent's tavern in Pennsylvania. When he arrived at the Tucson airport the elation of freedom was finally kicking in. Bidding goodbye to his good buddy Kyle, he boarded a United flight that was heading to the East Coast.

"Flying home." What does that mean? He was a kid who grew up in Pennsylvania among poor, tough, hard-working Sicilian, Polish, Irish and Lithuanian coal-mining fathers and dress-sewing mothers. He would soon see if the boy who left Pennsylvania to join the Army because he could not fit in and couldn't see college as an option would fit in as a young man in the world now. Maybe more importantly, for just how long?

It turned out Sal stayed until the following New Year, enjoying a Christmas with his mom, dad, and brother. He knew he would miss them a lot, but at least he could telephone them and write. On the other hand, his childhood pet and dear friend, Tippy, an old beagle, would never understand him leaving again. They would miss each other terribly. Sal packed up his orange Pontiac and drove back to Arizona, which, it turns out, was the home of his soul.

Sal never answered any of the letters from the Army Reserve requesting his presence at their monthly gatherings. Vietnam was in high gear, so as he drove back through the gates of Fort Huachuca, it was with some trepidation and apprehension. He had left Pennsylvania with $165 in his pocket, but now only had $37.30 left. He thought that if he stayed in his friend's room in the barracks and ate in the company cafeteria he could plan his next move and save some money. When he put on his friend Kyle's uniform to eat, he knew if First Sgt. Washington spotted him, it would end any plans for the future he might have.

It didn't take long for Sal to decide freedom was way too precious to squander hanging around an Army post. He said goodbye again, then started out on an odyssey beyond his imagination. At least the weather was turning out to be more tolerable for a guy driving a car with no air-conditioning. Luckily, he did have a trunk full of canned foods along with an 18-pound roast beef, thanks to a sympathetic soldier on K.P. duty back at Ft. Huachuca.

CHAPTER 2

FIRST VISION

D riving south, Sal realized he was coming up to the road that went to the top of Miller Peak. Two years earlier, he and Sgt. Kyle Kinney, along with their girlfriends, had left Sierra Vista in tee shirts on an 82-degree Christmas day and decided to drive up the mountain to find a white Christmas. As they rounded a curve in the road, they got stuck in a four-foot snowdrift. Two hours of digging later, they got out and turned around, glad to leave the lower temperatures up on the mountain. I guess you could chalk that up to a "be careful what you ask for, you may get it lesson, a White Christmas," that is. They were even happier to leave the screaming mountain lion they heard up there behind. It obviously had taken issue with them smelling up its Christmas day.

After reliving this memory, Sal decided to pull off onto the side of the road where he could sit under a big Oak tree to eat a c-ration can of date-nut bread. Little did he know this decision would change his life forever, because he was about to experience his first involuntary journey into another dimension:

It was a sunny and warm winter's day. Sal started to doze under the tree. As he drifted off to sleep, he slowly became aware of the voices of men speaking Spanish. He tried to place the dialect because it was familiar—more like the three years of high school, Spanish-language classes he took—Castillian Spanish. He could understand most of what they were saying. The leader was standing in front of him talking. He had led half his men on a reconnoiter campaign, looking for the Seven Cities of Cibola, the legendary cities supposedly made of silver and gold. They first found only a dry and barren desert as they looked towards the sunset. Turning in the direction of the sunrise and the horizon of blue-green mountains, they decided that must be the way the padre meant. This padre, Marcos de Niza, was a Spanish missionary priest who had traveled into the Southwest a few years before Coronado and came back from his adventure telling tales of the city made of silver and gold.

Sal realized the soldiers couldn't see him, but he could see and hear them. Some of the men were dressed in strange, shiny helmets with bright metal armor carrying lances and long swords. Their horses were very impressive and in good condition. He figured there must be 200 soldiers within view, some who were wearing leather vests. He figured there had to be 500-600 in all. There was a mixture of races, both Spanish and Indian, spread out among the trees and grass. The leader spoke of their six-month trip up from Mexico City to where they were now, a land filled with all the grass and springs. Not only did the padre tell of the marvelously rich cities, but also there was a Negro slave, Estevan, who also said he had traveled through these mountains and deserts for two years and had seen these marvelous cities. He was brought with this expedition to help lead them to these cities of gold.

When the army finally arrived the buildings they believed to be made from gold were only made of mud, rocks and logs. Instead of being welcomed by the inhabitants, they were fired upon, then pelted with rocks. The soldiers were hungry so they attacked the main village where they found a storehouse of corn and squash. They took as much as they could carry along with large jars of dried meat and berries. They were able to feed themselves, then return again to this place with its nuts, fruit and deer in abundance.

The Negro man said they must not have gone far enough and the cities were farther to "El Norte." They were preparing to set out again, now that they were rested and re-supplied with food and fresh mounts.

The general then spoke as if in conversation with Sal and said, "The real treasure is the land that makes a man want to return to it, and embrace it as his home forever. Lest you doubt this, witness that I, Coronado, and most of my men have chosen to be here for eternity."

Sal awakened from what he passed off as a strange dream. He shook his head and looked for a sign that someone had been there. He found none. He made a mental note to drive up to the mountains northeast of where he now was and stop at the Pueblos and villages of Zuni and Acoma in New Mexico. He felt he might have his dream again in that sacred area. It was curious to Sal how his vision put into words what his thoughts were: how this land of Arizona got into his soul and his desire was to always be here.

Sal stretched, relieved himself in the bush and started to sit back down under the tree. He heard voices again, but now as relaxed as he was, he thought he was still half awake, but these voices came from the present moment. The voices were speaking Spanish—Mexican style—and they didn't sound friendly. Four men were coming down the trail from the peak. Two were arguing about their share of the money for carrying "Las Drogas." Suddenly, one of the men pulled out a pistol and fired, hitting the guy he was arguing with. The other two ran into the woods the way they had come. The shooter was in a rage, screaming and yelling, warning them if they didn't come back, he would hunt them down and kill them like this "torpe mulo" lying there. Luckily for Sal, the Pontiac was parked down the hill, out of sight. He ran straight down, started it up and flew down the road before anyone realized he was nearby. He didn't even think about where he was driving to in his panic. By the time Sal calmed down he was nearly in Sonoita, which was halfway to Tucson and Nogales. He decided to stop at the Sonoita Café for a piece of their famous pie and coffee. And besides, no one was speaking Spanish there; he'd had enough of that for today.

It was late in the afternoon and Sally the waitress wanted to talk. That suited Sal. He started to mention the vision, but thought better of it and told her about the shooting instead.

"The Cochise County deputy was just in and bought two large coffees," Sally told him. "He was complaining that he had to sit in his car on speeder duty out on Route 82. Maybe it would be good if I called the sheriff's office and had them send him by?"

"Sure," said Sal. "Why not?"

About thirty minutes later, Deputy Larry Goodnight strolled in, happy to have something better to do than watch an empty road. Sal told him what he heard and saw.

"Well, you're a damn fool to be hanging around Miller Peak Trail," Larry said. "Don't you know that's one of the main mule trails for drug smugglers out of Mexico?"

"No!" Sal retorted sharply. "I didn't know it, and if that's true, why the hell aren't you sitting down there instead of up here watching the cars go by?"

Larry just shook his head and answered, "Don't know; this is where I'm assigned."

They set an appointment to have a detective take a statement from Sal the next morning in Tombstone at the café across from the Bird Cage Saloon. Larry called it in, then left to meet the ambulance and sheriff out at Miller Peak Road.

After Sal got an O.K. from Sally to park his Bonneville behind the café, he went to the men's room to wash up. He was all too ready to head back to Hotel Pontiac for a nap. By three a.m. he was slept out so he decided to take a walk. About two miles out, a thunderstorm rolled up over the Santa Rita Mountains and caught him without a jacket. Sal ducked under an overhang of a "Rancho Estados" development sales office to wait out the storm. Just as he started to think it was O.K. he heard a low growl from under the shack. "Naw...," he thought to himself. This can't be. But there it was again, though much louder. Obviously, this big cat had heard about Sal and his friends bugging his feline cousin up on Miller Peak two years earlier.

Sal jogged back to the safety of the Pontiac as quickly as he could. With his prior sleepiness totally gone, he was figuring he could get through another adventure-filled day. As he sat in the dry comfort of his car, he thought about today's good fortune: he hadn't gotten caught by Sgt. Washington at Fort Huachuca; he didn't get pulled in permanently when he visited another dimension; and he hadn't been shot by drug runners or even eaten by a cougar.

But maybe the best part of the day was Sally giving Deputy Larry Sal's bill for two cheeseburgers, two slices of pie, and many coffees. He was still alive, still had $35 in his pocket and he was free to do whatever entered his mind.

CHAPTER 3

MORE VISIONS

A t daybreak, Sal decided to head out to meet the detective in Tombstone. Knowing it was a long ride away, he asked the clean-up guy, Roy, to fill his thermos with coffee for the trip. No charge, of course, so it tasted even better. He headed out on Route 82 into Fairbank, which used to be a rip-roaring little town in the 1880s. It was still inhabited to this day, but mostly by ghosts. Sal parked and walked along the old road through what was left of the small settlement. "Hard to believe it was once owned by the Hearst Newspaper Family," he thought. As Sal sat on his car hood for a bit, he heard a voice whispering to him but saw no one. "Hey you, I'm Joe Goldwater. I have a pretty famous grandson, Barry, you know, heck of a politician and photographer. I also had a hand in starting the first shopping mall in Arizona."

With this happening again, Sal mumbled to himself, "Jeez, I gotta get my butt out of here, but I've got one more stop before Tombstone."

Sal drove down the dirt road to Charleston, which sat along the San Pedro River and was once a booming smelter town. It had lots of excitement, a few murders, nearly as wild as Tombstone in its day, but now it was deserted, with rusting old equipment everywhere. He pulled his boots off and sat under one of the biggest Sycamore trees around, sipping his coffee. He leaned back with his eyes closed, thinking about yesterday.

Sal was suddenly startled to hear a man's voice. He opened his eyes, but saw no one. "What's this?" he thought. Probably just the wind, but when he leaned back and started to relax again, he heard and saw men running wildly up and down the river. Some were up in trees, others behind trees shooting wildly. Then out of the mesquite and willows burst at least two dozen big bulls, shaking their very large, horned heads. Dust, screams and bullets were flying; a nearby wagon overturned. The mule that was pulling it got gored by a bull. Sal heard many shots from muskets, smoke and dust were everywhere, and he started wondering if the Apache ghosts stampeded the cattle to overrun the men.

After awhile, everything calmed down. One of the men that Sal first heard speaking looked in his direction and explained what was happening. Over 500 hundred Mormon men were forced to join the U S. Army under General Kearny by their leader, Brigham Young. If they didn't fight in the campaign against Mexico, Young said he would block them and their family's path to the "Promised Lands." This was their only battle up to now, and they had been forced to relive its humiliation over and over. It might have been penance for the later massacre of Methodist travelers at Mountain Meadows in southern Utah, which had been ordered by Mormon elders in Utah. Mormon men and Piaute Indians killed all travelers over seven years old so they could prevent any of the settlers from telling that they had been attacked over a five-day period by Mormons dressed as indians. The perpetrators did pillage and steal all the goods, money, animals and children under seven years of age from the wagon train. They murdered one-hundred-plus poor souls.

This man also added this may have been an act of revenge due to the fact that in the 1840's, a group of Mormons had been tarred & feathered, beaten, some even killed by "indians." The survivors were chased out of Missouri by Protestant gangs who were hell bent on persecuting these "out of the norm" Mormon people, because once again their own "Special" religious group had "God on their side." In fact, this man wondered why John Lee, one of the leaders of the Mountain Meadow atrocity, was

memorialized at Lee's Ferry Crossing, like some kind of hero, on the Colorado River. Word had it that Lee hid out after the killings, while these poor souls were punished over and over again. Although John Lee was finally captured, tried, and found guilty, he reportedly avoided his execution by a firing squad by wearing an iron chest plate under his large coat, the bullets knocking him flat to the ground where after dark he was allowed to escape into Mexico to live out his life.

The man telling this story was named Corporal Merrill, who said he loved the area so much that he had returned in later years to help found the town of St. David. He and the Cluff family took pride in establishing a beautiful place along the river that became the home for so many.

Sal was stunned into disbelief at what was revealed to him. He started to wonder if he was losing his mind. He walked away from the riverbank and got into his car to head for his meeting with the detective in Tombstone. He was sure that he best not mention today's adventure, hoping the sheriff's people found some sign of a struggle at Miller Peak. He couldn't help but wonder if maybe everything was becoming a hallucination. Thank God he'd stopped drinking long before he lost more brain cells.

CHAPTER 4

POLICE

s Sal pulled into Tombstone—the town too tough to die—he saw a sign directing him to "The World's Largest Rosebush" there in the heart of the desert. He'd have to stop later for that, he thought, as he parked in front of the Bird Cage Saloon. He wondered if Wyatt Earp would have been as vindictive at the O.K. corral if the Clanton Cowboy Gang had not stolen his favorite horse from in front of this very same saloon. That happened the day after he stated he was going to get tough on rustlers, about which most of the town looked the other way. The rustlers' money supported all the good things of Tombstone—gambling, drinking and prostitution.

When Sal walked into the Hot Muffin Café he spotted a buzz cut, mirror sun-glassed hombre looking him up and down. He strolled over and asked, "Detective?"

Detective Sergeant Joe Moreno nodded, "How did you know it was me?"

Sal smiled at the obvious and replied, "If the county is buying, I'm eating." That being said, he went ahead and ordered a big breakfast.

Sergeant Joe looked Sal in the eye and said, "Why did you make up such a goofy story?"

Stunned, Sal replied, "Didn't you boys find anything?"

"Sure," said the Sgt. "One half empty K-ration can of date and nut bread. The Ranger wanted to press littering charges against you for that. Why did you think wasting our time would be funny, young man?"

Sal had no answer to that. He decided to eat as quickly as he could since the breakfast was great even if the company wasn't. Sal was sure he couldn't tell the Sergeant the rest of the story or he might end up locked in the nervous hospital. Sal decided to stick to the story he had already told Deputy Larry, explaining to the Sergeant he did not know the trail was traveled for drug smuggling. And the killer yelled "torpe mula"; that was something he just couldn't make up.

"Clumsy mule is a phrase you might have picked up from the working girls in Nogales for all I know," the detective said, "That don't mean anything."

Sal smiled, thinking the only phrase he picked up down there was the phrase "Los Ojos Bonito"—beautiful eyes—because Sal had piercing blue eyes.

One more thing he did pick up there, he didn't care to recall.

"Wipe the smirk off your face, my friend," said Sergeant Joe. "We don't appreciate your little joke. Get out of my sight and out of my town or I will arrest you for littering, get you sentenced to 30 hours of community service, picking up trash on Route 92 from Sierra Vista to Naco."

Sal quickly headed for the door, as he had finished his meal, he thought to himself, "At least I've gotten two good meals out of my story. Of course, if I'm not careful, the next one's may be eaten behind bars."

CHAPTER 5

BOSS TWEED

Knowing he would want to come back to Tombstone after the smoke cleared, Sal headed up Route 80 on the Jefferson Davis Highway. He felt like so many others who had rode out of that town, very quickly, before him. But something told Sal to take the turn two to three miles out of Tombstone on Middle March Road right into Cochise's stronghold. It was probably a good idea to not bump into any of Cochise County's finest for a while.

Sal pulled onto a little-used track to find a quiet spot for a nap. He was driving a slow 5 M.P.H. when he spotted a stone foundation of what must have been a sizable home once upon a time. Half expecting to have an "other world" experience, he parked in the shade of a big Sycamore tree and got comfortable. He needed to figure out where to go from here.

As he barely drifted into a restful sleep, a fast-talking New York accent jolted him awake. Not knowing what he might hear or see next, he looked up. Standing by him was a portly, well-dressed, older man with a stogie in his mouth.

"Hey, how ya doin'?" he said to Sal. "I got a story for you. I'm the guy that ran New York City back in the 1860's & '70's. I came out here a lot by riding the train up north. I was 'the law' in the Big Apple. Sometimes though, I needed to get out of that city for my health, if you know what I mean. I would only stay here in the Arizona desert for about a month; after that it was safe for me to head back to the big city. This place got into my blood. I wanted and needed to be here; now I've been allowed to spend eternity here.

"I've done a lot of bad things in my life, but luckily, I did a lot of good that nobody but the supreme judges knew about. I started a lot of orphanages in New York, kept them supported when I took from the well-to-do folks and spread it around to the poor. I was a partner in the Brooklyn Bridge, even put a stop to the Orange Riots.

"You may be wondering how a chubby politician from New York City could survive and thrive with his house right smack in the middle of Cochises' stronghold in Apacheria, homeland of the fierce Apache. For one thing, I never had to worry about my enemies sneaking out here to ambush me. I had the best guards in the world. Who would dare come here without an invitation from Cochise or me?

"When I first got out here, we spotted an Apache boy lying off the trail. We had left St. David by wagon from Benson. The boy had been shot by Mormons in St. David during some horse-stealing raid, I guessed. He was bleeding and delirious. We patched him up and I put him back in the wagon, tied a white flag on a stick and rode up as close as I could to the big rocks up there. I just started hollering and fired my pistol. Then I left the mule tied to the buckboard and got out of the way. I watched from back here, about an hour later these two ghostly figures came and looked into the wagon.

"When I got up the next morning my guard man told me the wagon left during the night. Two days later when we woke up, there was the wagon with the mule still attached in the yard. In the back of the wagon were two deer, freshly killed, and about two pounds of gold nuggets. After that, whenever I was out here I would fill up a wagon with corn and flour and hook the mule to it. I'd light a signal fire and leave the wagon out front. Come morning the wagon was gone, but one to two days later it was back with something of value in it: turkey, deer or gold.

"I never gave them whiskey, ammo or guns. Once, after I left them beef jerky, canned peaches and blankets, they left a young, blonde, Mormon girl by the front gate. I'll never forget her mother's face when I rode into St. David. That's how I came to be able to make it in this spot. I'd have liked to bring that New Jersey guy, Thomas Nast from Morristown, who kept doing those cartoons of me, bring him out here in a wagon and leave it. He and his caricatures of me were driving me nuts—most likely the main reason for my downfall.

"So, how's that for a good story?" Boss Tweed asked, looking very satisfied with himself.

Sal surmised that this spot hadn't been a place where he could get a good nap, but he sure enjoyed the story just told him, coming directly from such an infamous political pirate.

"I just can't believe what my life is turning into," replied Sal. "Somehow, I opened a gate and now I seem to be able to flow between two worlds. I'm not sure if I'm hallucinating, but it sure feels real—the stories of people, I mean. I think I will head up to Benson to the library on Huachuca Avenue. I want to talk to Nicole there and check out some of these stories I've been given."

As Sal started to drive away, he thought about Boss Tweed. If he remembered his New York City history well enough, Tweed was the King of Political Corruption. He wondered if somehow that infection permeated the Arizona statehouse, considering the quality and criminality of some of the past Arizona governors.

CHAPTER 6

GOOD SAMARITAN

S al headed back up Route 80 towards Benson when he spotted a fellow on the side of the road with a flat tire. He pulled over to ask if he could help to discover the man had no spare. Sal was obliged to give him a ride to St. David, if that was the way he was headed.

Sal let the man in his car, but the man had with him his dog, "Little John," who was a St. Bernard as heavy as he. Little John weighed some 200+ pounds. Sal grimaced as he wondered if Little John was going to rip out his backseat, especially the way the dog was poking his nose and digging his paws into it. Then suddenly, Sal remembered the roast beef he had in the trunk, which was what the dog was smelling.

"What's your name?" asked Sal.

"Brother Alex," he replied. "I live at the monastery in St. David."

"Is it O.K. if Little John has a slice of roast beef?" he asked. "I have some in the trunk."

"Sure," said Brother Alex. "I wouldn't mind having a slice myself."

That settled, they headed up the road with a pound of beef in each of their hands, or paws as the case may be. Little John finished first, of course, so now Sal then had 200 pounds of drooling canine over his shoulder communicating, "Hey, you done with that, yet?" Sal missed his old dog, Tippy, whom he had to leave behind, so the attention actually helped lift his spirits.

"So, what are you doing with your life?" Brother Alex asked, starting up a conversation.

He seemed genuinely interested so Sal told him a little about his last few days. Brother Alex didn't seem shocked at all, as Sal half expected; in fact, Brother Alex began to tell him that even as a monk, he had had similar experiences.

By then, they were near the monk's turn off, so Brother Alex guided him the rest of the way. He steered Sal up a long driveway to a spectacular property with lots of big trees, green grass, flowers and some impressive stucco buildings.

Sal let Little John out of the backseat and ruffled his ears as if to play around with him. Noticing the rapport developing between the dog and Sal, Brother Alex asked Sal to sit awhile and talk.

"Would you like a cold drink?" he asked.

"I sure would," said Sal. "But non-alcoholic."

Brother Alex returned shortly with cold lemonades and a large bowl of water for his furry bear of a dog. After Sal had drank about half of his lemonade, Brother Al spoke.

"Sal, I think you really like my dog," he began. "If you have nowhere to be for the next three to four weeks, how about doing me a big favor and stay here to look after him? I need to leave tomorrow morning for San Jose, California to help out my folks. I'll be gone about 25-30 days. I would so appreciate your hanging around here and taking care of Little John."

"What about the other guys here?" Sal asked.

"Well, until I showed up here with Little John, the rule of the monastery was 'No Dogs,'" said Brother Alex. "They tried to get me to give him away, but where he goes, I go."

It turned out that Brother Alex was a first-rate stucco man and the buildings of the monastery were in dire need of repair. The monks needed Brother Alex's talents, so Little John stayed. But now, Brother Alex had to go back home to help out his folks and no one could be counted on to take good care of the dog.

"You can stay in my room and eat three square meals a day," encouraged the monk.

Since this was a better offer than the 73rd at Fort Huachuca, Sal agreed. "O.K. What do I have to do?"

"You'll have the run of the place, actually," said Brother Alex. "You can check out the reading room and the river bank. They are two of my favorite places. The only time you have to step quietly with Little John is meditation time, which is from two to four p.m."

Brother Alex guided Sal into the kitchen area where they had a big, healthy lunch with salads, fruit, home-baked breads and brown rice. Sal went out to his car to carry in the rest of his roast beef, then gave it to the cook to do what he could with it.

After lunch, Brother Alex, Sal and Little John dropped the monk's flat tire at a nearby Texaco station on Route 80. When it was fixed, they headed back to the highway to rescue the monk's car. On the way down Route 80, three coyotes dashed across the road making Little John very agitated, which he made known by whining. Alex mentioned he never had his dog fixed and this might be the time of year he gets the most excited. If Little John were to get loose and chase the coyotes, he would probably only last two or three days. His coat was too thick for running in the desert. The male coyotes would constantly attack him even though he out-weighed them several times over. Coyotes made their living killing everyday; chances were good that one could distract Little John from the front and another would hamstring him from behind. It was the same way they brought down deer.

Sal agreed to keep Little John close and under control when they got to Alex's car. Once there, they changed the tire and put the dog in the back seat. When Brother Alex tried to start the engine, nothing happened. He glanced over to the passenger side to find a partial bottle of tequila sitting there. Brother Alex lifted the hood of his car. Sure enough, the battery was gone.

"What do you think of that?" said Alex dryly.

Sal just laughed and replied, "I think that even 80 to 90 years later some things just haven't changed. We're in the shadow of the Dragoon Mountains where some people used to and still take what they need and give back what they think you want."

The trio headed back up Route 80 in Sal's car to the same Texaco station for a battery. The mechanic, Bud, laughed at their plight and told them the travelers from south of the border had helped his business grow steadily the last 17 years.

"This here road is the main route for the people and drug smugglers heading north," he pointed out.

Sal laughed out loud remarking he already knew something about that now.

Back at the monastery that night, Sal slept on a chaise lounge under a big Sycamore. In the morning, Brother Alex bid him farewell then gave a big hug to Little John. After the monk left, Sal threw a Frisbee for the dog for a short while. It didn't take long for the dog to find the shade of a tree as if to say, "Hey, I'm fat and furry; that's enough exercise for me."

CHAPTER 7

SHELTER

S al looked around the grounds and settled into the peace of the place. He decided his favorite spot was a rose arbor made of iron re-bar in front of the chapel—that is, after the dining room, of course. There were a few people staying at the monastery, maybe eight or ten men and women. Sal noticed a little sign in the dining room that said there would be a 12-Step meeting at 10:30 a.m. All were welcome. He de-cided it had been awhile since he attended a meeting Maybe it would be a good idea to go. He put Little John in Brother Alex's room and walked into the meeting. He wasn't surprised to find about half the monks and six visitors sitting around, drinking coffee and socializing.

"Hi, I'm Sal D.," he introduced himself. "I'm an alcoholic."

After he did this, a friendly monk by the name of Brother Bob D., invited him to lead the meeting. Being an open 12-Step meeting, there was a mixture of Alcoholics Anonymous, Narcotics Anonymous, Overeaters Anonymous, as well as Alanon members along with a few plain curious or bored anonymous "members." Sal told them a little of his story—what it was like, what happened, and what it was like now. He spoke about 30 minutes and asked if there were any questions. To his surprise, there were several.

"Did you want to stay sober?" asked one man.

"Hell, yes," Sal replied. "I love my life sober."

"Did you ever kill anyone while you were drunk," another one asked.

"No," said Sal. "But, driving with one eye closed so that the second middle line would go away put me one foot away from many head-on crashes."

After the meeting adjourned, everyone felt more connected. Sal was glad he decided to attend. He learned there was a meeting every night after dinner, even if there were only two or three people in attendance. He went back to the room and retrieved Little John so he could walk him, but most likely clean up after him. It took the best part of a 15-gallon garbage bag when cleaning up after a St. Bernard.

Sal helped himself to another terrific lunch in the monastery's dining room. Then headed for the reading room to see what interesting books he could find there. He picked up one book by a guy named Michael Harner who wrote about the Jivaro Indians. These Jivaro had lived along the Amazon in South America. Their Shaman would drink a concoction made from an herb called Ayahuasca which allowed him to go on a "out-of-the-body" journey to have visions into other worlds. Sal first thought, "Hell, I go to meetings to keep from doing that," but as he read further, he realized this was serious stuff.

"Man alive," he murmured to himself. "This is kind of what's happening to me, but without the Ayahuasca."

He toyed with the thought that perhaps he was special, and wondered if anyone else could see what he had been seeing. Sal decided he would go back to the Miller Peak trail the next morning to see if anything "paranormal" happened to him again. In the meantime, he thought he would travel the eight miles to Benson to check out its library. Someone there had to know something about that New York guy, Boss Tweed, and the Dragoon Stronghold of the Chiricahua Apaches.

When Sal arrived, he found a group of very pleasant female volunteers working at the library. The one named Nicole told him she would do what she could to help. Nothing came up in the index cards on Boss Tweed, but there was plenty on Cochise, Nana, Geronimo, Magnus as well as other Apache warriors and leaders. From what Sal could tell, none of the Calvary was able to force the Apache out of the Dragoon Mountains. It was just too tough for the troops to travel, though they moved regularly between Camp Huachuca and Fort Bowie on Middle March Road there in southern Arizona territory.

Sal remembered reading that over 25 percent of the U.S. Army and one-third of the Mexican Army spent nearly two years chasing Geronimo and his 30-40 warriors all over the Southern Arizona and Northern Mexico territories back in the 1880s. But, try as they may, they didn't even slow down his raids. Geronimo was able to steal horses, plunder wagon trains, and attack ranches at will. Most of the mines had to shut down until Geronimo just got exhausted and turned himself in for the third and last time. Though the government promised Geronimo he would be allowed to live out his life with his family near his birthplace, near Clifton, Arizona, they lied once again. He died in Oklahoma in 1909. Before his death, he was often found at the railroad station selling little "play" bows and arrows.

Sal couldn't remember a more feared, but respected Shaman warrior than Geronimo in all of American history. Even the great Teddy Roosevelt invited Geronimo to ride out with him at the head of his inauguration parade in 1905, along with five other great Native-American chiefs. If some of the fiercest Apache hadn't decided to double cross the others and work as scouts for the U.S. Army, guiding them to the secret hideouts, people might still have to live in fear of those renegades swooping out of the rocks and the side trails to kick their butts.

The last time Sal knew of an Apache raid was 1935, when some young Indian bucks decided to live by the old ways. Sal figured they scared a lot of folks along both sides of the border, especially those that remembered how violent it was, or even those who had just heard the stories from their older relatives.

Nicole told Sal there was a ranch near Tucson where the wife of a rancher had started a unique bookstore; maybe she could help him find something about Boss Tweed. Sal thanked her, thinking he didn't have enough cash to buy a book even if she had a book on him to read. He asked Nicole to keep looking and he would check with her again. Luckily, he mentioned he had Little John in the car so Nicole gave the big pooch a few biscuits the library kept around for such occasions. Little John was happy to see Sal but even happier to see the biscuits. It took a lot of fuel to keep that big lug running.

CHAPTER 8

RIVER

S al and Little John headed back to St. David to a solid dinner for both of them. Afterwards, they took a nice walk along the river. Both of them had no problem sleeping through the night.

The next morning Sal was up early, and though Little John needed a little prodding, they went for their morning walk. Once the dog smelled the aroma of bacon from the kitchen, he was ready to roll. Sal went over to the kitchen to score some early grub. Breakfast was served at 7 a.m., but though it was only 6 a.m., he got some biscuits, bacon and a big bone. He loaded Little John into the car, but passed on filling his coffee thermos until he got to Tombstone. The Hot Muffin Café brewed some high-octane coffee that suited him better.

Sal had just walked into the café when Deputy Larry hollered out to him. "Hey buddy, c'mere."

Sal looked across the room and there sat the deputy along with Sergeant Joe. "Uh, oh," he thought to himself. "This can't be good. Why didn't I scout out the cars in front, first?"

Both officers looked happy to see Sal, which kind of surprised him.

"You know," said the deputy. "We really need to know how to find you if we need to. What's your current address?"

Joe waved abruptly to Larry to shut him up and said to Sal, "Tell me where you were living last year around September."

"Pennsylvania," Sal said immediately, which knocked the wiseass smile off the detective's face. "Why do you ask?"

Neither officer answered, so Sal continued. "Look guys. I've been straight with you both. I saw and heard exactly what I told you. What's your problem?"

After a long pause, the detective said, "Your story bothers me. We didn't find nothin' when we went up there with the paramedics to Miller Peak Road. So Deputy Larry and I went back yesterday to search some more. Up the road we found a skeleton. In its partially intact jacket was a page from a newspaper advertising a bullfight in Hermosillo, Sonora. The paper was dated September 16."

The men asked Sal for an employer's phone number during that time period for an alibi. Sal gave them Quaker City Tree Service out of Philadelphia. He had worked for them six days a week from August to November of that same year.

"What does that have to do with this other deal?" asked Sal.

"There was a bullet hole in the jacket. Ballistic tests are being conducted to see what we can learn," he replied. "Your story seems to fit, but four months too late."

Again, the deputy asked where Sal would be if there were any more questions.

"At the monastery in St. David," Sal told them. "I'll be there for the next couple of weeks." Sal filled his thermos and decided to skip going to Miller Peak for now. This experience with the officers had left him with a bad taste in his mouth. Nevertheless, it was a nice, clear, breezy January day and Sal decided he and Little John should take a walk near the San Pedro River by way of Route 90. Little John was delighted to hop in the river to soak himself and his considerable coat in the cold water. Sal remembered a little canyon that was southwest of the bridge so they both hiked to it. He wanted to see if the caves located there still had owls nesting in them. They walked about a mile and a half then almost fell down the cliffs into the opening. Sure enough, Sal found three cave-like crevices that had white owls living in them. He didn't want to disturb the birds, just satisfy his curiosity. In the meantime, Little John found a sleeping skunk that he just couldn't leave alone. The dog found out quickly enough that he should let sleeping skunks lie.

From that time on for the duration of the hike, Sal tried to keep Little John downwind of him. They went back to the river to soak but it was to no avail. Sal and the dog then continued north on the river which, strangely enough, flowed downstream. The San Pedro was one of those rivers that flowed north out of Mexico into the United States. On the trail he passed the Route 90 Bridge again, fondly remembering a lot of good times he had there back in his Army days.

Sal looked around for the railroad cable car that nearly cost him his fingers three years earlier. Sure enough, it was still there. Sal shuddered as he looked down at his hands. Life would have been so much harder without his fingers, but fortunately, they had only been broken. He recalled how, after a long weekend of drinking and partying, he had rolled out alone on the cable car over the river. The bed was so dry that a fish would have to walk across the rocks to go down river. The other drunken soldiers he was with decided to rock the cable and Sal almost fell out. He grabbed the cable causing the pulleys to run over his hands breaking all eight fingers. He somehow managed to work his way back to shore by using his palms. The "spirits of the cable car" probably decided he hadn't suffered enough that day so when he returned to the campfire, another drunken soldier poked him in the stomach with a burning stick and said, "Here, this will make you forget your finger pain."

Sal shook his head at the memory of that experience. He thought perhaps that was what people must mean when they say to keep your memory green when it comes to drinking. He made a mental note to share this story at the next 12-Step meeting he went to. Little John suddenly ran up to him shaking his wet fur and skunk stink into Sal's face shocking him back to the present. They walked back to the car, but Sal regretted not having

a large garbage sack he could put the dog into Little John jumped up into the backseat.

Heading back to Tombstone, Sal remembered there was an abandoned airfield near Gleeson about five miles from Tombstone. It was now a ghost town, where the 232nd Signal Battalion was bivouacked. Sal had been part of a group of rowdies chosen to be the "aggressor army" for war games there. He was squad leader of ten men, all dressed in camouflage with blackened faces, and they carried carbines loaded with blanks. As they crept up to attack the 232nd, Sal spotted the silhouette of a vehicle in the moonless night. Thinking it was a sentry's vehicle Sal was able to sneak right up to the car and poke his blank firing carbine in the window while saying, "Got ya!" Sal would never forget the next ten seconds, when a young man raised up off a young woman, then pulled out a very large .44 pistol from under the seat to point it right into Sal's face.

"What the %$#! * do you want?" he yelled back at Sal, who tried to explain, while visibly shaking, the war games the Army was engaging in there. Sal began thinking that First Sergeant Washington probably knew something like this would happen when he picked Sal to head up the squad. In the following week, Sal redeemed himself by capturing the Communications Van and Headquarters of the 232nd along with their Battalion Commander. He also saved a three-quarter ton truck and his squad when a blank from one of the carbines set fire to the grass.

Sal figured that was enough remembering for one day, so he took Little John back to the monastery to see what was cooking—literally. They then passed the next two days hiking along the river, swimming in it when the day got too hot, reading a few books and trying to decide what to do next.

CHAPTER 9

ARMY MEMORIES

B oth Sal and Little John enjoyed a great dinner up until Brother Stan came over to Sal's table and said, "A deputy stopped by today and wanted to see you. I told him you left early this morning and didn't know when you might be back. He just said he'd catch up to you; then he drove off. Are you in any trouble?"

"No," answered Sal. "I've been trying to help them out with something and they probably have another question for me. It's O.K."

Satisfied with Sal's response, Brother Stan walked away. Sal thought to himself, "Why am I feeling guilty? I didn't do anything wrong." Of course, when you're an alcoholic you keep a certain amount of paranoia with you. There are such things as blackouts where you don't remember what you did the night before and pray all the next day that no one walks up to confront you with what you might have done during a blackout.

Sal sat there and thought about another experience he had last year, when he only had 21 days to go in the "Sergeant Washington Army." Sal had just found out that he would be a free man within three weeks. He was found guilty to having committed an Article 15, a punitive action one notch less than a court martial, for being AWOL in San Diego two months earlier. As punishment for that infraction he had to clean the Battalion Headquarter's Office every night for eight hours for two weeks straight. It gave him a chance to read a big binder containing the A.R.'s (Army Regulations). One regulation that caught his eye said a soldier could be released up to 90 days early for farming, if you were needed for planting or harvesting. Or, if you were in another occupation that was seasonally necessary, you could apply for early release. Sal's folks had a tavern and restaurant, so, after much hoopla with the Inspector General's office and his company commander he was granted an early out to bartend for his parents back in Pennsylvania. That was definitely a "First" for the Army's reasons for discharge. To celebrate Sal went to Mexico in an Army jeep and in uniform, along with his buddy, Sergeant Jake (Butterball) Billet where they got smashed on beer and tequila.

Even though completely hammered, they drove back to the Fort and ended up at a baseball game where his company was playing. Sal was relieving himself next to the jeep when a car pulled up alongside him. It contained a brand new lieutenant fresh out of West Point along with his wife and two kids. He had been assigned to Sal's company. The lieutenant commanded Sal to stop, and the next morning, Sal was informed he retorted to the lieutenant, "Once you start, you just can't stop!" The lieutenant grabbed a baseball bat and was going to slug Sal, so Sal picked up another bat and began to chase the lieutenant.

That was one of those blackout moments for Sal, and it took a lot of the fun out of drinking. He had been close to a court martial that time which made Sergeant Washington very happy since he had no liking for this particular soldier. Washington even told Sal, "I gots ya!" But luckily, after a few apologies and explanations, the lieutenant let Sal off with only another Article 15. That prompted a letter from the Army some months later, telling Sal Dusi he would not be receiving the "Good Conduct" medal due to the number of Article 15's he had accumulated: the number was 14.

CHAPTER 10

LIFE~CHANGING VISION

"Oh well," thought Sal. "Maybe I'll share that at my next 12-Step meeting too."

That next meeting would be in just under an hour so Sal had enough time to take Little John for a quick walk then take a bath, himself. After walking about a quarter mile, though, the two of them lay down under a big old Sycamore, and glimpsed a bald eagle that had been fishing in the San Pedro River. Soon, Sal became aware of a presence near him, besides the dog, and looked up to see a woman in a cobalt blue dress. She was adorned in silver and turquoise jewelry and was staring down at him. Before he could react, she spoke.

"I walk along the river every day and night for eternity, for I have spent my life helping those of my tribe that were in need: the crippled, old and orphaned of which there were many. My people's horrible state was due to poor diet, disease as well as the inter-tribal warfare and foreign colonization of my time.

"You seem to have been an aimless soul, but now you have the opportunity to assist a great many people in this world. If you want to make things easier for yourself in the future world, you would be well advised to find a way to do good—now—helping the less fortunate wherever you go.

"Many opportunities will present themselves; all you have to do is be receptive and take the right action when you can. I'm called ' Teralisa' by my people. Go in peace, we shall surely meet again."

Sal put his head down, ashamed to look up, as he remembered times when he had a few extra bucks, but declined to help people who were in need. He had wanted to hold on to all he could; otherwise he couldn't afford a bottle of booze, or a case of hooch if that's what it took, to keep his own little demons at bay.

When he felt the nerve to look up, he was alone with Little John once again. He figured now was a good time to walk back to the monastery and make it to that AA meeting. The group's discussion that night was not that stimulating, so Sal's mind kept drifting back to what the spirit had said.

As he lay in bed that night, Sal thought about what he could do to help those that were in need. One thought that came up over and over was how desperate Mexican immigrants who were escaping across the border carrying just their few belongings in a plastic bag. Sal thought about how many bodies were found on the desert floor after they starved or died of thirst, when all they wanted was to find a better and safer life. They were just like his ancestors who came to America carrying only one or two bags on a boat. Then an idea popped into his head. If a guy were to drive into the wilderness and set out jugs of water and maybe some canned or dried food under a tree, a few lives might be saved. He could mark the tree with a blue ribbon, so it would be noticed and Sal could find it again. He became determined to do this to start of fellowship for those unfortunate. After this idea occurred to him, he spent the rest of the night sleeping peacefully.

In the morning, Sal awakened with a light heart. He could feel he had turned a big corner in his life, from a recovering drunk and drifter, to someone with direction and purpose. Little John nudged him as if to tell him he also had a big purpose, getting outside right now! Sal laughed and brought the shovel.

CHAPTER 11

RED GAS

After enjoying a great breakfast, Sal packed up Little John into the car, along with 30 one-gallon jugs filled with water he got from the monastery kitchen. He also grabbed a bunch of candy bars and left-over muffins as well as a box of freezer bags. Driving south, Sal thought he was undertaking something huge for a guy with no money for gas. Then remembering how the Army provided him with drinking money for two years, he headed over to Fort Huachuca and the old buffalo-soldiers' barracks to see if all those Jerry-cans of gas he used to stash and resell were still there. Luckily, nothing had happened in that area since 1945 and the cans were still stacked up under the piles of tumbleweed he had placed there. Hoping the gas wouldn't varnish up in his carburetor and no one would see the red dye stains, he filled up and drove off. The Army had put red dye into the gas to deter soldiers from putting it into their vehicles.

"Take the right action and old H.P. (Higher Power) will provide," he said to himself.

Sal drove through Bisbee, remembering what an ass he'd made of himself one night. First, he had been at Sergeant Billet's house until his wife, Catherine, kicked him out. Then he went over to Sergeant Elias's house, who foolishly let Sal in, even as drunk as he was. Sal was thrown out again for suggesting to Sergeant Elias that it was O.K. for him to sleep in the bed with the sarge's wife.

Sal hoped this attempt to help others would balance out some of the stupid moves of his past. He drove south towards Douglas, which was across from Aqua Prieta, Mexico. Ten miles before town, Sal turned west. He remembered a migrant once telling him that many people crossed between Aqua Prieta and Naco in order to head to Tucson and Phoenix. After about five miles of very rough road, Sal decided to start dropping off his water three jugs at a time, along with a few candy bars and muffins in a freezer bag. Over the next six miles he did the same thing until he ran out. He also tied a blue ribbon on the mesquite trees where he left the stash hoping people would see it and investigate.

As he drove back out, Sal thought that this was still Cochise County. If Deputy Larry or Sergeant Joe were to see him here and ask what he was doing, would they believe his story?

"Oh well," Sal told himself, "doing good isn't always easy."

Driving back toward Tombstone, Sal decided to pull over outside the Mule Mountain Tunnel north of Bisbee to let Little John relieve himself. As he drove into Tombstone he looked for the giant rosebush he had heard and read about. He located it, but being the end of January he only got to see a naked giant plant with plenty of thorns. Deciding that he deserved a good, caffeinated cup of coffee, he headed for the Muffin Café.

Sal ordered from the smiling waitress named Lu, who was probably ten years older than he was but definitely pretty for her age. She told him she had worked at the café for the last nine years, ever since leaving a bad man, a bad marriage and a bad climate behind in Chicago.

"I just got off the bus out front and didn't bother getting back on for L.A.," she told Sal. "Things worked out pretty well, though. I am now the day manager here and I share a house with a man who manages The Bird Cage Saloon.

Sal shared a little bit of his own story with Lu: that he got out of the Army, got out of the state, came back here again, now out of the cold

weather back East, out of cash and maybe out of his mind. As he got up to leave and take the last swig of his coffee, another waitress whacked him in the back of the head with a tray full of dishes, sending his coffee cup flying. He turned towards the waitress, who snapped at him rudely, "For Pete's sake, stay out of the aisle."

He got no apology and no smile. "What a nasty witch," he thought to himself.

Lu quickly apologized for her. "She's usually like that," said Lu. "But she has the owner, who is also the night manager, convinced that she is a real asset. She shows up at 4 a.m., never missing a day, so I can't dump her as much as I'd like to."

Sal decided it was time to bug out for the monastery, but before leaving, he told Lu what he was doing for the migrants. Intrigued, she said, "Too bad you can't use all the food I throw out everyday." Sal bid Lu goodbye and got ready to head up Route 80 to the monastery, but not before letting Little John leave a large offering in the ditch next to the car. Sal heard a nasty voice behind him, so he turned.

CHAPTER 12

NEW ACQUAINTENCES

"Pick that up or spend the night in jail." Sal looked at what had to be the male twin of the nasty waitress. This twin "brother" was wearing a town constable shirt and hat. He got out a one-gallon plastic bag and scooped up the dog's imitation of a giant, soft ice cream sundae then threw it into the waste can. He silently hoped that the refuse container was the constable's favorite place to lean as he guarded the ditches, witches and bitches of Tombstone, thinking of that nasty waitress. Once the sun baked that waste can it would be a very unpleasant spot to be around.

Finally, Sal started up the Pontiac and drove up Route 80 before any more unpleasant episodes intruded on this bittersweet day. At least the gas worked well enough to keep the old Pontiac on the road. The constable hadn't seen any of the red dye.

When Sal got back he told Little John they were going for a walk along the San Pedro. Having already missed lunch, he grabbed an apple, a chunk of cheese, half a loaf of rye bread and a jug of lemonade. That seemed the right combination for a hike.

The two ramblers headed down to the river and made it three miles when they surprised a family bathing and splashing around. The family all started to run, but Sal spoke to them in broken Spanish, telling them he was no threat. By gestures, and a combination of a little English and a little Spanish, Sal figured out the San Pedro had become the El Camino para trabajo—the road to work. These Mexicans told him many people, especially families, came this way so they didn't risk that their children would die of thirst when they traveled north. They camped in the salt cedars, tamarisk and weeds along the river, picking berries, cactus and anything else they found that could sustain them. Sal took the opportunity to tell them about the jugs of water and food he had started leaving under trees. They gratefully told him he would become known as "Santo Salvadore" for this good work. He would find families all along the river that were in great need of food and blankets, and as the weather became warmer, the water would be life saving. No one trusted in the safety of drinking the river water except in a dire emergency.

Sal gave the family his cheese and bread and wished them "Vaya con Dios" since it was time to head back to St. David. As he walked with Little John, he thought about how to collect food and blankets for the families passing through the area. Fortunately, the Benson library let him place two big boxes by the door: one for blankets and one for food.

By Monday, Sal had 23 blankets and almost 225 pounds of canned goods. Now he needed to deliver the food down by the river. He wondered if he should call his good buddy Sergeant Washington to see if he'd loan him ten guys and a three-quarter ton truck. But it just wasn't worth it to let the man ever find out where he was. He would probably, somehow, find himself in a lot hotter water than the San Pedro in July if he did.

That night, Sal began to think about what he was doing and why. It was one thing to drop off water to save people from dying, but was he stepping over some boundary with the food and blankets? These people were cold, hungry and scared; what was he doing that was so important or unlawful that he couldn't spend some time and effort helping them out? Remembering the spirit and her words of advice, Sal felt he was now on the right path.

The next morning after breakfast, Sal planned out his delivery system by breaking up the river into four sections. Starting approximately three miles above the border he could drop three blankets and 5-20 lbs. of food in a plastic bag at one-mile intervals. He hoped the travelers would only take what they needed. He also remembered to leave a couple of can openers that had been donated by the supermarket in each bag. He also included items for the children: some crayons and paper he had managed to scrounge up from a kindergarten teacher he knew in Sierra Vista.

Sal was getting excited about the noble journey he had embarked on. He could hardly keep from racing out the door. He realized he could help a lot more people if he had a specific plan, instead of acting compulsively. The boxes from the library were a good idea that worked, so why not expand the collection area? He decided to gather some big boxes and place them at all the other libraries, medical clinics, and even gas stations. Even if someone took food and blankets out of the boxes before he got there, he would still be accomplishing his mission to help people in need.

CHAPTER 13

IT'S HAPPENING

T hinking about what Lu had said about all the food she threw away, Sal realized that every diner, café and restaurant probably threw enough food away to feed 10 to 20 people. But it would be a challenge to get this food before the pig farmers did. The farmers who picked up scraps from the kitchens at Fort Huachuca always got to the restaurants early. It was time for him to remember his A.A. lessons: (a) one step at a time; (b) avoid grandiosity; and (c) "the power to change the things he could." In keeping with the important maxim, "First Things First," he decided to make a list of all the food possibilities.

Sal was so excited in making his list that he could barely stay still long enough to write all the places he could remember for food throwaways: The Military Inn in Sierra Vista, Kelly's Bar, Holiday Inn, the Bowling Alley, and the Commissary at the Fort. Broken boxes, bags, dented cans, and overstock were all game. Tombstone had many possibilities, too, starting with Lu and the Bird Cage. He was sure they would know other establishments that might be willing to give him leftovers, maybe more if he was lucky.

Before he headed for Tombstone, Sal wanted to stop at the St. David Texaco to see if he could put a collection box there to catch all the campers passing through on their way back to Tucson and Phoenix. To Sal's delight,

Bud the owner, was happy to help.

"You build the box and I'll store the overload in my storeroom until you can pick it up," Bud said.

This excited Sal even more. Most alcoholics have a great many ideas, but it's the poor planning and hesitant or unsure implementation that usually dooms them. However, Sal was already acting on his idea and it was actually working out. He headed into Tombstone to talk to Lu and have some good coffee.

Arriving there, he made sure to sit in Lu's section and not the witch's. When Lu saw Sal come in, she brightened up and immediately brought him over a cup of hot brew.

"How are you doing, Sal?" she asked cheerfully.

"Doing real well," he answered. "How about you?"

"The witch was late this morning so the boss might be willing to let me get rid of her if she causes one more problem," Lu smiled. "At least that will give us a chance to improve the attitude around here."

Sal told her about the idea he had to use the thrown-away food. She agreed to start saving everything she could for the needy. She also agreed to speak with her boyfriend, the Bird Cage manager, to see if he would shake some stuff loose from over there as well.

Sal felt like things were really jumping now. "Do you have anything you could give me today?" he asked excitedly.

"Pull around back of the kitchen and I'll see," she replied.

When Sal did, the dishwasher of the Muffin Café loaded day-old muffins, breads, and various foods into Sal's car. He also gave him ten quart containers of milk. With a quick yell of gratitude, Sal took off for the river.

As Sal wrestled one-handed with Little John to protect his booty, he wondered how he was going to get the food to the people. He decided to carry some with him until he found some travelers and then convince them to come to his car and carry the food back to their camps themselves. With his arms full of food, he and Little John took off down the trail. About a half mile later, Sal met up with some people who were hiding in the bush.

"Hola!" he yelled as friendly as possible. It took a few minutes but a man from the group finally approached.

"Yo tengo comidas, para tu familia," Sal spoke haltingly but correctly in his high-school Spanish—"I have food for your family. "The Mexican nervously accepted the food and carried it back to the brush where at least 15 hungry people popped out. After receiving many "Gracias, senor," Sal told the man there was more of the same in his car. If he would come with Sal, they could have more food. The only thing Sal asked of them was to share the food with others they met along the way who were also in need.

A few men followed Sal and Little John back to his car to help him retrieve the supplies. Sal told the men that whenever possible, he or someone else would be at the bridge on Route 90 with food everyday before noon. Sal hoped the people staying in the bushes would pass this information along to the next travelers.

Sal knew he had to accomplish his good deeds without Immigration Services finding out, and that could be a big problem. As he drove back to St. David, he thought how ironic it was that the illegal immigrants were staying about 100 feet from the cable car where his fingers had been broken. He wondered if that meant anything.

After a late lunch at the monastery, Sal told the cook what he was doing. The cook informed him that he ordered part of the monastery's food from the Tucson Food Bank and he thought he could break loose some supplies to help out. Sal explained the people couldn't cook so whatever he gave them had to be ready to eat.

Sal started to realize he might have started something that could get out of hand. He would certainly need help to do all of this, and need it soon. As he looked at his "To Do" list, he saw that gasoline was right under the food, so he drove back to the Texaco station to fill up as well as let Bud know how the first day went. He told him how dire his money situation was. To his surprise Bud offered to chip in 20 gallons a week and repairs when necessary. That put Sal's mind at ease, since picking up the old gas at Fort Huachuca felt like a disaster just waiting to happen.

CHAPTER 14

APACHE

S al took Little John with him the next morning while he dropped canned goods and a few blankets off at the bridge on Route 90 by the San Pedro River. The word was out that the travelers could look under the bridge above the waterline to find supplies. After leaving his goodies, Sal decided to head over Mule Mountain to Bisbee to see if there was any opportunity to score some food for his endeavor. As he started back on Route 90, he spotted a figure on the side of the road. Thinking he might be a "border crosser," Sal pulled over to tell him about the cache of supplies under the bridge. As he stopped, he realized it wasn't an ordinary traveler. He wore a bandana on his forehead and a handsome turquoise necklace around his neck.

Sal opened the passenger door and asked the stranger if he would like a ride. The man got in and muttered "Thanks for stopping."

"Heading home?" asked Sal to make some conversation.

The man turned and said quietly, "What you are seeing out there is all my home and the home of all my people for the last 450 years."

"What do you mean?" asked Sal.

The stranger grunted his reply, "I am Apache, to use your white words. My people were here for hundreds of years, living, hunting, raiding and trading. Now we are no longer free to live our own way on the Red Trail.

We must live the White Way."

Sal told the stranger what he was doing, intending to make himself, a white man, look a little more favorable to the native's eyes. The man looked at Sal with coal black eyes and said, "Do you think this makes me happy? You are only helping more outsiders to come into our homeland that Yusan (Apache God) gave to my people to live on as He intended."

Sal had always thought the Immigration Services were the only ones who wouldn't like what he was doing. He hadn't thought others might not like it as well. The negative proverb of damned if you do, damned if you don't came to mind.

"What's your name?" asked Sal.

"Call me Nahteste," he replied. "You?"

"Sal," he replied.

"Do you think it was right to free the Blacks?" Nahteste asked.

"Of course it was," Sal answered.

"After you Whites did that, you sent the Blacks out to our country." Nahteste started a narration. "The Buffalo Soldiers chased us off our lands and made us Red people prisoners on the worst land around. Do you think Red people should now love the White or the Black people? The Brown people—Mexicans—the ones you help, they invited Cochise's father and many other Apache elders to their villages for fiestas. They all were to celebrate the peace that was mutually agreed upon between the two peoples. The Mexicans gave them much food and drink, and when they were drunk, they killed them. So, no! I am not happy that you help these people invade our homeland."

Sal tried to argue that America had guaranteed the rights of all Americans—Red, White, Black or Brown—to live and work where they pleased. "If this is so," countered Nahteste. "Please tell me how many Indian people you have met working in stores, restaurants, factories and hospitals? Go to San Carlos Reservation and what you will see is the once-proud Apache sitting in front of their American-Government "housing." Tell me if you see a smile on anyone's face. No, my friend, we have not prospered by the great European Expansion and I am sad, sick in my heart."

Sal remained silent, at a total loss for words. This was not what he had expected to hear on this bright and beautiful morning. Then Sal, himself, suddenly exploded.

"No!" he raised his voice. "I refuse to have you put me down for doing good deeds for anyone. I stopped to see if I could help you. I am driving you out of the desert as a favor. What are you doing to help your people or anyone else?"

The two men were warriors, each in his own battle, but now the two were fighting each other. "Hunger, thirst, cold and heat; these are my new enemies," said Sal. "If I am helping anyone, they can be Black, White, Red, Brown or Yellow for all I care. How can you say I am doing a bad thing?"

Nahteste was quiet for what felt like a long moment. When he finally spoke his tone of voice was less bitter. "Yes, Sal, you are doing a good thing and I do not have the right to criticize. I have seen so much suffering among my people brought on by others that I have nearly given up hope. What you are doing helps me to realize there are things to be done even on a small scale. If we can change one child's life, who knows what they will grow up to be or how they will affect others? Keep doing what you are doing. I will try to follow your example and help others, too."

Nahteste was silent once again as he let the words sink in. Then he said to Sal, "Please leave me at the intersection of Route 90 and 80. I must get to Tombstone to sell some silver. Maybe our trails will cross again. I would like to see how your good deeds have worked out."

The men clasped hands then Nahteste got out of the car. Sal was sure the man was not out of his life for good. Driving south on Route 80 he thought to himself, "I didn't expect to have that conversation today. I bet Nahteste would not like to know the road he got out on was once called the Jefferson Davis Memorial Highway."

CHAPTER 15

NEW FRIENDS

little before reaching the tunnel through the Mule Mountains, Sal began to see steam coming from under the hood of his Pontiac. He quickly pulled over to look for water. By luck, there was a ranch house with a large water tank just over the embankment about 200 yards away. He walked up to the house and spotted a handsome gentleman sitting at an easel painting a picture of a large dead Cottonwood tree. The painter nodded at Sal as he glanced up the road to Sal's steaming radiator.

"Howdy," he nodded to Sal. "Seems like my job in life is to give out water to travelers in need." He laughed at his private joke before grabbing two watering cans. He then unscrewed the sprinkler heads from them and filled up both.

"Come on," he said to Sal. "I'll carry one for you. Let's get that car running right."

On the way to the car, the gentleman told Sal the reason he laughed was because he had lived 14 years in the Chiricahua Mountains. During his time there, he had provided water to the thirsty people who were crossing his property, heading north to the States for work.

"There's a much-used trail behind my house here that goes from Naco, Mexico up to Tucson, so I put a big old stock tank out there with a tin dipper, and ran a pipe out from my tank. Now there's always fresh, cool water for the travelers on their way north."

Sal couldn't believe his ears. This guy was doing almost the same thing that he was beginning to do. What were the chances that his Bonneville would stop in front of this ranch? Is this the spirit's work? The man introduced himself as Irv, and Sal burst out with his story.

"I can't believe it," Sal said. "I am trying to do the same kind of thing."

"Well, why not let this old car of yours rest here awhile?" asked Irv. "We can go to the house and see what my Bonnie's got put up for lunch."

Sal would never turn away a good meal, so he was happy to be treated to fried chicken, corn on the cob, and hash brown potatoes. Irv's wife, Bonnie, was also an artist, painting inside while Irv painted outside. They told Sal they had lived in Colorado for a long time, even built their own home out of logs and stone. When they wanted more isolation they ended up in the Chiricahua Mountains along Cherry Creek looking after a big, old ranch for some rich Easterners. Now they felt the need to be closer to civilization so they moved over to Bisbee. They were actually thinking about moving to Sedona next since it was a better place to sell art. There were already too many hippies in Bisbee doing their own artwork.

"I have an idea," said Sal. "If you don't mind, I would like to drop off some food and other emergency supplies at that stock tank of yours. If someone's in need there would be something in place to help them."

"Sure!" Irv and Bonnie said in unison. "We'd be glad to have you do it. In fact, just drop it off on our porch and we'll take it down there for you. A little walk would do us good."

They asked Sal where he was headed. Sal told them he was searching for more sources of supplies around Bisbee. "Then I'm headed over to Naco just to look at where so many of these immigrants are coming across," he said.

"Before you go," said Irv. "I'd like to tell you a funny story about Naco, Mexico and Naco, Arizona. There was a bit of a battle between Mexican rebels and the government Federale troops back--awhile, 1915 if I'm not

mistaken. The Mexican Federale General owned a very fancy automobile. He decided the safest place to put it would be on the American side of the border, in Naco, Arizona. So he stored it in a big, old barn there.

"To ensure a victory against the rebels, 'El Generale' hired an American pilot, Mike Latvy or Kelly or something. This General had his own plane he wanted this Mike to fly, so in this broken-down heap, the General fixed him up with four bombs to drop on the rebel stronghold. Latvy took off with his load, as onlookers from both sides of the border watched. He then flew over the rebels, but they responded to this with heavy rifle fire. Since he never expected such a quick reaction, the American pilot got so excited he couldn't get the bombs to release. All four bombs finally did let go but too little, too late. Alas, our flying ace wannabe was now dropping his bombs over Arizona territory. More precisely, he was directly over that big, old barn, and "El Generale's" grand car. He ended up blowing that barn and car into oblivion.

"When our hero saw what he had done, he just continued flying away. Can you believe that? He didn't even bother to stop for his payment. Surprise, surprise, Ha! I heard that later one of Phelp Dodge's Company's higher-ups from the Bisbee Lavender Pit Copper mine ran into the same pilot up in Alaska where he was soon to become a famous bush pilot. Interestingly enough, that occurrence was the only aerial bombing in the continental United States right up to present time."

Sal thanked Irv and Bonnie for their help, for the lunch, for their future help and for the great story. Then he bid them "Adios!" and headed for town.

As Sal turned up Brewery Gulch he saw a sign on an old warehouse that read, "Cochise Food Bank." He parked and went inside to see if anything useful could be done there. The woman that serviced the counter looked very familiar. Sal then realized it was Catherine, the wife of his drinking buddy, Sergeant Jake Billet.

Sal re-introduced himself to her, then quickly added that he had been sober over seven months. He told her he was staying at the monastery in St. David and was attending 12-Step meetings every night. He got ready to duck out in case she was still mad over the crap he pulled when he was drinking. But she kindly told him that the past was the past.

"I wish Jake would stop drinking, too," she told Sal. "Our life would be a lot better if he did."

Sal agreed. He then proceeded to explain what he was doing. After listening to what he had to say, Catherine told him the Food Bank received loads of foodstuffs, but then donations would dry up for awhile. She agreed to call the monastery if she received enough goods to share with him. As far as the water situation, though, Catherine told Sal there was a large commercial laundry operation just outside of Bisbee where they used a tremendous amount of bleach. He might be able to persuade them to wash the bottles and fill them with water. Obtaining enough water jugs was a big problem for Sal. This news made him feel elated, as well as morally supported. Catherine gave him the directions to the laundry in Warren. Afterwards, the two said their goodbyes to each other.

"Tell Jake I said hello," said Sal as he was leaving. "I guess he should be getting discharged pretty soon from Fort Huachuca." Catherine answered in the affirmative: "In a couple more months."

Sal wondered why his phone call to Jake last summer from Pennsylvania had never been returned, but he was glad Catherine was no longer mad at him. "Oh, well," he thought to himself. "It's better to give resentments than to get them, at least that's what my sponsor told me..."

CHAPTER 16

JUGS, TORTILLAS AND BLANKETS

Sal followed Catherine's directions that led him to a large, rundown stone building. There was a big sign that read, Borderland Commercial Laundry, so he parked and went inside. Once in the front entrance, a secretary greeted him. He explained his situation and why he'd like some help.

"Wait right here," she said to Sal. "I'll have to ask my boss."

When the secretary returned after a few moments she told Sal her boss wanted 20 cents each for the jugs. Sal's expression dropped and the secretary said, "You don't have any money, right?"

"You're reading my mail," Sal replied with a smile.

The secretary told Sal to follow him, and she took him in back to meet Damian Ortiz, the manager.

"Sal wants to explain what he needs the jugs for," she told her boss.

After hearing the explanation, Damian said, "Look, when my people crossed over no one helped them. Why should I extend myself to you and your 'project' now?"

Though taken aback, Sal said, "Wouldn't it be important to your folks if someone had been there to help? And by the way, is Kelly Ortiz of Kelly's

Bar in Sierra Vista a relative?"

"That's my Dad," said Damian. "Why?"

"I spent a quarter of my time with him during my two-and-a-half year stint at Fort Huachuca," explained Sal. "He always told me how proud he was of his kids. Three of them graduated from the University of Arizona at Tucson, if I remember correctly."

With that new information, Damian changed his tune. "O.K., you can have the jugs for free. Once a month we weed out all the stained, torn and worn blankets, so if you want, we can pile them up for you to take to the travelers as well."

Sal was overjoyed with this unexpected windfall and thanked both Damian and his secretary. He decided to leave before they changed their minds.

Now driving towards Naco, Sal saw a new supermarket. He pulled around back and saw a big, jovial Mexican-American supervising the unloading of an 18-wheeler. His nametag said "Juan Gonzalez, Inventory Manager." Sal introduced himself, told Juan about his newfound purpose in life then asked for some help. Juan told Sal he could get him quite a few dented and stained canned goods; maybe he could grab some ripped bags of beans and flour, too. Juan added that the store had put in a tortilla-making machine that broke about every fifth tortilla. The store manager's ego wouldn't let him rehire the two tortilla baking ladies, so the market would most likely have broken tortillas forever. If Sal would like, Juan would be happy to have them collected into a large bag and saved for him to pick up.

"Would I like it?" Sal exclaimed. "You bet! When can I start getting tortillas 'to go'?"

"Give me five minutes," said Juan. "I'll see what's up."

When they got over to the baking area, Juan showed Sal the three large drums full of cracked and broken tortillas. "Take as many as you like," Juan said to Sal. "We just dump them in the garbage for the pig farmers to haul away."

Sal was able to fit nearly half of the three drums' worth into his car, placing them around Little John, who would have his fill soon enough. Sal made arrangements to stop once a week to pick the tortilla pieces up and any other donations that might be available. He then drove down the hill, looking across the border into the Mexican state of Sonora. How lucky he was to live in this land of plenty, he thought. No wonder people unlucky enough to be born on the wrong side of the fence were willing to endure cold, heat, thirst and hunger to get to this amazing land called the U.S.A. It was so different from the Mexican side in so many ways.

Sal recalled a New Year's Eve two years earlier when he and a group of drunken soldiers drove down to Naco's red-light district. As they walked up to the Blue Moon Bar, a man came running out who was being chased by the owner waving a .45 pistol. The owner fired and displaced a sizable amount of the man's cranium. Sal and the others stopped in their tracks, quite stunned at the bloody and violent spectacle. The local Policia showed up and the shooter told them he thought the man he shot was someone else, someone who had been bothering his wife. The Policia in charge just said, "Oh, it was just a mistake. O.K. No problemo!"

The working girls of Naco must have liked the man because they constructed a stone memorial, which they paid to have built, right in front of the local Catholic chapel . Surrounded by the bars and brothels, Sal remembered how he had sat in that little chapel contemplating his own life.

Sal decided he wasn't going to cross the border today since he had Little John with him. There was no telling what would happen on the Mexican side without dinero to pay off the border guards. Instead, he drove to the Naco, Arizona side to visit the wash where two years prior he and four friends were flipped while driving a red, Vauxhall station wagon during a flash flood in the area. "So much for shortcuts, "he thought to himself now. It took a lot of old Jose Cuervo tequila to make that traumatic memory disappear.

Having had a very productive day, Sal decided to drive up Route 92 and over to the San Pedro bridge to drop off the tortillas. Tomorrow would be another day; who knew what that would bring? When he arrived at the river, it gave him a chance to soak down Little John again, who was still wearing a bit of eau de skunk.

CHAPTER 17

BIKERS

That evening's 12-Step meeting was a pretty pleasant diversion from Sal's new career. Three bikers from Camp Verde, Arizona arrived for a few days' retreat. One of them shared a saying Sal had never heard, but promised himself that he would remember. "I didn't want to be one more of the row of fools on the row of stools," he had shared. Sal chuckled over that one until he fell into an exhausted sleep that night.

Morning arrived quickly, and after Sal finished his chores with Little John, he headed to Tombstone to see what the day would bring. He walks into the Muffin and sits down at the counter, Lu brings his coffee quickly, and then glancing around, he spots Nahteste in a corner booth. Sal picks up his coffee and walks over to talk with the Apache.

"Good morning, pardner!" called Sal. "How have things gone for you in Tombstone?"

Nahteste nodded and answered, "Some good things and some bad."

'O.K. then," smiled Sal. "Tell me your story today."

"I got up here yesterday, as you know," answered Nahteste. "Got a nice price for my silver. I decided to hitch a ride back to my cabin, and just as I got out to the edge of town, standing on the side of the road, the constable pulled up. He got out of a Lincoln Town car and told me to get off the road—they didn't allow hitchin' in their town, least of all a pigtailed, welfare-abusing half-breed. I lost it and shoved him against his car, calling him a fat-ass slob and a racist pig. I figured I was about to get shot when a loud voice came from inside the car telling him to back off, that he had asked for my reaction to his racist slurs.

"Then the mayor of Tombstone stepped out of the vehicle. He told me to walk away and not hitch in their town again. So, I decided I'd get a cheap room for the night, which is why I'm still in this town. I'd say my trip was 50-50, good and bad. As long as I have some loot in my pocket let me buy you a big breakfast."

Sal wholeheartedly accepted and said, "I love the Muffin café." He waived Lu over and introduced her to his new amigo. He decided to tell his breakfast benefactor that things could be worse.

"When Sheriff John Slaughter of Tombstone went out after bad guys, he rarely brought back anyone alive," said Sal. "Luckily, that man's long gone, because he wouldn't stand for any of that hitchhikin' stuff in his county."

"Yeah," said Nahteste. "I'd like to have seen Constable Lardo hassling Geronimo. Actually, that reminds me of something. If the American government really wanted to put a stop to the drug traffic over the border from Mexico, why don't they go up to San Carlos Reservation and deputize a group of Apaches from there? Turn them loose with a few horses, surplus jeeps and radios and those drug dealers would quit coming into Arizona. Hell, I'd sign up myself, just for the fun of it. We'd all get some pride back along with putting a dent into what's killing our young people."

Nahteste thought for a moment before continuing. "Drugs and gangs," he said. "I hate to keep singing the same song but the white man sure brought us a lot of nasty stuff to deal with."

Sal stayed quiet and let the words sink in. "This could be a very good idea," he thought, but he wondered whom to approach to get help with drug addiction among the Apaches. There could be a coalition of the Yuma, Papago, Pima, Apache and Yaqui Native Americans on both sides of the border. It would be a formidable group if it were organized properly. Probably never happen, though; not enough opportunity for bureaucracy.

Sal told Nahteste he would give him a ride home so he didn't have to risk another confrontation with Tombstone's finest. When they got in the car, Nahteste said, "Whoa, it smells like the constable back there."

· As they headed south, Sal asked Nahteste if he was serious about stopping drug dealers.

"One hundred percent serious," Nahteste answered. "I'd do whatever I could without ending up in jail myself. Any ideas?"

"Yeah," nodded Sal. "Let me run this by you. I know a deputy that would probably be interested in some extra arrests under his belt. Could you bring a few buddies into this adventure?"

"I have two nephews staying at my place," said Nahteste. "They beat up a couple of truckers who were hassling them at the Safford Diner where they wash dishes. Can't go back home for a while, but they need something constructive to do down here. I know they'd be up for anything to stay busy."

Nahteste added that over the years the Mexican government would send their captured banditos up to the northern border to serve as soldiers to get them away from more "genteel" citizens. He asked Sal if he ever considered what the southwestern U.S.A. would be like if the Apaches hadn't kept the population of the Chihuahua and Sonora areas so slight.

"It'd probably still be part of Mexico," said Sal. "Maybe California would too. You sure can come up with some good stuff for me to ponder, dude. So, where do I drive you to? I know you said Route 92 toward Naco, but where's your cabin?"

"About ten more miles," Nahteste said. As they passed the turn off to the infamous Miller Peak Road, he said, "You know, Sal, we are now passing through Miracle Valley where they filmed parts of the movie, 'Oklahoma.' It looked more like Oklahoma here than there. They also filmed the movie 'Red River Valley,' which was actually set in Texas, about three miles from here."

Nahteste instructed Sal to take a right turn after Palominos, and they ended up at an old wood cabin on a little hill overlooking the San Pedro. "Let me tell the boys you're here," he said as he got out of the car. "I need the boys to see me; I wouldn't want you getting scalped or worse."

Nahteste winked, but Sal was sure that this little hilltop could be dangerous for someone who didn't belong there. Nahteste came back after a few minutes and indicated no one was around. Sal nodded his O.K."I need to get back to St. David anyway and follow up on a few things," he told Nahteste. "Think about what I said and I'll stop by in a few days to see what we can come up with together.

CHAPTER 18

VIGILANTES

When Sal arrived back at the monastery, the three bikers were still there. Everyone had dinner together, and afterwards there was an open AA meeting with some interesting sharing. Two of the bikers and one affluent visitor shared they had been addicted to heroin. Sal had never spoken to anyone who had been on heroin before, so he asked if they could talk together after the meeting.

The bikers, Sal and the visitor grabbed some coffee and leftover cake then started talking. They told him how horrible it was to be strung out, living their lives just for the next fix. Sal realized how much worse it was to be under the spell of heroin than booze. The bikers told Sal they wanted to help others hooked on heroin now that they were clean, so Sal asked them what they were going to do to help.

"I lived in upstate New York for a while in a college town," said the visitor. "I was friends with a bunch of hippie-commune guys who sold marijuana along with working various odd jobs. If someone came to town hooking college students and younger kids on heroin these commune guys would warn them the first time they caught them at it. If he continued to deal heroin they would beat him up. The third time, they would kill him, burying his body under rocks in the river. Word got out and no one was selling heroin anymore in their town."

"Could we meet tomorrow morning and talk?" asked Sal. "I have an idea."

The next day after breakfast they all walked down to the river with Little John leading the way. Two of the bikers had been soldiers discharged just in the past year. They were planning on hooking up with a couple of army buddies that were living in Sierra Vista by Fort Huachuca. Sal asked if he could accompany them to explore an idea he had. They agreed, and after leaving Little John in Brother Alex's room, they all went together in Sal's car.

When they got to Sierra Vista, the bikers said they were to meet their friends in the American Legion Hall. Once they entered the hall and sat down, they had some real coffee. Sal got comfortable with the men he was introduced to. They said they were part of a group of retired soldiers called "Idle Warriors" looking for action to stay busy. Sal told them about Nahteste's idea and wondered if somehow they could work together to stop some of the drugs getting into America from across the Mexican border. The "Idle Warriors" figured it could be a good way to put to use all their military training. With that, Sal said he would arrange a meeting between them and Nahteste so they could do some planning.

Sal left the bikers and drove the 15 or so miles to Nahteste's cabin. When he was about to get out of his car, a young man walked up to him and stared. Sal admitted later he was pretty scared at the sight of a six-foot, six-inch Apache warrior with a shotgun motioning for him to stay in his car. Sal quickly explained that he was Nahteste's friend and just wanted to talk with him. He was then led inside to where Nahteste lay sleeping. As they woke him up, Nahteste laughed and said, "Well, White man, do you think my nephew could scare those drug mules back across the border?"

"Absolutely," Sal said without hesitation.

Sal and Nahteste drove back to Sierra Vista to meet with the other soldiers. The Idle Warriors told him how they set up sandbags on top of their trailers to use as gun implacements to protect their homes, families and cars from the drug mules crossing the border. Nahteste laughed out loud at their ingenuity.

"Me and my nephews used to hide in the trees and step out in the dark with guns scaring those guys so they would drop their loads and run back south," said Nahteste.

"I think you guys could work out a good program," said Sal. "I have enough to do with what's on my plate and I'd like to get back to St. David. I'll leave you guys to work out whatever you want to do together."

"Great," one of the ex-soldiers said. "We'll talk awhile then give Nahteste and whoever else needs a ride back to wherever."

Sal headed to the monastery to take Little John out for a walk before he made a mess in Brother Alex's room. That night when he bumped into the bikers, they just winked at him and smiled. Sal smiled back, thinking he had enough to do saving the poor souls he was feeding; he didn't need to know anything about what these guys had planned. One of the bikers, named Jersey, had given Sal a big cigar, which he later took down to the river to enjoy. As he puffed away, Little John splashed in the water. "So ends another exciting day," Sal thought to himself. "This is the new 'Life of Sal.'"

When Sal got back to the monastery, he scrounged up some wood, borrowed some tools and had Brother Amos help him build a drop-off box for the gas station. That afternoon, he filled 30 jugs with water, put the box in his trunk and headed over to Bud's Texaco. Then he drove past the Immigration Service check point and placed the jugs in the desert not far off the road. This was the path that travelers used to keep from getting lost. Upon his return, he left Little John in Brother Alex's room again, went to eat, then return to his room to retrieve his four-legged buddy for his evening walk.

CHAPTER 19

JUSTICE

The next morning, Sal went to the Muffin Café for some coffee, but especially for Lu's sunshiny smile. "When you're done, pull around back and load up again," she told Sal. "And by the way, the witch got caught pocketing all the tip money so I was allowed to fire her."

Sal and Lu had a good chuckle and Sal said, "I thought you cleaned the windows, it felt so much brighter in here."

Once Sal loaded the goodies into his car, he was off to the bridge to drop off his booty. After that, he headed to Bisbee and the commercial laundry where he picked up 45 one-gallon jugs already filled with water. He took those near Douglas and placed them under trees. On the way back, Sal stopped at the supermarket and picked up two large bags of tortillas and 30 dented cans of assorted vegetables. Juan even gave him several can openers, which he said, "fell off the truck." Sal took all these supplies back to the bridge then returned to St. David.

"I'm starting to feel like a route salesman," he mumbled to himself. Whenever Sal turned off Route 80 onto the monastery's driveway he felt like someone was staring right through him; even the hair on the back of his neck felt like it was rising up.

Opening the door to Brother Alex's room, Sal was met by an odor he couldn't believe—dog poop and skunk. He realized he was taking too long to get back and now was paying the price. Sal headed over to the kitchen for a bucket, hot water, a mop and some vinegar so he could quickly pay his penance. But first, he took Little John for a walk. He couldn't believe what he saw when the big pooch let loose another cowpie-sized pile. "I am definitely feeding this mutt way too much," Sal said to himself out loud. "From now on it's doggie diet time for the canine brother."

At that evening's 12-Step meeting, the bikers and visitor friend were absent. Sal thought, "That's a funny thought I just had: abstinence makes the heart grow fonder. Never heard that in the rooms."

It had been a long day so Sal fell asleep as soon as his head hit the pillow. But in the morning, Sal was awakened by a low growl and a tapping on the door just as the sun announced its arrival. Groggily, Sal answered the door, putting his boxer-shorted butt between Little John and whoever was knocking. To his surprise, there stood the three bikers, two ex-soldiers and their new buddy, Nahteste, grinning and laughing.

"C'mon man; we need to talk about last night," they told Sal.

"Let me get dressed," he answered. "I need to walk Little John, so I'll meet you at the Benson Truck Stop for some high-octane coffee. I can't even listen until I get some caffeine in me."

Forty-five minutes later, Sal pulled into the Truck Stop right next to the shade of an 18-wheeler. The giggling bikers were sitting in a booth in the back of the restaurant. Sal was anxious to hear their story, especially since it was an unusual sight to see these big and bad dudes giggling at anything.

With two carafes of coffee already on the table, Sal helped himself to a cup then said, "O.K., spill it before you guys wet your pants."

Jersey, the biggest biker started the tale. "Well, after meeting with Nahteste and some of the Idle Warrior guys we headed down in three cars to meet his nephews. Wow! They're big! We now have a vigilante group of 12 men, all ready to play hardball. Everyone's armed, from 1911 Colt .45's to pump shotguns, even one old M1 Garand rifle!"

Sergeant Mike, one of the founders of the Warriors who had become the accepted leader of the band, then took over the story. "As long as we were all together and down close to the drug trails, I said why don't we go out and see if we can do a practice run? Everyone agreed and Nahteste told us there was a path through Montezuma's Pass, where Coronado first came in the 1500s into what is now Arizona. He was sure the drug smugglers used that trail to connect up with the vans and cars at the trailhead to transport the stuff to Tucson and Phoenix. So if we hung out kind of unseen along there, he thought we could have a little fun at the banditos' expense.

"We headed out on foot since it was only a mile and a half from Nahteste's place. I placed my troops along the trail and in the trees. We weren't going to shoot first since we didn't want to draw any attention to ourselves until we get a little more settled on our plans. But we're still planning on teaching these guys a lesson so they don't come through here anymore.

"Just as the moon started to come up, we heard cursing and laughing men coming up the trail from the border. We're trained fighters so we can't believe how noisy they're being."

Unbeknownst to Sergeant Mike, two of the tough clowns of his squad—Nick and Don—had plans of their own. Nick let the group of seven men walk past him, loaded with bundles on their backs. Then Don stepped out into the path in front of them with his shotgun pointed at the group. The smugglers crashed into each other and started falling over themselves in sudden fear.

"I told them the path was now closed," said Don with a smirk. "And I don't want to shoot them but if they drop their packs and head back to Mexico I'll let them live. This time."

Meanwhile, Nick had snuck up close behind them with half-a-dozen, cherry-bomb-like, M-80's fused together. The lead smuggler spoke English and told Don there was no way they were going to drop their load.

"You'll only get one shot off," said Don as the others started to spread out. "Besides, if we go back without our load our bosses will shoot US."

The jefe started to pull out his pistola just as Nick lit the fuse on the fire crackers. Don jumped behind a huge Oak tree just as the M-80's exploded. The banditos thought they were all about to be executed so they dropped their packs and bolted back down the trail. They left heroin plus a very nasty smell behind.

Sergeant Mike came running down the trail to see Don and Nick hugging each other in appreciation. "What the hell kind of gun was that?" he growled to his men. "And I thought I said there'd be no shooting. What's going on?"

The two clowns stopped laughing long enough to explain to the Sergeant what they had done. They had to go over the story a few more times as all the Idle Warriors came into a huddle. Everyone agreed it was a dangerous stunt, but nevertheless it was funny as hell.

Sal chuckled softly as he heard the men recount their story. They continued celebrating until Nahteste's nephews asked the obvious: "What do we do with the drugs?"

"This stopped all the fun," said Jersey. "There had to be more than $100,000 worth of heroin there. This about broke up the group on our first picnic 'cause some of us wanted to burn it and some—if the truth be told —thought it'd be a shame to waste it."

Luckily, Sergeant Mike had plenty of experience dealing with groups of men. "I told them to pick it up and get off the trail before we had a firefight that wasn't of our own making," he said. "No telling if the smugglers had reinforcements across the border. We started out, leaving an obvious trail up towards the trailhead, and then we split up, backtracked and slipped over to Nahteste's place. Once we all gathered there, we piled all the packs on the ground."

Sergeant Mike remarked at that point that Tattoo noticed the rich visitor from the monastery was missing. Two soldiers went back to look for him, but 45 minutes later they returned empty handed. Not one to leave any man behind, Sergeant Mike took half a dozen men and spent the next two hours searching the area.

The soldiers went to the trailhead where two vans were parked. What seemed to be a very agitated older guy was just standing there looking into space. When the drivers of the two vans saw the soldiers in camouflage walking up, they took off in a hurry. But the old man was hopping mad.

"I can't believe someone stole my old jeep," he complained to the soldiers. "It wasn't that great anymore, 'cause the steering and brakes were shot but it's all I had to come out here to hike. I always try to get off the mountain while it's still light, but I found some old ruins and forgot the time. When I got back here, my jeep was gone. Leaving the key under the mat wasn't very smart but I didn't want to lose that one key on the trail and get stuck out here." The old fellow told the soldiers he only lived about three miles away at the religious community in the valley by Hereford, so he figured he could just walk home at this point. He wasn't sure why he even used the jeep, come to think of it.

The soldiers decided to leave before the old guy started asking them questions. Sergeant Mike and the other Warriors began to think their rich visitor must have seen the profit in the pack he was carrying and decided to go another route.

'We still had six heavy packs with drugs in them," said the Sgt. "Losing that much heroin would give the smugglers something to think about. So we all agreed that burning the drugs was the right thing to do—no matter how sad the Biker Boys looked."

Nahteste had a large burn barrel he used for trash so they got it going hot and threw the heroin into the flames—backpacks and all. Standing out of the breeze they all watched way more than a $100,000 worth of drugs go up in smoke. That heroin would have screwed up many a young person's life just so some greedy dealer could profit. Agreeing it was a good night's work, the soldiers and bikers went to the American Legion Hall for a late dinner. Then the bikers were able to get a ride back to the monastery from one of their friends where they found the old man's jeep parked and the rich visitor's car gone.

"That's one of the finest adventures I've ever heard," said Sal. "It has it all—humor, violence, danger, larceny and a moral: Don't Deal Drugs."

Again, they all laughed until they almost wet themselves, eventually getting curious stares from the truckers sitting around them. But the truckers could see how tough the bikers looked so they left them alone. As they started to leave, a waitress carrying a tray suddenly knocked Sal in the back. He looked up and couldn't believe his eyes or ears, as he saw the witch cursing at him for getting in her way—one more time. But this time, Sal was ready for her. He bent down and picked up a plate as he falsely apologized, making sure the manager was watching. Then he whispered in her ear as she came closer, "What?" yelled Sal. "Fifty dollars for a quickie in your car? Are you crazy? You aren't worth that!"

The manager quickly came over and told the witch to clear out. "I knew you were trouble when you first came here from Tombstone," he said angrily.

"I'm sorry for all the trouble" said Sal to the manager. And with that he left, as one of the bikers paid the bill. Together, they left for St. David, satisfied that the good guys were ahead, for now, on all fronts.

CHAPTER 20

RESCUE

S al drove back to the monk house and as he drove, he started thinking that he had never known there was so much fun to be had in
Cochise County. He had been stuck for two and a half years under
Sargeant Washington's thumb at Fort Huachuca, but all that had
changed now. It looked as if his life would be full of adventure from here
on out.

Just as Sal rounded the curve that would bring him to the bridge, he
noticed a big skid mark that wasn't there when he had headed up to Benson. He saw steam or smoke coming from below the bridge, so he pulled
over to investigate. He saw a car flipped on its side in the deepest part of
the river. Realizing someone must still be inside the car, he ran down the
embankment. The water was only 18 to 24 inches deep in the water hole
the car had settled in, so Sal was able to get onto the car and get the door
open. He held it ajar with his shoulder as he reached in to help an elderly
woman who was hanging by her waist from the safety belt, unconscious.
Sal leaned deeply into the passenger side to unhook her.

Fortunately, there was only steam coming from the engine so there
was no danger of an explosion. Sal took his time so he could carefully ease
the small woman past the steering column and up to his shoulder. He
carried her out of the car and water then gently laid her under one of the

nearby Sycamore trees. She had quite a lump on her forehead from the crash, so Sal was worried about what he should do. Just then, he heard a shout from the bridge. A passerby asked if they needed any help. Sal told the passerby to call an ambulance.

Sal took off his shirt and dipped it into the river to put on the elderly woman's head. About 20 minutes later, Sal could hear sirens approaching, and the woman started regaining consciousness.

"Be still now," said Sal so the woman wouldn't try to get up. "Help is close by."

The old lady looked at him in wonder and said, "Are you an angel?"

"No," smiled Sal. "No, far from it; just happened to be in the right place at the right time."

The woman smiled a little as the paramedics climbed down to her side. They loaded her on a stretcher and carried her up to the ambulance. Sal walked alongside her stretcher to see if she wanted help taking care of her car.

"Please do," the woman answered. "And what is your name, young man?"

"Salvadore Dusi," he answered. "I'm staying at the monastery in St. David."

"See," she said. "Angel or monk—close to the same thing."

The ambulance then left the scene while Sal stood there wondering what he should do next. He wasn't sure how to take care of a car that was half submerged in water. So with a shrug, he headed for his buddy's Texaco station. Bud owned an old wrecker that he kept out behind the station. He told Sal that if Sal helped, they could get the car out of the river now. Sal agreed so the two headed out to the bridge.

Sal could tell Bud really knew his stuff; he had the car out of the water within a half hour. It was back on its wheels and up the embankment where they could haul it to the station. As they did so, Sal made sure he gave a big bowl of water to Little John, who had been very patient waiting and watching all the human goings-on.

At the station, Sal removed 12 cans, a box of donuts, and two bags of potato chips out of the donation box and headed back to the monastery. Once back, he decided he better sit down for a couple of hours and think through everything that had happened—his life was getting very busy.

He took a tablet from the reading room out to the bench by the pond and sat down to write in two columns: What do I have? What do I need? He was happy to note that he was getting more and more food, and plenty of water, so that left the problem of delivery. Under the 'Needs' column he listed a bigger vehicle. This would maximize his ability to deliver more food to more people. But then he briefly admonished himself not to become too grandiose; he needed to stick with what he could accomplish.

Thinking about what route people take to get to Tucson, Sal pinpointed where it may be the driest terrain, which was out past Huachuca City and Sonoita. He took 20 jugs from the kitchen shed and filled them with water. He packed the stuff he picked up from the Texaco station's donation box, plus what cook at the monastery gave him. He had an additional six loaves of bread and three pounds of sliced American cheese as well. Sal laughed to himself, thinking the first American thing these people would be getting was American cheese.

After loading up his car, Sal and Little John set out for Route 82 and what's jokingly called Rain Valley. He knew canned goods, bread and cheese would help the travelers as they walked parallel to Route 82 over to Route 83 toward Tucson. This path would put them through the Empire Ranch and mountains.

Well, thought Sal, since I'm over here I might as well check on Sally and her great pies. Once he had dropped off his manna from Sal, he drove down to Sonoita to thank her for her kindness in listening to him when he was so freaked out about his Miller Peak experience. It was hard to believe it had only been eight days since that event.

At one point Sal realized he was driving too far to drop off his goodies, but then he remembered an old railroad track he had crossed through Fairbanks on Route 82. He figured that track was probably used as a path by the travelers. It could also be the western boundary for his drop offs. He could then make Gleeson his eastern boundary, half way to Douglas from Bisbee could be the southernmost drop and his main drop off point would be under the bridge at the San Pedro. Having made his first real command decision, he happily pulled into Sally's pie place with great anticipation.

Sally came right over to Sal's table, smiling brightly at his appearance. "Well, who is chasing you today?" she asked teasingly.

Sal looked into her eyes wondering how much she actually knew.

"Deputy Larry was in here two hours ago," she continued. "And he told me a lot about what's been happening with you."

Sal shrugged a bit sheepishly and decided not to tell old Larry about the Idle Warriors deal. He couldn't be trusted to keep his mouth shut. Sally put a cup of coffee down in front of Sal along with a fresh slice of peach pie she said had just been taken out of the oven.

"I'm buying," she winked at him. "I love the stories about you."

"Thank you," said Sal but he thought to himself , "You don't know the half of it." After finishing his coffee and pie, Sal thanked her again, then remembering that Little John was waiting in the vehicle, asked for a bowl of water.

CHAPTER 21

THE FORT

As he left the café, Sal decided to stop at the Fort Huachuca Post Commissary to see if he could score some canned goods and other items. He also wanted to see Chaplin Cliff, whom he had had a few good conversations with when he was still a soldier stationed at the Fort.

At the Commissary, Sal found the assistant manager, Don Gleeson, who had also been stationed at the Fort a while back. Upon discharge he decided to apply for a permanent job in the Commissary. Sal explained what he was doing and to his delight, Don wanted in.

"Sure," Don said. "I get a lot of damaged goods. It'll save me from having to run it to the dump. Pull up to the dock in back and I will load you up."

Sal couldn't believe how much Don was able to give him. He couldn't fit it all into his car even though he filled the trunk and the front passenger seat. Little John was taking up the entire back seat so Sal promised Don he would come back within the week for the rest. He bid him "Adios" then headed for the Chaplin's office.

Fortunately, Sal lucked out seeing that the chaplain was in his front yard raking the gravel in the driveway. He re-introduced himself and explained to the chaplain what he had been doing.

"What do you think, Chaplain?" asked Sal. "Do you agree or not?"

"Sal, you are doing God's work," replied the Chaplain. "When Jesus and his followers traveled their road they depended on the generosity of others to support them. Is there anything I can do to help?"

"I seem to be getting enough food products," said Sal. "But delivery is becoming a problem."

"Let's go sit on the patio and have some lemonade," he smiled at Sal. "We can talk about it there."

The two men conversed about the base and all its problems with drinking. The soldiers felt a lot of guilt for going to the red light sectors in Mexico, followed by the car accidents while driving back drunk. An additional problem was how to keep the wives' of the deployed soldiers busy, so they didn't get themselves into trouble with the single men on the base.

"Maybe I could try organizing some of them to assist you in your endeavors," mulled the Chaplain.

"That is an excellent idea," said Sal. "How soon could you meet with them to work something out?"

"If you give me a number where I can reach you, I'll speak to a few of them to see if they are up for helping you with the deliveries," he answered.

Sal gave the chaplain the number at the monastery and bid him goodbye. He then went over to see if Sargeant Kyle Kinney was around. To his dismay, the sergeant was out on the range testing some new equipment.

CHAPTER 22
THE ATTORNEY

D riving out the main gate, Sal stopped at Kelly's Bar to say hello and tell him how much his son was helping him. Kelly didn't seem too interested, but he said just the same, "Good to lay eyes on you; didn't think I would ever see you again—at least not sober."

Sal left Kelly cleaning up his bar, and thought, "Oh yeah; I know I was a problem drinker and usually wasted half my paycheck in here getting that way. I wonder if that's where the saying 'wasted' came from."

As long as he was in the area, Sal decided to drop all his goodies at the bridge on Route 90 before heading home. When he got to the bridge he blew his horn. Two travelers peered out from the trees and he waved them over. When they approached, Sal explained what he was doing.

"Travelers before us left a small sign," said one of the men. "It said to look under the bridge for supplies. We are happy to meet the man helping us out."

"I'm sorry for not having can openers," Sal said.

"It's O.K.," they replied. "We have knives to open the cans."

The Pontiac was now empty except for Little John and Sal, so Sal decided to head to Tombstone for a good lunch. He arrived in the town too tough to die and parked in the shade before heading to the Muffin Café.

Noting there were no police vehicles out front, Sal sat at the counter to catch one of Lu's smiles.

Lu came right over and asked Sal if he was ready for the day's special. "We're offering a big plate of leftovers," said Lu. "And it's on the house."

"I'm in total agreement with free," said Sal. He proceeded to tell her about his encounter with the witch. She laughed so hard the other patrons in the café were beginning to stare at them both. Luckily, the owner wasn't around to give them the evil eye.

"I don't have anything for you to pick up today," said Lu. "But you could go over to the Bird Cage because my boyfriend has been saving some food items for you."

After Sal finished his lunch, he pulled behind the Bird Cage and knocked on the back door. Terry, Lu's friend, came out and told Sal to hang on because he had a couple of boxes of food for him to take. As Sal watched the goodies being loaded into his car, he thought, "Wow, this is getting to be a community project I've started."

Sal thanked Terry for the donations and headed back to St. David. He was very pleased with himself for the way things were turning out. That lady spirit must be happy that she appeared to him by the river, jolting him into action. Sal was now sure that helping others was a lot more satisfying than sitting around drinking and being no good to anyone—especially himself.

Sal stopped momentarily at the Texaco station to say "Hi!" to Bud. It turned out he had some interesting information to pass on: "That old lady that crashdrove her car into the river, her attorney from Tucson was in to see about the car's condition," said Bud. "He said I was easy to find since I am the only garage around St. David. He said he would pay me to fix up the car as best I could and to call when it was ready to be driven back to Tucson. I agreed and before he left he gave me his card to give to you whenever I saw you. He wants you to call him."

In his drinking days, this sort of information would have frightened Sal, not knowing if he had done something stupid in a blackout that would get him into trouble. But now he knew he was O.K. since he was sober. He felt completely comfortable calling the attorney.

Once back at the monk house, Sal took Little John for a walk and shovel detail before putting him back into Brother Alex's room. Then he headed over to the office to get permission to use the phone. When he called the lawyer, the man told him his client, Mrs. Crane of the chewing gum company, wanted to meet him so she could thank him in person. Their meeting could take place at the attorney's office. Sal agreed after the lawyer told him Mrs. Crane and he would pay for a tank of gas to make the trip, so Salvadore made the appointment for the following day, got directions and hung up.

"Wowee," thought Sal to himself, "a simple thank you over the phone would have been fine, but it can't hurt to have a friend on your side that's rich. I'm just glad she's not the reason for another white cross on the side of the road."

As long as he had permission to use the phone, Sal decided he would call home to Pennsylvania to see how his folks were doing. He had to call collect. But when his mom answered, agreeing to accept the charges, she was obviously overjoyed to hear from him. Sal thought it was good to hear her voice as well. She told him that everyone was doing well; both Dad and brother were working hard. Sal told her he found work, but he needed to explain it in a letter, which he swore he would write soon. After Sal hung up the phone, he grabbed a tablet and walked over to the pond to write his mother a long letter. There was a lot to tell her about his "borderland," good-deed adventures.

That evening's AA meeting was only so-so, but there were a lot of new visitors to meet. When the meeting ended, Sal hit the sack.

CHAPTER 23

TUCSON MEETING

The next morning, Sal satisfied himself with a big breakfast then figured it was time to head to Tucson to see what this appointment with Mrs. Crane would bring into his life. First he walked Little John, but left him in Brother Alex's room with a big ham bone and an even bigger bowl of water, not bringing him along for the ride. Once he arrived at the attorney's, he was escorted into a large conference room where the lawyer, Mrs. Crane, and most importantly, a big carafe of real coffee awaited him. Mrs. Crane had a big bandage on her forehead, but she told Sal the doctor said she would be fine.

"I'll probably have headaches for awhile," she said. At that point, the attorney shook Sal's hand and thanked him for his heroics. They passed a little time with some small talk until they became more comfortable with one another.

"I'd like you to tell me a little bit about yourself," said Mrs. Crane. "What are you doing with your life?"

Sal hesitated a moment while wondering how much information he should share. He knew this was a very prominent attorney. Sal intuitively knew he might get into trouble for helping illegal aliens, so he asked, "Is what I tell you going to be confidential?"

"It will be if you give me one dollar," replied the attorney.

"Why? What for?" asked Sal, a little stunned.

"Once you put me under retainer, the attorney/client privilege is invoked," he replied. "Then you can say anything to me and I cannot repeat it, even in court."

"Do you want to know everything I have been involved in?" asked Sal as he slapped a dollar on the table.

"Most definitely," they replied. "There is a good reason for this."

Sal proceeded to explain everything that had happened since he had returned from Pennsylvania. When he finished, Mrs. Crane asked her attorney if he would please have his secretary take Sal to lunch for an hour so they could speak privately. Though Sal was starting to wonder what he had gotten himself into, he relaxed when a very pretty woman approximately his age walked into the conference room. They instructed her to take Sal to a nice restaurant but to return in one hour.

Sal was quite taken with the secretary, whose name was Mary. She told him she was working full time for the law office while she was in law school at the University of Arizona. After a wonderful meal, the hour was up, so they walked back to the office. Mary then escorted Mr. Salvadore Dusi back to the conference room. The attorney, Mr. Mayhew, and Mrs. Crane were smiling broadly. They asked Sal to be seated so they could talk with him about something very important.

"Mrs. Crane feels very indebted to you, Sal," explained Mr. Mayhew. "After listening to your tale, she would like to extend an offer to you."

"I was born into money, son," Mrs. Crane took over the conversation. "And I have felt guilty for living the good life without accomplishing much beyond the junior league sponsorship I have. You have done more in a short time, starting with $37 in your pocket than I have in my whole life with millions in a trust fund. I feel you were placed in my life to give me an opportunity to do some good, too.

"If you would be so kind, please explain to me what you'd do if you had whatever money you needed to accomplish your goals as they present themselves, to expand them to bring more joy to people. If you could relieve the hardships of more people out there that are having a tough time, what would you do?"

Dumbstruck, Sal was unable to voice his opinion. Both the attorney and Mrs. Crane laughed and apologized for making Sal speechless. "It is not our intention to put you on the spot," they said. "It's just that it's a marvelous opportunity for much good to be accomplished. No one will ever get hurt, only helped."

"Can I have a couple of hours to collect my thoughts?" asked Sal. They then agreed to meet back in the conference room at 3 p.m. to discuss the offer further.

Sal walked out of the room and stopped long enough to thank Mary for the great lunch, and to ask if there was some place he could go to sit and think. Mary told him there was a park one block past the restaurant where they ate lunch. Sal promised to be back at 3 p.m. then walked to the park in a daze. He found a bench and thought to himself, "Jumpin' Jehoziphat! Who could have seen this coming? I thought with my military training I was coming back to Arizona to be a telephone lineman or something similar."

When the time drew nigh, Sal returned to the law office where he let Mary escort him back to the conference room. A third gentleman had joined the party, who happened to be a banker from Valley National in Tucson.

Mrs. Crane, attorney Mayhew and Rob Weaver, the banker, sat awaiting Sal's ideas.

"There is a great need not only for the border travelers' plight but also for the Apache Indians, still on reservations, who just sit idly accomplishing nothing meaningful day-in and day-out," said Sal. "I would love to help them all. If I had the financial support, along with your guidance, I could find a way to do just that. I have talked with several of the travelers who have told me they would prefer to stay in Mexico, but there is no work available to them. They say it's very frightening to leave home and sneak into America with their families just to survive."

"Sal, would you be willing to come back after you have had time to think about what it would take to accomplish some of your ideas," asked Mrs. Crane. "We could also think about how we could help, not just financially."

"Of course," replied Sal. "Anytime."

"If you can return next week, we can have some thoughts on programs we would like to fund," said Mr. Mayhew. "And you can also tell us what you would like to do first."

With that, Mr. Mayhew handed Sal a check for $300. It was to cover car expenses; he could deposit the check in Mr. Weaver's bank, which was two blocks from the office. Once again, Sal was dumbstruck. He watched silently as the attorney instructed Mary to walk Sal over to the bank to assist him in opening an account.

As they walked together, Mary struck up a conversation. "They really seem to like you," she said. "They told me they intended on helping you accomplish some dreams."

"I can't believe what's happening," he replied. "There's been a lot going on the last few weeks." Sal proceeded to fill her in as they went into the bank to open an account. Sal deposited the check but kept $50 to cover his gas and some food. As they walked back to Sal's car, Mary handed him a piece of paper with her phone number written on it.

"Call me anytime if you have questions or just want to talk," she told him.

Sal thanked her and drove away, musing that he didn't need the car to get back to St. David; he could float back. Sal decided he better not tell anyone of his good fortune. He thought he'd do a lot of thinking about things first, so he didn't disappoint Mrs. Crane and her adviser.

CHAPTER 24

BYE BIKERS

‡——‡——‡——‡——‡

O nce back at the monastery, Sal took Little John for a walk by
the river and sat down for a" skull session." Knowing there were
so many things he could do to help people as long as he had
the backing, he had to plan carefully so he didn't blow it like
he had everything else in his life. A long time ago he had been offered a
chance to enter the Officer's Candidate School in the Army, but he decided at the last minute to throw the opportunity away. He had never been
able to deal with the discipline it took to improve himself. Now he had a
chance to do good and become a man his family could be proud of instead
of someone they were glad to see go away.

Sal realized that he was sitting under the very same Sycamore tree
where he had had the vision that set him on this journey. He wondered
where it all would lead. He knew he was doing what the spirit woman
wanted, helping his fellow man along his path. But who knew that it
would be such a wonder-filled trail? He had told himself before: when you
help others in need you help yourself.

As Sal pondered these thoughts a plan started to formulate in his
mind. He gathered up Little John, and realized that was a lot of gathering,
he laughed and headed back to the monk house for a well-cooked and
delicious dinner.

That evening at the 12-Step meeting the three bikers appeared, looking very pleased with themselves. Sal decided he better not mention these guys' program to anyone, including Attorney Mayhew, a representative of the law. After the meeting, he and the bikers went over to the pond to discuss their activities. Sal's biker buddies proceeded to tell him yet another great story.

"We've become pretty tight with the Idle Warriors as well as the three Apaches," they told him. "We planned out a couple of strategies to intercept the drug mules. We found and ambushed two different groups not far from the boundary line, getting them to drop their packs and run back to the border."

They did all that without firing a shot, but learning from their first experience, they used the power of the M-80s to startle and disperse their quarry. One of the ex-soldiers still had good contacts on the base, which meant he had access to some new weapons called "Flash-Bangs," a type of grenade being tested that was more effective than M-80s fused together.

"We found we only needed one per interception," they told Sal. "It was enough to achieve the objective of scaring the hell out of the drug mules, get them to drop their packs and high tail it back where they came from."

Sal told them that since he wasn't part of their group, he would rather not know about their modus operandi. He was committed to helping people, not scaring 20 years off their lives. This led to a heated discussion about Sal not being in the right mind when it came down to dealing with these wetbacks.

"I guess I'm not," Sal defended himself. "I'm trying to help these people on their way to a better life. I just want to make sure they've got wet throats."

"Every load of heroin we burn saves the lives of many college kids," he was told. "It saves inner-city minorities as well as regular folks from having to go through the hell that we've experienced from using the narcotic since it was so easy to get."

'I agree that what you're doing is a good thing no matter how bizarre," admitted Sal. "I just don't want to be involved. It's better I don't know any more than I already do." They all agreed with Sal, shook hands, wished each other good luck and told Sal they would be gone in the morning.

"Hey Jersey, before you go tell me how you came out here to Arizona. I've wondered about you because I ended up out here too. "Sure Sal, I was in college, University of Maryland, actually, having a blast: fraternity, parties etc. I worked the summer between classes as a bouncer in Washington, D.C. A beer truck driver asked if he could leave his rig parked for the weekend in the back of the bar's parking lot; I said sure but leave the keys in case I need to move it. That night two buddies and I drove it up to the campus, where we made a big sign saying '$5.00 Per case of beer.' We sold out in less than two hours. As you can imagine there were repercussions. Ha! That was the end of my big college career. I hit the road on my Harley-Davidson, which I was able to buy with the money earned from the beer sales. Ended up in Arizona, hooked up with my two road-riding brothers here and never looked back.

Sal headed to bed, thinking how blessed he was to be smack in the middle of some great adventures. He laughed to himself thinking that there must be millions of crazy stories out there in this wide-wide world. Looked like he was living in a crazy, kooky "story" himself, but he was lovin' it.

CHAPTER 25

THE WIVES

W aking up refreshed and ready for another exciting day, Sal took Little John for his morning constitutional, otherwise known as "one big shovel load." He went up to the dining hall and had himself a great breakfast. He saw Brother Casper, the acting manager and director of the monastery, and walked over to him to ask if he should pay for his room and board now that he had a little money in his pocket.

"That's not necessary," said Brother Casper. "Brother Alex eats more than you so right now we are ahead. But when you leave, please notice the contribution box by our Reading Room."

Sal thanked him then shook his hand. Brother Casper mentioned that the biker guys had paid up last night and headed down Route 82 early this morning. He knew 'cause he had heard their bikes as they "roared" down the highway.

After Sal fed Little John, he decided later today he would drive down to Tombstone for a leisurely lunch. He straightened his room, then washed Little John's blanket and hung it on the fence outside to dry. He loaded up the dog into the Pontiac then rolled out in a southernly direction. On the way, he decided to stop at the Texaco station to see Bud.

"I am semi-employed now, working on a project for Mrs. Crane," Sal told Bud.

"I'm not surprised," he said. "When God built the Earth it was Mrs. Crane's family that held the mortgage, so I just knew things would go well for you for saving her life. You're her hero."

"I can't believe the way things are working out," said Sal. "I only intended to help others, but now I am being helped even more. Have you heard of the Serenity Prayer? 'God grant me the serenity to accept the things I cannot change; the courage to change the things I can; and the wisdom to know the difference'?"

"I will have 17 years in the A.A. program this May," laughed Bud. "I've even met and shook hands with Bill W. when I visited New York City in '56." (Bill W. [Wilson] was co-founder of A.A. along with Dr. Bob back in 1935.)

Sal shook Bud's hand. "There. Now I've shaken Bill W.'s hand, too." They both laughed and parted company for the day.

Once at the Muffin Café, Sal relaxed into a big bowl of four-bean chili but he was really there to get a smile from Lu. "O.K. Stinky Little John," he thought to himself. "It's payback time now that I've gassed up on the chili." This payback would do, specially since the dog could smell 1,000 times better than any human. While Sal finished eathing, Lu told him that the cook's lasagna hadn't sold out this past weekend.

"If you'd like, I can pack it up into two containers to give to your travelers," she told Sal. "Would you like it?"

"Sure," said Sal. "I'll take it with me 'cause I'm traveling down there now. One of the Mexicans showed me how they make forks out of the cat claw bushes in place of eating utensils."

Sal loaded up the lasagna along with three-dozen, day-old corn muffins then headed down Route 80 and 90 to the welcome bridge. Sal recalled how one summer he and another drunken soldier were standing in the river with water to their ankles when they realized the water had reached their knees in just minutes. Five minutes later, a wall of water came down the San Pedro out of Mexico rolling tree limbs and garbage past them. Luckily they had scrambled up the embankment, scared sober as they watched in awe at the power of the flash flood.

Once Sal placed the surplus food carefully under the bridge, he tooted his horn. Almost immediately he saw a lone figure moving through the bush. He wondered how many people came through the area in a week and whether the little offerings he was leaving made any difference. Thinking it was the best he could do for now, he settled on knowing it would improve with Mrs. Crane's help.

Sal drove to the west side of the San Pedro River where he could see humungous Cottonwood trees beckoning. It would be a good place to walk Little John, sit down and just think. As he watched the dog splash in the river and drink muddy water, he found a spot to get comfortable under a tree. Little John joined him as soon as Sal had settled in for some pondering. After only a short time, he saw the "Lady In Blue, Teralisa" approach him. As she did, he realized that 15-20 miles wasn't far for a spirit to travel. She smiled at him reminded him that he was on the right path.

"Helping the poorest around you will bring great rewards in the here and now, but also in the hereafter," she said. "Have you thought about the native people barely getting by on their reservations, the little bit of land the White Man left them with?"

"I hadn't," he replied. "But I was told in no uncertain terms that I should be."

"Then do your best to assist them," she said. "Your reward will be great. They need much help, especially the children."

Sal looked over at Little John to see how he was reacting but he was snoring, so he figured he was the only being here that was aware of the Blue Lady's presence. Looking back up from the dog, Sal realized the woman had spontaneously disappeared. But he now knew what he had to do going forward. He remembered in a private mentoring session with his captain, the Company Commander, at the Fort. He'd been teaching him how to lead others, how to develop a group so that it could become a force multiplier. Being only eight miles from the main gate of Fort Huachuca, it was worth the drive and a visit to see Chaplain Cliff.

After Sal pulled into the Fort, and up to the chapel, he saw the chaplain getting out of his own car. Sal walked up to him. He asked if Chaplain Cliff had a little time to talk.

"Sure I do," said the Chaplain. "I was hoping to see you back here soon. I've been busy on your project and I have some good news. Let's go onto the patio where we can have a little more of that lemonade while we talk."

Chaplain Cliff began to tell Sal that he had organized ten of the wives from the Fort. "Wow," Cliff laughed. "I sound like an old-school, polygamous Mormon gathering up ten of his wives. I sure don't know how the Mormons did it, though; I'm in trouble with just my one and only wife half the time."

"In any case, they would like to help with this project you've taken on," the chaplain continued. "They asked if they could get into any trouble doing this; I told them it was a possibility, but it was God's work and if need be, I would get all the chaplains on the base to vouch for their good character. They said they're ready to go so lead on, Sir Sal. Your entourage awaits."

Though Sal felt he was getting in deeper by the minute, he asked the chaplain to organize a meeting so they could plan everything out. Chaplain Cliff told him that Mondays were the best day for him to be available, so next Monday would be perfect. The meeting was set for 10 a.m. when the wives would have their children in school. With the time to meet was set, Sal left the base. This time, though, he didn't need to "tap" the gasoline reserves.

CHAPTER 26

NAHTESTE

It was now time to get over to Chief Nahteste's house to work on another plan. Salvadore was definitely in the mood to help the unfortunate, but the truth of the matter was he was helping his own unfortunate self even more. "I really shouldn't think that anymore," thought Sal," now that I have Mrs. Crane on my side."

Driving down Route 92 he thought about how much he enjoyed the area—Ramsey Canyon with its birds and coatamundi (kind of a mix between a racoon and a monkey), Miller Peak with its deer and mountain lions, and Miracle Valley, which was so peaceful, along with Hereford (was this place really where this breed of cattle began in America?).

Before he knew it, Sal was turning up the driveway to Nahteste's cabin, hoping the nephews recognized his car before shooting any bullets or arrows at him. It wasn't more than 80 years ago that riding up this same trail could easily get one tangled up with some of the meanest, toughest Apache warriors the world had ever seen. Now he was planning on partnering up with three of the toughest Native Americans who were only two generations removed from Geronimo's lineage. He sure couldn't have done this in Pennsylvania, he thought, even though two Sicilian mafia families ran the little town where he grew up. Each version of fighters could have given the other a run for their money.

Sal was suddenly startled when Nahteste leaned into his back window and grabbed his hair.

"Hmmm," Nahteste grumbled. "How much would this scalp bring?"

"Only some wet pants," Sal thought.

Sal wondered to himself how cowboys could sleep on the ground with only their horse standing guard when Geronimo's warriors were out and about.

Nahteste laughed and let go of Sal as he said, "Not much for this scalp: too much dandruff."

Sal meekly smiled, still a little shaken by the sudden assault.

"Let's go talk," Nahteste motioned to Sal to get out of the car. "You didn't come out this far just to get a thrill, White Boy!"

Once they had gotten some coffee and were sitting on a log bench by the house, Sal started explaining a part of his plan. "Thanks to your tongue lashing about the Apache's plight, the latest visit from the spirit woman and the generosity of some folks in Tucson, I am ready to do some good on the reservations," said Sal.

"I am very pleased and proud of your good intentions," Nahteste answered. "I'll do whatever I can to help out."

"So what educational services are available to the children at the San Carlos and Fort Apache reservations?" asked Sal. "How could they be improved?"

"Four or five of the Apache women have actually left the reservation to be trained as teachers at the Cochise Community College," he said. "I am sure that at least two or three would be willing to return to the rez to help better educate the kids there, because many of them live too far from the schools."

"My idea is to have some teachers go out to the boonies and quickly train some mothers to start home-schooling the kids," said Sal. "They could set up pocket schools in the far reaches of the rez. I know I can provide textbooks and supplies as necessary, eventually bringing in artists to capitalize on the natives' natural talents to make saleable art objects.

They would teach them to produce articles that could be sold at art shows off the rez."

"That would be a good start," said Nahteste. "We could get my people enthused with the idea of education. An education would make it possible to earn one's own living, thereby improving self-esteem."

"Is there much drinking on the rez?" asked Sal, already anticipating the answer.

"That is probably the biggest problem facing the men that still live there," Nahteste replied.

"Well, in a few weeks I'll have turned over some of the duties of distributing the food and water to the Mexican travelers," said Sal. "I'd like to go up to the reservation to see what could be done about some of Native-Americans' issues."

"O.K.," said Nahteste. "I'll contact my sister, who has returned there to help my mother and grandmother; she might have some good ideas."

"Then I'll come back next Monday afternoon," Sal told Nahteste. "And we can discuss this in more depth."

Nahteste started to tell Sal about the recent ambushes he was involved in, but Sal quickly interrupted and asked him to keep it to himself. Nahteste understood. Sal then walked Little John who left a large deposit at the end of the driveway just to show his displeasure at his protector's being playfully "ambushed" earlier.

CHAPTER 27

SATISFACTION

S al decided to drive over to Bisbee and see if the tortillas were ready to be picked up. He pulled around back of the grocery store. Juan Gonzalez just happened to be there having a smoke.

"Hey Sal," waved Juan. "I have a bunch of stuff for you. Stay right here and I'll get it."

"Well Juan, hang on," said Sal. "I need all the space in my car for water jugs so I'll come back in a couple of hours if that's O.K."

"Sure, buddy," Juan replied. "I'll have it ready for you then."

Sal headed for the commercial laundry where he picked up 36 gallons of water as well as 15 old blankets. Thanking Damian, the owner, he headed towards Douglas to drop off a few of the jugs and blankets. The high desert could be very cold late at night, especially during the winter months. Sal left three blankets at each drop off, along with the water. Now he'd have room for the food he'd get from Juan. Once done, he headed back to Bisbee to pick up tortillas and about 100 dented cans of food. With the car crammed with food and Little John, Sal headed to the bridge.

Sal chuckled to himself when he discovered there was no food left from his drop earlier that day; he tooted his horn and left everything he had, including the blankets. With his good deeds done for the day, Sal then headed back to St. David. The only eventful thing that happened during his trip back was a parade of tarantulas crossed the road. When Sal stopped to let them pass he almost got rear ended by a motor home with a very grouchy driver. Sal got out of his car to point out why he had stopped. The driver moved on, grumpily, after the spiders crossed safely. On his way home again, Sal was quiet except for a couple of bean toots, which Jersey called "barking spiders," a small payback for Little John's skunk smell.

Once back at the monastery, he fed Little John and just made it in time for dinner in the dining hall. An excellent meatloaf and mashed potatoes reminded him to finish his letter to his mother.

The 12-Step meeting was O.K. that night; a couple of tourists were in attendance. They said they were headed down through Aqua Prieta to Copper Canyon in Mexico for two weeks. Sal warned them that he had learned that drug labs were all over in the mountains there. They'd better be careful, as the bad guys were known to shoot first if any strangers ventured into their areas.

After walking and shoveling after old Little John, Sal headed for the sack. It had been a great day that produced many possibilities for the future. He marveled again at how true it was that when you help others you were really helping yourself.

CHAPTER 28

OLD AND NEW FRIENDS AND MEETINGS

I In the morning after a fine breakfast, but lousy coffee, Sal walked
Little John and decided to visit Bud at the Texaco station. Bud was
notorious for his strong coffee, so after Sal helped himself to the powerful brew, he got Bud to stop mechanizing and talk to him.

"Bud, I have a thought," he began. "Would you be willing to drive over
to Fort Huachuca a couple of times a week to lead a meeting?"

"Yeah, I guess," Bud said after hesitating. "I've been hiding under the
hood too long. It'd be good to hear some stories to keep my memory green.
When can I start?"

"I'll try to put something together this coming Monday," Sal replied.
"What time could you get there to run the meetings?"

"Well," said Bud. "I close the garage at 6 p.m. so 7:30 would work for
me."

"O.K.," Sal said. "Let's aim for that. See you next week."

Sal pondered a thought after finding out from Bud there were no open
meetings between Benson and Bisbee. Maybe a quick stop in Tombstone
would pan out for him. He felt he was chasing down another windmill, but
he wanted to see how this idea might turn out. Seeing a Christian church

on a side street, Sal pressed the doorbell at a small cottage that was attached to the chapel. A tall man answered and introduced himself as Reverend Thompson. Sal quickly explained what he wanted to do, and though
the minister was skeptical, he said, "Don't really like having a bunch of
drunks in my church basement. But if we can help them turn their lives
around, I guess it's worth it. If you can get my wife to assist you with the
coffee and snacks, and you'll clean up after so it's ready for Sunday school,
then you can do it. I assume you'll want to do it on a Saturday night when
the town is packed with bikers and drunks?"

"Saturday is great," agreed Sal. Then the minister took him around
back to meet the reverend's wife. As they both saw each other, they were
taken aback. It was Jenn Jenkins, a woman Sal had spent a couple of evenings talking to during Helldorado Days, two years back. Helldorado was
one of Tombstone's craziest festivals.

"Whoa!" said Sal. "How did you become the preacher's wife?"

"After talking with you I just couldn't or wouldn't take any more abuse
from my husband at that time," she replied. "It was time to set out on
my own." Jenn had been married to Jerry Jeff Jenkins, a striving Country-
Western musician. "Let him sing his songs around the country," she continued. "I wanted to settle down and start a family. I left him right then
and there in Tombstone and worked in the motel for a while. Soon I met
the Reverend. Got myself divorced, remarried and pregnant all within the
last two years."

"Whoa!—one more time," said Sal. "One never knows what's on the
path of life, does one?"

"Well, sit down and have some lemonade and muffins I just took out
of the oven," said Jenn. "Then you can explain to me what I can do to help
you."

Once Sal explained what he was doing and that he wanted to get an
A.A. meeting going in the area, Jenn agreed to do everything she could to
help. The reverend excused himself after giving them both his blessing.
They were about to do God's work in his church. He now was ready to get

out of the way and leave them to do it. After looking over the church's basement, Sal was pleased.

"This is great," he said. "It has a bathroom, a little kitchen, tables and chairs, and all we need is a big coffee maker. By next week I can arrange for at least one of those."

Jenn gave Sal a big hug with tears in her eyes and said, "You know, it's what you said that night that changed my life. I was either going to start using heroin like Jerry Jeff or kill myself. Thank you so much. What I remember the most is a little saying you told me you read in a book on alcoholism someone gave you: 'To thine own self be true.' I tell myself that every day. Saying it has let me believe in me once again."

Sal was embarrassed and uncomfortable with all the praise, but he was still able to respond. "I have learned even more about just that lately by helping others. Loving service is what God put us on this earth to do."

Both Sal and Jenn agreed to get the basement area ready and pass the word out that the first AA meeting would be held in three weeks. It would be on Saturday nights at 8 p.m. and run about two hours. It would also be open so anyone could attend—alcoholics, drug users, family members, or anyone interested in learning more about becoming sober, or dealing with someone who wasn't.

As he left, Sal started to think about all those years he had spent at St. Mary's Parochial School and Church growing up. He hadn't believed in all the church hoopla made up by old men, but just maybe he had an angel guiding him on this path. At the very least, there was a kind spirit leading him along his way. He had read once in a magazine that "to go with the flow" is how many people were able to cope with their lives, whether they were bored housewives or high-pressure stockbrokers. It sounded good to him, since it was basically what he had been doing. So far so good, as the man that fell off the bridge yelled to the fisherman in the boat. Sal hoped he wasn't heading for a hard landing himself. But if so, at least he was leading his own life as well as he could: helping instead of hurting anyone.

Sal turned to Little John and spoke, "How 'bout we head to Fairbank, where that big hole in the river is so we can swim a bit?" Little John didn't reply so Sal took his silence as agreement. He drove southwest from Tombstone and began chuckling to himself as he realized the local cops had been leaving him alone. It meant to him that he was now one of the "good" guys. Maybe I should get a white hat, he thought. Then they'd know for sure.

After splashing around in the river, Sal and Little John laid down under a big Cottonwood to nap. Of course, once again, it wasn't long before the blue-skirted spirit, Teralisa, came along with a friend. He was a big Apache, who even looked like a painting of Cochise Sal remembered seeing in some bar. The big guy spoke slowly to Sal.

"You're a good man, doing good deeds," he said to Sal. "If there were more like you we would have lived in peace together. I tried, but some men lied to me, then the Army killed part of my family and tribe for nothing, they accused us of kidnapping and killing when we were actually working for a peaceful co-existence. That led us to fight ten more years for no reason except that White Men slowly kept taking our homeland away, little by little, lying all the time."

The big warrior then said to Sal, "I will say my words: You do good. I say this for you to ponder. The White Man looks at the world and thinks everything is for and about him, that he is in charge of everyone. The Apache say all is equal, and if in balance, Hozho, it is good. This is as the Great Spirit wanted. Maybe that is why we could not get along; the White Man had superior numbers. He killed off so many native people with his diseases that we had no natural defenses for. He forced us to give up our ways and our homes. Now our people live like beggars on their own land. It is out of balance. Not good. I am very sad to see such strong people wasting away."

"What you say, you must now do," the powerful warrior continued. "Help educate our people; it is a very great thing. 'The Dinetah,' the people, must learn to be in balance with the White world, yet try to keep some of their own Red values. Don't kill what isn't to be eaten. White man kills the deer, then leaves the meat to rot and but then takes only the horns?

Enough talk. You, friend, go do good." Then they both were gone.

Sal shook himself in order to come back to reality. He thought once again that he was either losing his mind or learning incredible lessons. He had never even hallucinated like this when he was extremely drunk. It was scary but at the same time very exhilarating. He wouldn't give up these experiences for anything. With his good deeds done for the day, Sal then headed back to St. David.

CHAPTER 29

SAL CALLS MARY

S al grabbed Little John and headed back home for the day. After
dinner, he asked to use the phone so he could call Mary in Tucson.
That was something he hadn't done since high school: call a girl.
He stammered as the phone connected. Mary picked up the line.

"Hello," he said clumsily. "This is Sal."

"Oh, I'm so happy you called." Salvadore was delighted to hear her say
that. "I've been thinking about you. How are you?"

"Doing fine," he relaxed. "You O.K?"

"Yes, thanks," Mary replied.

"I'll be up on Tuesday if that's O.K." Sal said with high hopes.

"Of course," said Mary. "I was also told to tell you if you called that Mrs.
Crane and Mr. Mayhew would be available whenever you could come up."

Sal began to feel a little self-important so he took a stab at asking for a
date. "Would you go to lunch with me when I come up on Tuesday?"

"Yes," Mary said. "I would love to."

Sal gave Mary his number at the monastery then bid her adieu until
Tuesday morning. He was elated with her response when she said she was
looking forward to seeing him soon. He practically floated a foot off the
floor as he went back to his room. One of the monks walked by him and
said, "You're in trouble now, smiley!"

Sal laughed and thought to himself, "Oh yes, I definitely am."

That evening's 12-Step meeting was just mediocre, but to Sal every one was a success if going to a meeting kept him away from a drink for one more day. Plus, he never really knew how many others were helped by attending AA regularly. After a short walk with Little John, Sal hit the sack with the hope of good dreams about Mary instead of spirits.

The next morning, after Little John's constitutional and clean up, Sal went to the dining room to eat. One of the monks Sal hadn't yet met asked him for some assistance in the flower garden. Feeling grateful for all that the monastery had done for him, Sal readily agreed. When they got to the garden, Brother James showed Sal the rebar rod he had bent into arches. He needed Sal to hold it up so he could weld it into place. Making small talk as they worked, Brother James told Sal how he had ended up at the monastery two years prior.

"After getting out of the Air Force at Luke Airfield near Phoenix I sold vacuum cleaners," he began. "I made so much money I only had to work two days a week. It gave me a lot of time to drink, so eventually it was too much of an effort to get cleaned up and walk door-to-door. I decided to go on a big bender down in Mexico. It was by God's grace that I stopped here first, on the way to Aqua Prieta. The Brothers invited me to spend a few days here, and because I was bored I did. I had a few bottles of Jack Daniels in my car, but I checked out a 12-Step meeting anyway, just to see what it was like."

Brother James explained that he was half drunk when he attended the meeting. He had promised himself he would be full drunk within two hours once he left the AA meeting. But by luck or Divine Intervention, the speaker was a former Marine by the name of Tom. He explained that when he got out of the service down in Yuma, he went to Mexico and wandered in a tequila fog for one-and-a-half years.

Tom had many brushes with death. One night he went into a chapel after being pursued by an angry police chief. The cop was in a jealous rage after he caught his wife succumbing to Tom's charms. He said that by luck, he only had to jump one story when "La Policia" pulled up in front of the house. He bailed out of the wife's window, ran for his life then ended up sleeping on the floor of a confessional in the chapel. He was awakened by the sound of soft singing on a Sunday morning. He looked through the slats of the confessional door, where he laid eyes on a beautiful angelic senorita that was sitting, kneeling, and standing only three feet away from him.

"He thought to himself that that was who he should be spending his time with," said Brother James. "Not other men's wives that act as rotten as he. Then as the sunlight came through the chapel windows, a beam of light shone on this woman and something melted in his heart. Right then and there Tom said he prayed to God to give him the strength to become the man he thought God wanted him to be. He would stop drinking. Now, he does only good works."

Tom then committed himself to a Salvation Army detoxification facility in Phoenix, dried out and got healthy. After that, he wandered around the southwest doing odd jobs to earn gas money and food. He'd stop at churches and do work for them as well as parishioners who needed an extra hand, and he'd speak at as many 12-Step meetings as he could find.

"I haven't found my senorita, yet," he had shared. "But with the help of my Higher Power, I've certainly found peace of mind."

Brother James said that Tom's story hit him in the gut as if he had been sucker punched. He felt both nauseated and elated at the same time. He asked Tom if he could speak with him afterwards, and Tom told him that quite often, the meetings (or talks) people had after the main meeting were often more important than the actual meeting. Tom and James ended up talking together until the sun came up.

It was funny how sharing experiences, tears and confessions could bond two people together. When they parted company, James went in to see the head monk, Brother Casper, to see if he could stay for a while. He was willing to work for his keep and be as useful as he could be. Brother Casper told him he was more than welcome, as long as he poured out the bourbon he had seen James sneaking out by his car. Since James felt no more need to drink, he agreed. Now it was two years later, and he had two years sober. He couldn't be happier.

"I found God, found peace and I finally found James," Brother James said. "I've stopped running from demons I couldn't name, demons of my own guilt-ridden mind. Just like I heard you say in a meeting, "I have found the enemy, and he is me." I like me a lot better now, for the first time in my life. I feel like I'm accomplishing something, making this world a little better place to be. I'm not hurting anyone else along the way."

Sal thought to himself that the monastery must be some kind of incredible "good energy" vortex. A lot of good seemed to emanate from these grounds.

"Say, Brother James, would you like to help get a meeting started in Tombstone?" Sal asked.

"Sure," he replied. "I don't know exactly what to do, but I'm willing to help in any way I can."

"O.K." said Sal with satisfaction. "We'll work it out, following the instructions in the Big Book of AA. But first, let me get a large coffee pot because we can't have a meeting without that!"

"O.K." said Brother James. "While you're in Tucson go to that 12-Step store called 'Awakenings' and buy a bunch of big books and 12-Step books—and any other literature they have. If they have any medallions for lengths of sobriety, we should give those out, too."

Sal agreed to make the purchases the following week, then told Brother James about his friend Jenn, who as fate would have it, allowed them to meet up again.

"There are no coincidences, Sal," said Brother James. "I'm happy things are falling nicely into place for you but more than that, I'm glad the rebar is staying up."

Since Sal was never what he considered "handy," Brother James assured him that when the morning glories and different-colored vines blossomed, the rebar would look terrific. They enthusiastically parted ways, mulling over all the things they had to do to show others how they found the peace that was never in a bottle, regardless of how many they poured down their throats.

When Sal returned to Brother Alex's room to retrieve Little John, there was a note under the door jamb. It said to call a Cristo Sanchez in Bisbee; there was a number. Sal was puzzled, but he walked Little John first, then went to use the phone. This time he ran into Brother Casper, and gave him $10 for the use of the phone with a promise of more money if he needed it for the phone bill.

When Cristo answered, he was a very pleasant man who told Sal that Damian Ortiz from the commercial laundry told him what Sal was doing to get water to the travelers. He offered his help, explaining he had a factory that made water bags, the kind made out of canvas. They were the kind you hung on the front of the car to cool down the water by evaporation as you drove. Cristo was having a problem with one of his sewing machines and had ended up with a lot of defective bags he couldn't sell, even though they still held water. Sal was delighted to hear this news, so he asked Cristo how he could get to his place. They agreed that Sal would come to the factory the next day.

That was another "Wow!" for Sal. He thought that having an angel spirit work with him was turning out to be great. Sal figured he would need to eventually talk to Brother Casper to explain his actions. Because of them, he thought he might have to find a new place to stay, which he did not want to do. He hoped that when that conversation took place, they both would be in agreement.

CHAPTER 30

PIZZA MAYBE

---·····---

I n the meantime, Sal decided to call Chaplain Cliff at the Fort. When
the Chaplain answered, Sal told him he was going to be in Bisbee the
next day, and he wanted to stop by for a chat. The Chaplain invited
Sal for an early dinner, so they decided to meet at 3 p.m. At the rate
he was making appointments with people, Sal figured he better get an
organizer to mark down the times and dates for everyone he had agreed to
meet. Plus it would help for all the things he needed to do. He grabbed an
old tablet until he could get to Tucson where he was sure Mary could show
him where to get the supplies he needed.

Sal needed lunch so he decided to drive to the Benson Truck Stop and
treat himself to their extra strong coffee. He knew it was much better for
him than strong red wine or plain old beer. He remembered a night at the
N.C.O. Club at Fort Huachuca that was referred to as "Falstaff" night. The
bottled beer was ten cents a bottle and he drank 44 bottles in approximately four hours and still made it back to the barracks. Those were some
crazy times. Drinking coffee and not booze was his thing now; the worst
that could happen is either not being able to sleep or getting the runs.

Sal walked into the Truck Stop, glad the witch was gone, because she
would probably have put floor cleaner in his coffee. He found an empty
stool between two big truckers and ordered his lunch: two cheeseburgers,

fries and an unlimited amount of coffee. The trucker on his right decided to start up a conversation.

"Whom do you drive for?" he asked Sal.

Smartass that he was, Sal replied, "Bonneville Freight, short hauls—water and food."

Then Sal laughed at his private joke. "Really though," corrected Sal. "I'm just kidding. I'm a civilian, not a trucker."

"You sound like a guy from the Northeastern Pennsylvania Valley," the trucker kept up the conversation. "The way you talk."

"I am," said Sal. "Near Scranton."

"Yeah?" said the trucker. "I'm from West Scranton. Did you play football? When?"

Sal told the man what year he played and the trucker replied. "I'm a little older than you but you guys always had a good team."

"Do you remember Old Forge and how they used to file their cleats sharp and then try to step on your fingers," Sal reminisced.

"Oh yeah," said the trucker. "But we cold cocked a few of them for doing that. Last game they carried their quarterback off the field in a stretcher. But man, they had the best pizza in those mafia joints back then."

"Yeah," Sal laughed. "Besides my family, I miss the white pizza the most."

The trucker finally introduced himself as Dominic from West Scranton. "A lot of the times I haul refrigerated 'reefer,' trailers that have frozen goods in them," said Dominic. "If I can do it, I'll bring you a couple of white pizzas next time I haul from there if you'll give me your number."

Sal gave Dominic his number and secretly hoped he would get a call. When Sal's food finally came, Dominic left, and Sal was left to ponder coincidences again.

After lunch, Sal went over to the library to see Nicole and pick up what people had put in the donation boxes. He thought he might also get a book on the San Carlos and Fort Apache Reservations. Fortunately, Nicole was happy to help, and she gave him a book that told the history of the Indians up to the 1950s. Sal thanked her, and loaded up some donated goodies in his car. Heading back to Route 80 and his temporary home, Sal figured he would never be bored. It was a good thing he had opted out of the Army or he'd be in the Vietnamese jungle right now being shot at. He figured he was more useful in the world doing what he was doing than being a pawn in some kind of deadly game between world powers.

Since it was such a beautiful day, Sal decided to get Little John and head to the river to chill out. Lying down on the banks of the San Pedro River next to a wet and smelly dog, Sal began to write on his tablet. He started to think that dropping bags every few miles might not be the best way to distribute the food and water. After all, a lot of the Mexican refugees went right along the trail but just didn't find the food or blankets. If he could find five or six well-traveled trails that they used extensively, he could concentrate on them. If Chaplain Cliff's ladies wanted to expand on that, they were welcome. That would be a great thing if they did 'cause it would free him up to get involved in other beneficial endeavors. Fort Apache and San Carlos reservations were only part of the projects he wanted to initiate.

CHAPTER 31

SUPERSTITION MOUNTAINS

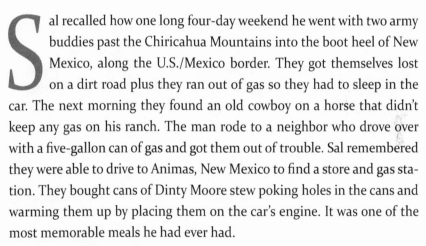

S al recalled how one long four-day weekend he went with two army buddies past the Chiricahua Mountains into the boot heel of New Mexico, along the U.S./Mexico border. They got themselves lost on a dirt road plus they ran out of gas so they had to sleep in the car. The next morning they found an old cowboy on a horse that didn't keep any gas on his ranch. The man rode to a neighbor who drove over with a five-gallon can of gas and got them out of trouble. Sal remembered they were able to drive to Animas, New Mexico to find a store and gas station. They bought cans of Dinty Moore stew poking holes in the cans and warming them up by placing them on the car's engine. It was one of the most memorable meals he had ever had.

With a full tank of gas, Sal and his friends decided to drive into the Superstition Mountains and maybe find the Lost Dutchman's gold mine. On the way, they drove the Apache Trail, which has a 2,000-foot drop on one side with no guardrails. They drove 40 miles with the doors open, ready to bail out in case of an emergency. There was a song, "40 Miles of Bad Road," sung by Phoenix resident, Dwayne Eddy. That tune had to have been inspired by this stretch of road.

Once in the Superstition Mountains, the craziest thing happened to them. They drove as far as they could on a primitive patch of road, got out of the vehicle and walked a path through the desert. They kept going through a couple of passes. Fortunately, each man carried one of those two-and-a-half-gallon water bags like the ones Cristo told Sal he could pick up from him. Eventually, they came to an area where people were camping. They saw some kids playing and a woman working in a large vegetable garden near a spring. Thinking the people were gold miners working a claim, the three Army musketeers yelled out to them.

"Hi! How are you doing?" they tried to be friendly, but they startled the woman and the children enough to send them fleeing into their make-shift homes. One of them set off an alarm of bells, which called to other women to immediately gather in defense. They came forward with their rakes, hoes, and shovels at the ready.

"We are so sorry," offered Sal to the women. "We're just three Army guys out hiking around. We didn't mean to bother anyone. Sorry!"

One of the older women stepped forward and spoke for her group. "If you don't bring problems you won't get any from us," she said. "Just know that you have rifles aimed at you right now."

"No problem," said Sal. "We'll leave right now if you like."

"Sit down at the picnic table and we'll see," she nodded to the men. The three looked at each other and wondered what they had gotten themselves into. But once seated, the children came outdoors once again. They stayed their distance, but they looked relieved.

The lead spokeswoman, whose name was Janet, reminded Sal of an Amazon. She said to the men, "Do you have some money you could loan us?"

The three men laughed and replied, "How will you pay us back, turnips from the garden?"

"Just give me an address," replied Janet. "Sometimes our men find gold nuggets and we are flush for awhile. Right now, we're broke."

The men talked amongst themselves and decided they could afford

$100. That much could be chalked up as a loss if it came to that. Sal spoke for his buddies and said, "We'll loan you the $100 on one condition. You have to tell us your story about this place."

Janet agreed as long as Sal and his buddies didn't spread the story around. After promising to keep their mouths shut, Janet began her tale. "Twenty some years ago, six German soldiers escaped from the concentration camp the U.S. government had near Phoenix during World War II. Five of them made it into the mountains without being seen, and those five still live here, but are afraid to go to town in Apache Junction or outside these mountains. Over the years I and the other women stumbled on to these guys when we were out hiking or riding. We decided to stay with them, to return and become their "wives." I and some of the other women regularly travel into the world. We go mostly to Mesa where there's a coin shop run by an old German refugee. We take some of the nuggets we find. He always gives us a fair price. The money allows us to buy plenty of groceries, which last quite a while."

When Janet and the women were done shopping, she told Sal that the coin man's son gave them a ride to the end of the dirt road. The husbands, who were watching for her return, helped their wives carry the provisions back to camp.

"I know it sounds crazy," said Janet. "But one of our women is an elementary school teacher and has set up a classroom to educate our children. We love the solitude; no worries about the kids getting into trouble except for the occasional scorpion or snakebite. Luckily, we also have a nurse and one of the men used to be a medic, so we are well taken care of here."

Janet told the men they got their $100 worth of story. She asked for an address to return their loan, then the three got going. "Our guys don't really trust us speaking to other men out here," she said.

Sal gave her his address at his mom's house and wished them all good luck. "I hope your experiment turns out well for you all," he said as the three of them left the way they came. There was more than one "Wow!"

muttered by Salvadore Dusi on the walk back to their car. The three had vowed to say nothing for at least a few years about what they just experienced.

"Well," said Sal to himself after that trip down memory lane. "I hope they're still doing well." With that, he laid back down in the water to cool off before taking Little John back to his room and feeding him. He was looking forward to a good dinner, and a good meeting.

CHAPTER 32

THOU SHALT NOT JUDGE

That evening, a couple of the visitors attending the 12-Step AA meeting were from Tucson. They were staying at the monastery for a few days to relax, read and rekindle their serenity. They shared their experiences in sobriety with those in attendance. Sal felt recharged listening to them share. He asked them if they happened to know a Mrs. Crane from Tucson.

"That old rich biddy?" they exclaimed. "She has more money than God and she keeps it all. Why doesn't she make good use of her wealth by helping others?"

Sal just smiled to himself and walked away to get some low octane coffee. People are always so sure and so quick to judge others, he thought to himself. If we point a finger at someone's faults there are three fingers pointing back at us. But they would never know just how much good Mrs. Crane's money is doing, because she insisted it all be kept confidential. Sal had kept to his word and was keeping all his actions confidential. The important thing was taking the right action, which would bring the right results.

CHAPTER 33

CHRISTO HUGS

T he next morning, Sal awakened early, but lay in bed for a while
thinking. His days were completely full now, more than they ever
had been when he was in the Army. Today, he thought, he needed
to stop in Tombstone, pick up food from Lu, drop it off at the
bridge, back track to Bisbee and see Cristo, pick up water bags, take them
to Irv to put out by his water tank, then head over to Chaplain Cliff's to
try and convince him to start a 12-Step meeting at the base. It would be a
full day, which meant Little John would have to ride along. At least there
would be enough food in the car to keep him happy.

Sal hoisted himself up on his feet in anticipation that there were a lot
of thirsty and hungry folks counting on him. He quickly ran over his itin-
erary: walk the dog, scoop the poop, drink the lousy coffee, skip breakfast
until he could get to the Muffin Café. "Let's get on the way for the day, shall
we?" he urged himself. His enthusiastic self-coaching worked. Off he and
Little John went.

Once Sal arrived at the Muffin Café, he waved to Lu who was on the
other end of the counter. He gave his order to a very pretty girl who was a
little younger than he—oatmeal, bacon and rye toast—and keep the coffee coming. This waitress was obviously a new hire. The young gal smiled
at Sal, then turned in his breakfast order. Lu stopped by to visit once she

was done helping another customer.

"That detective was in here again asking for you," she said to Sal. "Are you in trouble again?"

"Not that I know of," answered Sal. "Jeez, I hope not. I'm way too busy to be bothered by the law. If he comes in again tell him to give me a call at the monastery. I'm pretty easy to find. That or just look for the car with a horse in the back seat."

Though the coffee was great, Sal lost his appetite at the news the sergeant was seeking another question-and-answer session with him. "Well," thought Sal, "I'm doing a few different things, and if they make me stop one or two of them I've still got plenty to keep me busy. Plus, I can train others to pick up where I may have to leave off."

Sal was thinking, with Mrs. Crane on his side, he could still get a lot done. He was sure a well-placed phone call would ease his way if it came down to that. Lu told him to pull around back to load up on food. She said he might as well go across the street and pick up there, too. He left a nice tip for the pretty girl, happy to have some money in his pocket to share, then bid the waitress "good luck" with her new job.

"Watch out," smiled Sal. "Not everyone here is as nice as I am. And sometimes your co-workers are really the ones to look out for." Sal and Lu laughed at their private joke, then Sal grabbed the toast and bacon leftovers off his plate to give to Little John.

Once he had loaded up the car with donations, he headed over to the bridge to drop them off. After looking at the time, he headed over to Bisbee and the address Cristo had given him. He couldn't believe the coincidence once again, a couple of years ago when he was coming back from Naco, Mexico, he and two other guys ran low on gas near Bisbee. Luckily, the car owner had a siphon in his trunk and knew how to use it. The car that provided them the gas to get back to the Fort was parked right in front of Cristo's factory. Sal decided it was probably best to keep his mouth shut about that incident. He pledged silently to himself to leave Bud $5 for anyone who needed help with gas if they came to the station needing to get an emergency gallon.

Sal was surprised when he was introduced to Cristo; he expected a little guy from the sound of his voice on the phone. But Cristo turned out to be about 400 pounds. He looked like a Mexican Sumo wrestler. He didn't shake Sal's hand, instead he picked him up with a big bear hug, saying in a small voice, "Very proud to meet you, amigo. You're a very good man doing what you do."

Sal was very happy when his feet hit the floor and he could breathe once again.

"From now on, call me Crisco," the big man smiled. "All my friends do. I can't imagine why."

Sal heard a girlish giggle sneak out of Crisco's mouth. "Oh, boy," Sal thought to himself." This could be tricky. I need to tell Crisco how excited I am about Mary, and how I plan on making that relationship a priority." "I had no idea that water bags were so much in demand," he said instead.

Crisco led Sal into the back of his work area, where he was glad to see seven or eight women working away on big industrial sewing machines.

"It's dropped off some," said Crisco. "But we still sell over 10,000 a year. Luckily for you we have more than 200 rejects that still hold water." Sal was only able to fit 42 of the water bags into the Pontiac. Little John took up most of the back seat. "That dog is the canine version of me," Crisco laughed. "He's a Chihuahua they over fed at the monk house," Sal replied. "Very sad; no more lap dog," Crisco giggled as he hugged Sal to the point of suffocation. Sal was glad to get on the road with his water bags and lungs still intact.

CHAPTER 34

TUMBLEWEEDS

Up the hill at Irv and Bonnie's, Sal pulled into the driveway to see them both on the porch with easels. Sal definitely noticed the serenity on their faces; he mused that that was a picture he could show at a meeting to demonstrate how it is when you finally are at peace with yourself. It really doesn't matter how much money you make if you can just get happy with your lot in life, no matter what that is. As Bonnie and Irv spotted Sal, they waved him up to the house.

"Have a seat by the little table," said Bonnie. "I just took a pan of blueberry muffins out of the oven."

Sal was grateful since he was hungry 'cause he hadn't had the chance to eat the big breakfast he had ordered earlier. After polishing off most of the pan, Sal told them about the water bags he had in his car. Both Irv and Bonnie were delighted to hear it, since they were always worried about the 90-some miles of high desert the Mexicans had to cross before they got to Tucson. Without a good source of water, it was dangerous. The bags would help a lot, especially if the travelers found a cattle tank or two on the way where they could refill their bags. Sal agreed and asked them to put out a couple of bags each day. He would deliver another load in a week or two.

Sal thanked them for all their help, grabbed the last two muffins along with a bowl of water for Little John before he headed out. He was on his way to Fort Huachuca to see about the meeting Chaplain Cliff was going to set up. As he drove away, he thought about how happy he was to have gas money. His adventure would have gotten tough to do without money, so having "angels" on his side was a big help.

Driving into town, Sal noticed how much Sierra Vista had grown. It had only been four years since he had arrived there, but the town had expanded in just a short time. He figured that with the great weather, lots of work for people on the base, plus the businesses that supported the soldiers and civilians, and, of course, the military retirees looking to be close to the commissary and inexpensive healthcare, this area was destined to keep growing. It wasn't like Pennsylvania, where he felt he was smart to leave, even though he missed his family and friends. If things kept working out the way they were, maybe he could start his own Dusi Dynasty out here in the desert; one never really knew where his next adventure was coming from. Maybe even with Mary, he fantasized. But then, Sal shook his head and told himself to slow down. After all, he had only gotten through one lunch with her, and even though this was the new and improved version of Sal, there might be enough of the old guy to scare any sweet, normal girl away.

As Sal pulled into Chaplain Cliff's driveway, the reverend came around from behind the chapel carrying a tarp full of tumbleweeds. He waved at Sal, saying, "O.K., I think I have enough for a nice salad later."

"Yeah," said Sal. "Those are some of the most aggravating weeds known to man. In Pennsylvania, we have burdocks, but they can't hold a candle to these guys. Some of the old Sicilian women even found a way to make those burdock leaves delicious—fry them in an egg and flour batter. I wonder if they could work a little magic with these guys."

"Be worth millions for that recipe," said the Chaplain.

They laughed together and headed for the shaded patio and lemonade.

"Have you ever seen anything in the Bible about Jesus and his Apostles being served lemonade during their travels?" asked Sal. "When you're hiking in the desert and it's hot, forget about making wine out of water; lemonade is the ticket."

"No, never saw anything like that in the book," laughed the Chaplain. "It might be a secret, one might call a heavenly recipe."

Sal agreed that the Chaplain's wife did have the perfect recipe for lemonade. He wanted to thank her for stocking up the refrigerator with the refreshing drink so he and her husband were able to enjoy it while they talked.

"Well," the Chaplain said. "What is it you want me to get involved in now? I mean, besides guiding my ten wives into one of your schemes?"

"O.K.," Sal nodded. "When I was stationed here, there wasn't much to do besides drink. And I admit no one held my lips open and poured. We had the 3-2-1 Club for us lowly peons, the N.C.O. Club for higher-up soldiers and the PX with its dollar pitcher of beer. Of course, there was also Kelly's and M.I. off base. So I'm thinking that since AA is what helped me become a sober and useful citizen again, what if we started an open AA meeting here in the basement of your church?"

Sal watched for the Chaplain's reaction but continued talking. "As busy as you are, you would not have to do much," explained Sal. "Unless some of the soldiers requested counseling—after all, that's your primary job, I believe. I already have a man with 17 years sobriety willing to drive over from St. David to lead the group. I know where to get the money we'd need to purchase the essentials like a large coffee maker, cookies and snacks, Big Books, 12-Step books, and sobriety medallions. The meeting would become totally self-sufficient in a short time. Everyone kicks in a dollar per meeting if he can."

"From what I can tell," continued Sal. "There may be more happening spiritually in the basement of this church than there is happening upstairs. No offense, Reverend, but it sure helps if we get some of the guys going back in the right direction."

"Give me a minute to think about it," said the Chaplain. "Let's see; it won't cost anything from my budget, you'll clean up after yourselves, you'll provide everything you need to hold the meetings, and a bunch of sinners will learn where the chapel is. Plus, I'll get to meet and greet most of them, right?"

"Yes sir," answered Sal. "That is certainly true."

"Well then," smiled the Chaplain. "Let's do her. Sounds like a win-win all the way around. When shall we begin?"

"I'll be in Tucson next week," said Sal. "I'll buy the coffee maker, the books and literature we'll need to get started. Then I'll speak with Bud to coordinate a start date. I can tell you by Monday when we meet with your wives club."

"Let's have another pitcher of that heavenly lemonade, shall we?" said the Chaplain. "Then we'll contemplate what we have begun."

Dinner that evening turned out to be one of Sal's favorites—sauerbrauten with spatzeles and carrots. Chaplain Cliff's wife was born and raised in Germany, which is where he met and married her. They were kind enough to allow Sal to take some leftovers and a big bowl of water out to Little John. He was starting to think that domestic life seemed pretty good actually. If he finally got around to it, he just might like it an awful lot. Back inside, the Reverend's wife served them some coffee and delicious pastries she had made that day. Sal was as stuffed as he had ever been in years.

"Grab your coffee, Sal," said Chaplain Cliff. "Let's go out to the patio and enjoy some great cigars. They came from one of my parishioners who was recently transferred from the Caribbean. He told me they were Hemingway's favorites. Don't mention where I got them—especially to any officers." "I'll be darned! Things just get better and better," thought Sal.

"O.K.," said Chaplin Cliff. "Bring me up to speed, please."

CHAPTER 35

STRANGE EGGS

S o Sal did just that. He even told the Chaplain about Mrs. Crane without actually revealing her name. He insisted the information be held in strictest confidence. Chaplain Cliff was astonished at how much Sal had accomplished in such a short period of time. He was especially intrigued with Sal's plans to work with Nahteste out on the twin reservations.

"You know," said Chaplain Cliff. "I have an idea I think was inspired by Heaven. Let me run it by you. A fellow student at the Bible Seminary where I attended dropped out after two years; he went on to earn a degree in Education. Then he finished his doctorate in Divinity. He's a good friend of mine who is a teacher and a minister, but without a flock. What if I can get my friend, Johnny, to come out and assist you in setting up a school program on the reservations? He might want to ask the tribal elders if he could also build a small church so he could begin his ministry. But that request would come later."

"That sounds like a fine plan," said Sal. "I really don't know how Nahteste will go for it, though. He hasn't been inclined toward believing what White men say. Maybe after Johnny has gained the confidence and respect of Nahteste and the tribal elders, he would have a better chance for a positive response."

Sal thought for a moment before continuing. "Keep in mind the Dutch Reformed Church has a history with the Apache," said Sal. "Most of it's good. But I am not one to know how interdenominational jealousies work. We certainly can use all the help we can get, and if Johnny is willing to assist in setting up some programs without assurances of it becoming more, I'm sure I can convince Nahteste to give it a try."

Chaplain Cliff agreed to contact Johnny and run the idea past him. He told Sal he could probably have an answer for him by Monday. Once that was known, Sal would then try to get Nahteste on board. With a shake of the hand, Sal set out on his way to St. David, satisfied with a great dinner and the chance to get an AA meeting started on the post.

When Sal arrived back at St. David, that AA meeting was already half over. Instead of interrupting by walking in, he walked Little John then tucked himself in for the night. "Another busy day," thought Sal. "I couldn't handle a job if I had one."

Once morning arrived, Sal walked Little John then decided today he was going to head to Tombstone for the day. He would stop for breakfast and then find Nahteste to see what kind of reception he'd get with the idea about the "flockless" priest. He was already sure Johnny would come out and be a part of their greater plan. When he walked into the Muffin Café, Lu waved him over to a booth in her section. She excitedly sat him at a table and said, "Sal, just wait until you hear this story!" She quickly placed his coffee cup in front of him then sat down in his booth.

"This morning, I had to be here real early for a special delivery of frozen meat the cook ordered, which would be dropped off at 3 a.m.," she began. "That's also when we close for an hour to prepare for the next day's customers. Well, over at the Bird Cage they had closed up and sent this drunkard packing. He pushed his way up in here even though we told him we were closed. He was very obnoxious, drunk and demanding. I told him the cook had already shut down the grill and we were just waiting for some supplies to be delivered. He kept arguing that he was hungry and he needed breakfast. So cook said to me he only had one egg left along with a chunk of Limburger cheese in the fridge. I told him to scramble it up in a pan. It would serve the drunk right for bothering us so late. So I served it to him with a smile on my face. After he took a bite he asked—'where do you get your eggs?' I said, Oh, in the little hen house out back—why? Then he said, 'do you have a rooster?' I told him we didn't. He said, 'you'd better get a rooster, there's a skunk doing your chickens!' When the drunk finished his meal he left me a $5 tip! Cook and I laughed the rest of the night."

Sal almost spit out his coffee at the punch line. They both laughed and Sal said, "I'll listen for that story in a meeting in case he ever makes it to a church basement."

Sal laughed again then said, "Now I feel like having a cheese omelet, but please make it mozzarella—not Limburger."

When Sal finished his omelet, he walked out of the café with day-old muffins for Little John, plus an assortment of baked goods to drop off at the bridge. At that moment, the constable was walking in the door of the café and held it open for Sal to carry out his boxes.

"That's a big take-out order," the constable nodded to Sal.

"Oh, I have a lot of dog to keep fed," Sal answered as he walked briskly to his car. "Damn," he thought. "Even that big lug is starting to be nice. There's hope for everyone, I guess."

After dropping the food under the bridge, Sal drove towards Miracle Valley. He recalled another occasion of an Apache encounter he had in the past. When he and three other young soldiers were driving from back East to Fort Huachuca for the first time, it was a very hot day in April. They were about 30 miles west of Roswell, New Mexico. They were in an old Pontiac with no air conditioning, and since they were "green horns," they didn't know enough to have water with them. As they came over a hill, they spotted a sign that advertised "Ice Cold Cherry Cider" for two dollars a gallon. Burt, the driver, whipped the car into the driveway, stopping by an old stone well. As they climbed out of the car a very desiccated Apache Indian came out of a trailer asking what they wanted. They responded they each wanted a gallon of the cider. The old Apache's eyes grew wide as he watched them chug down their ice-cold cider, and laughed as he collected their money, saying, "Good stuff, huh?"They agreed and drove on. About 15 minutes later, everyone started yelling to stop the car. They jumped out and all of them bolted into the desert where there wasn't a single bush to hide behind. No one cared. Everyone did what he had to do with cars whizzing by and shocked faces of tourists aghast at the sight of the four soldiers with their pants down around their ankles.

It so happened that Sal drove through the same area last winter on his way back from Pennsylvania and was amazed to see little Juniper trees growing where they had emptied themselves, fertilizing the desert. They could call it "Apache's Revenge State Forest."

CHAPTER 36

"BIG REZ" PLANS

S al was hoping that Nahteste didn't have any revenge planned for him this time. He figured he would keep the story to himself about the cider so he wouldn't give Nahteste any ideas. Sal needed to remember how angry Nahteste originally was when he heard what Sal was doing for the travelers.

As Sal pulled into the driveway, he saw Nahteste and his two nephews pushing an old truck up the drive. "Now I see why you guys are so strong," Sal yelled out to them. "Interesting exercise program—roll the truck down the hill then push it back up!"

Nahteste grimaced, almost laughed, but said instead," Just shut it. Do you have jumper cables?"

"Sure," said Sal. He was happy to lend a hand, especially since it might make the discussion go a little more smoothly. Sal tossed Nahteste a can of ether spray, which he kept in the car's trunk because of cold Pennsylvania winters. Using both, they started the truck and the nephews took off to who-knows-where-ville. Sal did not want to get nosy with these guys.

"Let's grab some coffee and sit in the shade," said Nahteste as he settled in. "What's up, my friend? You look like a man with something on his mind. Spill it—you've already gotten me into more fun than I've had in a long time."

"Well," replied Sal. "I've been thinking about how to get some education onto the two reservations. I may have stumbled onto something. I need you to be O.K. with it first though; your people's past history notwithstanding. I have a friend on the base, Chaplain Cliff. I explained to him what we want to do to help your people. He told me he has a friend that is a degreed teacher who would probably be willing to come up here and set up some school programs."

"Why do you look so nervous if that's all you've come to tell me?" asked Nahteste.

"Well," said Sal slowly. "There's more."

"Yeah," nodded Nahteste. "There usually is when a White man and a Red man make a deal. Go ahead; what else?"

"This teacher—Johnny—is also an ordained minister," said Sal. "Like my friend Chaplain Cliff. He doesn't have a congregation, yet, and if things go well with the school he would probably like to build a church and start his own ministry on the rez."

Sal waited for Nahteste to explode, but instead, he remained silent, looking deeply into Sal's eyes. Then he said the most unexpected thing Sal could have imagined. "You know, this might be the best thing to happen on the rez in a long time," Nahteste slowly nodded. "A do-gooder White man that can start a school for the younger children, and work with the older kids to keep them out of the gangs and off drugs and booze. I know you expected me to be upset with this idea, but actually, it may help everyone up here. If this Johnny can help teach the mothers how to home school when the roads are impossible to travel—which is half the year—the kids'll learn some discipline. He could try to get the older kids to come to church, at least for a while before they realize it's just a way to keep them controlled. This just might work. We all know that nothing else has."

Sal was delighted to hear the positive response from Nahteste. He hoped Johnny was willing to get on board. The area was such a beautiful place; at least on the Fort Apache reservation there were lakes, streams, deer, and elk. The western Apache got a better deal than most of their

Red brothers. The White Mountain Apache were allowed to stay on some of their own ancestral lands. The Chiricahua were taken to Florida and Oklahoma, and half of the remaining band that settled in Oklahoma was still there to this day. The other half was on a reservation with the Mescalero and Jicarilla Apache bands in New Mexico. Some families were also on the San Carlos reservation, which was not as beautiful an area as Fort Apache. Their ancestral lands were now a part of America's National Forest system, at least preserved so they could travel, camp and perform their ceremonies without interference. Nahteste was a Chiricahua Apache like his ancestors—Cochise and Geronimo.

Bidding him a warm good-bye, Sal left his friend in good spirits. It looked like their plan for bringing help to the reservations was becoming solid.

CHAPTER 37

ADIOS BIKERS

S al decided to call Mary even though it was only Thursday, so he could try to arrange an earlier meeting with the attorney and Mrs. Crane. Sal stopped on the outskirts of Sierra Vista at the Cabin Tavern to get change to place the call. Mary seemed delighted to hear Sal's voice and she told him she would ask Attorney Mayhew about his schedule for Friday. Sal asked her to call the monastery when she had an answer from the attorney's office, figuring he would be back home by then.

Sal then walked Little John to the edge of the parking lot, but alas, Little John did not leave a big deposit. Sal and Little John headed back to the monk house. After putting Little John into Brother Alex's room, he headed for the main building. As he entered, the phone rang. One of the Brothers answered the phone and looked up at Sal to say, "Oh yes, he's right here."

When Sal took the phone he became quite happy to hear Mary's voice on the line. She relayed the message that he could have a meeting with Attorney Mayhew at 1:30 p.m. on Friday.

"Great," said Sal. "And may I take you to lunch before the appointment?"

"Sure," said Mary. "I'll be ready at noon. Pick me up in front."

Sal hung up and said to himself, "Well, they say if you quit drinking things will get better, but I had no idea how much better they would get."

No bottle had ever made him feel this good. He knew he would never go back to that life. It was so much better being totally present in the moment and not acting goofy. Once more, he felt like his feet were barely touching the ground as he walked back to his room. He decided to take his notebook and sit down by the pond to plan out what he needed to buy for the upcoming meetings. He needed to ask Mrs. Crane for some money. He definitely wanted to see more of Mary.

It was so peaceful at the monastery. Sal understood now why the brothers gave up their previous lives to be here. No hot cars, no cool house or jobs that they had to work all year long to earn two weeks of vacation. In this fantastic environment they got 52 weeks of solitude, peace and quiet for doing a day's work—stress free—and enjoyed the companionship of like-minded people. Even though Sal didn't think he was ready for that lifestyle, he really understood its lure. Right now, his calling was to help as many people as he could, especially now that he was getting assistance from many different directions. That was all O.K. with him, because he really needed the help.

Sal realized the heroes he held in the highest esteem were the ones that spent their lives doing things to help others: Lincoln, Jesus, Gandhi, Bill W., Doctor Bob, St. Francis of Assisi, and J.F.K. Even though he was not of their stature, he was willing to help wherever he could. It would make his life worth living. He was no longer on a path of conning people to fund his way to more drinking and carousing. If he could just keep using his God-given talents to assist and contribute to others he was equally sure he would eventually be able to look back on his life with few regrets.

"Wow," mumbled Sal to himself. "What is it about this place that makes me think such heavy thoughts?" His reverie was suddenly broken by the sounds of loud Harley motorcycles pulling in to the driveway. He looked over and saw his three biker buddies he had guided into new adventures. Sal stood up and waved them over. The look on their faces spoke volumes, and as they shook his hand, they told him they were heading out for a while at least until things cooled down.

"O.K." said Sal. "But should I ask what's happened?"

"You may have been totally correct in backing away from what we were up to," said Jersey. "Maybe there's a good reason to leave law enforcement to the law."

Sal gave them a curious look as Jersey continued. "We did our usual setting up of an ambush down on the border, but this time things got way out of hand. We saw six guys coming up the trail with packs on, but before we could stop them, all hell broke loose. Rifle fire started hitting the trees all around us; we then saw other guys with rifles firing in our direction. One of our soldiers was hit in the arm so we opened up at the 'outlaws' to give us time to retreat towards Nahteste's place. Just two hours before this melee we had seen you leave his house, but we know you didn't see us. We were hiding out under the cover of trees for this ambush. One of the soldiers said he saw two of the riflemen go down from our fire before we got out of there." Jersey said they bandaged up their man and headed back to Sierra Vista so he could be treated at the base hospital.

"Nahteste and his nephews were not part of the deal this time," Jersey continued. "But he quickly packed up his stuff anyway. He said to tell you he'd be at his mom's place on the rez. He would not come back to his house for a while. So it's best that we'll be going now, ourselves. Things are too hot for us here. We'll probably head up to Sturgis, South Dakota or maybe Canada for a while.

Jersey and the other bikers started securing their rides for the trip and said, "Watch your back, Sal; we think the drug guys will be looking for revenge over our actions. You should be O.K., and the soldier will say he was hurt in a hunting accident. We wish you luck, maybe our paths will cross again."

Jersey told Sal they planned to attend A.A. meetings wherever they went 'cause they sure weren't going to do any drinking or drugging. With that, they headed up the road and out of sight.

"Holy frijoles," thought Sal. "Peaceful and serene? Things can sure change fast around here." Sal was thankful he had backed out of that mess before he could possibly become more entangled. He was thinking his guardian angel was watching out for him again. Putting away his journal he decided to walk Little John, then mosey over to the dining hall before he attended that evening's AA meeting. He decided that maybe he should talk about gratitude tonight.

The meeting that evening turned out to be a good one; everybody was happy to share their stories of gratitude. A man named Cooper caught Sal as the meeting broke up and asked him if he had heard the bikers roar out of the monastery that afternoon.

"Oh yeah," said Sal, replying as nonchalantly as possible. "They just stopped in to say good-bye. They were getting back on the road. California I believe they said is where they were headed next."

Time to hit the sack, Sal told himself as he left the room. It's been another fun day in my new life, especially now that I can recall everything that happens.

CHAPTER 38

MARY SMILES

F riday morning could not have come quick enough for Sal. He dressed in his good clothes then headed out for Tucson after a good breakfast at the monastery dining room. He pulled in at the truck stop for some real coffee, then rushed right back onto Route 10 so he made good time and arrived at the Law offices before noon. Mary gave him a big smile as he walked in the door. Together, they walked to the restaurant where Sal and Mary had lunch before, that memorable day when they first met. They spoke of many things and it was nice getting to know one another.

"I love my classes at the University of Arizona," said Mary. "I am really excited about studying to become a lawyer. I want to help others, maybe even be an attorney in the free legal aid center."

"I really respect and admire how you can work all day at the law office and then attend classes at night," said Sal. "Will I have to call you 'Doctor' some day, after you earn your doctorate in jurisprudence?"

They laughed together at that one. Sal got warm all over to see the way her eyes smiled and glowed whenever she laughed.

"You know," said Sal. "Me and my buddies used to come up on weekends from Fort Huachuca and stay in the transit barracks at Davis Monthan Air Force Base here in Tucson. We would go over to the University

Student Union Building and look at all the rich kids attending college. We were trying to get our education from the Army. Now I realize that the students we saw there were probably more like you: working their way through college to get a degree and better their lives. They weren't that much different from us, just no uniforms."

"Well, thanks for saying that, Sal," replied Mary. "I appreciate how you and many others are willing to risk your lives for our country."

"I never really thought of it that way," said Sal. "I just considered that I couldn't force myself to attend another four years of classrooms and studying after high school so I took what I thought was the easy route. I signed up for one year of electronics while I was in the Army because I thought it was the coming thing. But after four months I hated it. There were too many little adjustments and calculations in that field. I refused a lie-detector exam so I got out of the class and was offered less intense training. I guess I'm just not cut out for academics, but I do have good people skills. I believe I need a career that I could do well in without a lot of studying."

"From what I see and have overheard it seems you are doing a lot of good already," said Mary. "Maybe you're destined to be in a field where you can help others and yourself."

"Well, I never dreamed there would be this much satisfaction in helping others," agreed Sal. "Maybe I've been put on the path of social work. I guess we'll see where this all leads. Could be if I was born 100 years ago I would have been an Indian agent like that guy Clum. He was probably the best Indian Agent the Apache ever had. He did a lot to help the people. Unlike so many of the others that were and maybe still are only there to steal what they can from the Native-Americans' government funding for themselves and their friends."

They laughed, and Mary added, "I know I have definitely met someone who is destined to be known as a 'Great Defender of the Down Trodden.' Sal, I am very glad to have met you; I hope we can remain good friends as you pursue your dreams and I pursue mine."

Mary took his hand and squeezed it. As she did so, Sal's heart jumped in his chest.

"Just remember, Sal," she said. "Being born blessed with having a good heart may be more important than being born rich. Mrs. Crane is the richest person I have ever met, but I've heard her say to Mr. Mayhew that you have brought more joy into her life in a short time than anyone else she has ever met. That shows me how important we can be in some people's lives if we practice generosity of spirit."

Mary smiled that smile that warmed Sal's heart as she held his hand once again. This time there was no mistaking the electric shock it sent through him. He blushed and hoped she didn't see it.

"Let's get back to the office," Mary said. "I know it wasn't easy for them to clear their schedules to meet with you today."

Back in the office, Sal sat around the big conference table with Mrs. Crane and Attorney Mayhew. They smiled at him and said, "Well, let's hear what you have been up to this week."

Sal proceeded to tell them what he had accomplished: new A.A. meetings were established, a possible teacher to start schooling at the twin reservations, a group of women from Fort Huachuca to pick up the slack with delivering food to the Mexican travelers, the water-bag story, as well as exploration of some new sources for supplies. They were delighted and asked what they could do to assist him.

"Well," said Sal. "We will need a variety of things to get the meetings going, plus books, school supplies for the Apache kids, some means of a salary for the teachers, and well, have I overstepped my boundaries?"

Mrs. Crane was the first to speak. "Everything you have started sounds wonderful to me," she said. "I am prepared to assist you with the financing of all these endeavors. What is it that you need first?"

"The AA-meeting supplies are the immediate need," said Sal. "We need books, coffee pots and other literature. I know where to get the books and I'm sure there's a restaurant-supply business in Tucson for the coffee pots."

"Let me get Mary to help you with that," interjected Attorney Mayhew. "Maybe you could pick up the pots while you are up here today?"

"You have my permission to promise those teachers a fair salary," said Mrs. Crane. "So please, get that started, too. I will fund them to get it going for as long as necessary." Mrs. Crane thought for a moment then added, "I have a thought, Sal. I sit on the board of the medical center and one large expense we have is all the different medical kits. I'm wondering if we could somehow have the people on the reservation pack those kits. The medical center could save some money and we could provide ongoing work for more than a few people up there."

Sal got excited at the prospect. "That sure sounds like a win-win, Mrs. Crane. What can I do to follow up on that?"

"I believe it would be a good time for you to ride out to the reservation and meet some of the leaders," offered the attorney. "Don't take the word of one man on everything."

"Spoken like a true lawyer," Sal smiled. "Listen, verify, and then decide. I have no argument with that idea. I'll head over there within the week. I might even go there this weekend, but it probably better wait until after Monday when we have the meeting at Fort Huachuca."

"Well, Sal," said Mrs. Crane. "You have things to buy before you go back to St. David. Here's another $500 to cover the expenses for now. Is that enough?"

Sal smiled and thanked her profusely. "I always expected to see wings on the angels I met," he told her. "But you two surely qualify anyway. Thank you for all you are doing to help all those underprivileged people out there."

Attorney Mayhew told Sal he was sure Mary had found a place to purchase his coffee pots so she would give him directions to the restaurant-supply business. She also had information on the 12-Step store, Awakenings. Once he had touched base with the Elders on the reservation, Mrs. Crane and Attorney Mayhew wanted Sal to return and give them an update. Sal agreed, shook their hands and went to talk with Mary. She had everything he needed, including the promise to see him soon.

"I'll call you during the week," he told her.

"I'd really like that," Mary replied. "I'll look forward to it."

Mary held Sal's hand for a moment and once again he felt an electrical charge run through his arm. "Oh boy," he thought to himself." I am really in trouble." Sal stammered a good-bye and went out the door.

CHAPTER 39

CARRY THE MESSAGE

—⊁—⊬—⊁—⊬—⊁—⊁—⊬—⊁—

S al didn't have to drive far to get to the restaurant-supply business. It was just over on Speedway. When he told them what he was doing, they gave him a discount on the pots, silverware, cups and plates.

From the restaurant-supply place it was only five minutes to the bookstore. He was able to purchase 48 A.A. Big Books—two dozen for each meeting—24 12-Step books, four packs of literature and some medallions. He was particularly interested in the 90-day ones, which he felt were the most important. Helping keep someone sober for three months was huge; there was a lot for the newly recovering alcoholic to deal with within those first 90 days. Sal also bought a dozen Al-anon books in case family or friends of the addicted showed up. After paying cash for everything he was down to $128. He knew it was O.K., though; everything he had purchased was necessary and he still had nearly $200 in his checking account from the first check. With his newly purchased treasures he headed back to St. David.

The next morning, Sal decided he needed to make his rounds. It was time to put out water plus pick up and deliver food donations to feed some needy travelers. As long as he was going through Tombstone, Sal decided to have his breakfast there. He loaded up Little John into the Pontiac and hoped to score some goodies from the kitchen for his food route.

Once at the Muffin Café, Sal saw Sergeant Joe's car parked out front. Sal figured he would have to speak to him sooner or later, so he went inside. He was hoping that maybe the good sergeant would buy breakfast again. As he entered, Sal waved to Lu and mouthed that he wanted some coffee. Then he sat down at the same table as the sergeant who introduced Sal to another detective by the name of Bill Conrad.

"Bill's assisting me on an investigation out in your territory," said the sergeant.

"What does that mean?" asked Sal as he looked at both of the officers.

"Well, I wanted to talk to you again about that Miller Peak area," said the sergeant. "I've been charged with doing what I can along the border to slow down the drug runners coming into Cochise County. Last night there was a new development down there. We both are a little stumped. We're hoping you can shed some light on the situation in Miracle Valley."

Sal looked innocently at the officers as the sergeant continued. "We were called out last night to an explosion in the Valley—somebody's house burned down. While we were poking around trying to get a handle on what went on during the night, we found about 100 shell casings from at least nine different guns. I laughed when I told Bill about you. I said maybe that weird guy Sal can conjure up what happened, and here you walk in. Strange coincidence, don't you think?"

Sal sat speechless, thinking at least he didn't order a big breakfast because he had lost his appetite again. Sal decided to drink his coffee before he told them what he knew.

"First let me ask you a question," said Sal. "Do you know whose house was blown up?"

"Yes," said the sergeant. "We spoke to a neighbor and they told us some Indians lived there. Why?"

"Well," said Sal. "Maybe I can help you out. I picked up a big Indian one day near Tombstone and gave him a ride down that way; a big ole' Navajo, had a lot of silver jewelry that he planned on selling. He told me he was leaving the area—it was just too dangerous. He told me there were many nights where someone tried to steal his truck from his yard at the house he rented, so now he was hitching because they stole the battery from the truck. The part you'll probably find interesting is that one night he heard gunfire and thought that rival drug gangs were fighting with each other. Maybe that's what happened with all those shells."

Sal took a big gulp and asked the next question carefully. "There weren't any bodies in the ashes of the house were there?"

"No—no vehicles either," answered Bill. "The place looked empty. I guess they left before the real craziness started."

"Maybe it would be a good time to check out the trail," said Sal. "Maybe you could set up an interdiction and catch some bad guys bringing drugs into the county. Maybe take old Larry Goodnight off the radar and plunk him down that way to grab some banditos? Better give him a fast partner, though; looks like Larry would have a tough time running cross country."

The sergeant didn't find Sal's remark funny, but he did agree that Sal had a good idea about ambushing the drug mules. He let mention that Larry wouldn't have to catch them if he could get them to drop their packs.

"That would put a nice dent in the drug bosses' wallets," said the sergeant. "You know, Sal, I'm always glad to talk to you. I hope I'm never forced to arrest you. You seem to be in the most interesting spots way too often."

Sal gave a little shrug as the sergeant continued. "I'd like to let the county buy your breakfast," the sergeant said. "What do you say?"

At this point Sal felt he had dodged another bullet and felt hungry again. "O.K." he nodded. "That would be great; thanks. Always glad to help." Sal quickly called Lu over to place his breakfast order.

After the officers left, Lu came over and asked if everything was all right.

"Yes," Sal said. "Surprisingly so. I can continue my errands and so far, no problem."

"Good," Lu said. "I have some stuff for you. Pull around back when you're done. Joe already paid, and told me he had your breakfast this time but if you aren't careful the county will be buying you three meals a day."

CHAPTER 40

CHORES

S al pulled into the rear of the café and loaded up all the offered
goodies. He believed he had time to drop food and water at the
spot past Bisbee so the travelers would have something to carry
with them. The commercial laundry was open; they gave Sal 44
gallon jugs filled with fresh water. They also gave him nine blankets. Sal
bid them adios and headed down the highway towards Douglas where he,
in short order, put out the jugs. On the way back north he headed to the
Naco highway, stopping to see Juan.

Sal was able to fill his car with bags of cracked tortillas. He had to
even pack them around Little John, but the dog was happy to give up some
space in return for a few to munch. Sal drove through Bisbee and started
thinking there sure was a lot of activity in this out-of-the-way place. Bisbee had the largest open-pit mine in the world, billions of dollars in copper were taken out of the ground, which meant millions were spent in the
bars at Brewery Gulch. With all the travelers coming to Bisbee's Sacramento Hill Mine to find new work back in the turn of the 20th century. It
was ironic the miners came from thousands of miles across the Atlantic
ocean, from Wales and England to work in the mine, instead of the Mexicans who lived only a few miles away. It sure was a crazy world in Sal's es-
timation; he didn't doubt that some of the Mexicans walking through the

Bisbee area then and now would end up traveling thousands of miles to help landscape the homes of the Phelps Dodge Mines' bosses, who owned the mines, yet lived in New York State.

Sal saluted Irv and Bonnie as he drove by. He couldn't help but wonder how many goodhearted people were aiding the travelers along their way. He also wondered how many of them perished in the desert without finding that help. Sal was glad he was able to do a little for them because he was sure his grandparents had received some kind help when they came all the way from Europe to the United States. The phrase "pay it forward" came to mind, and that was exactly what Sal was trying to do. With Mrs. Crane's help, who knew what could be accomplished.

Sal put two bags of tortillas under the bridge, then drove up the dirt road to Charleston and Fairbank. There he dropped off the rest of his bounty, including three blankets at each stop. With that completed, Sal decided he and Little John deserved a good soak. He opened the car door and raced the dog to the big pool by the little bridge. While he floated in the water, he had a fleeting glimpse of bodies moving through the brush. "Vaya con Dios!" he whispered under his breath, "Buena suerte!" (Go with God and good luck.) Sal felt especially sorry for the small kids after miles and miles of walking through the heart of Mexico, then still having so much dangerous territory to contend with in this country.

Sal was glad he could do a little to ease their journey, and he was also glad he had told Sargeant Joe to be aware of the drug trail below Miller Peak. Though the men carrying all that poison may not be necessarily bad, their bosses were. They couldn't care less about young Americans whose lives were ruined by the crap. Sal was secretly glad he had only drunk booze; that had been hard enough to quit, but heroin was a whole other ball game.

"Go get them Deputy Goodnight," Sal chuckled to himself. He got out of the water and crawled up the embankment to lay under a big old Cottonwood. His lordship—Little John—took up a spot next to him. "Hey, Little John," Sal spoke softly to the dog. "This sure is the good life, isn't it?

Eat, swim, sleep, ride around; I think I'm probably more fun than Brother Alex, huh?" The dog gave a slight moan and fell asleep.

As soon as Sal relaxed, he felt a presence beside him. He heard a soft voice telling him to go to the reservations and see what the situation was for himself. He was to travel the road from St. David to the Dragoon Mountains of Cochise; then he was to go up to Dragoon and Route 10 to drive to the reservation. He was gently told he would be rewarded if he did as he was told.

"I am very satisfied with what you have done for the down-trodden," Teralisa said to him. "Keep up the good work. You are on a very wonderful, rewarding path of love for your fellow man."

Little John suddenly shuddered, rolled off a red anthill and jumped up. This startled Sal as he jumped back into the water. Sal looked where his mentor spirit had stood a moment before, but she was gone. Luckily, Sal realized that the same ants that had disturbed Little John were now only inches away from his bare legs so he followed the dog into the water. He chuckled to himself that his guardian angels even protected him from bugs.

Sal decided to take little John for a short walk to the Indian ruins nearby to dry off and snoop around. He hadn't been through the ruins in a couple of years. He could see the area was just as he last saw it, but with a little more graffiti. It was a shame people couldn't leave these sacred places alone, and let them stand for future generations to enjoy. He wondered how many of the ruins, which weren't protected by the government, would still be around in 100 years. Pothunters ripped open a lot of graves to steal relics; and the so-called scientists took the skulls and bones of the ancient ones back to museums to sit in boxes in their basements and collect dust. He thought that if he were a Native American, he might be inclined to go to some fancy cemetery in New York or Connecticut to dig up a couple of graves and say he was doing research. Maybe he could tell which of those White folks brought Small Pox to their land to kill off 90 percent of the native ancestors. He just didn't understand how the "Powers That Be" rationalized that it's O.K. for the White man to tear up Indian graves, but it would be unthinkable for Indians to tear up White men's graves.

Sal figured the prison sentence he would receive might be worth the publicity of bringing the crazy situation to the notice of the American voter. With that thought past, Sal knew it was time to head back to St. David. There was a lot to do there, and plenty of tasks to plan out, things that he actually could do something about, like the Serenity prayer says, "Do something about the things you can and accept the things you can't ."

Back at the monastery, Sal realized he missed lunch. He was famished so he found himself hoping the evening meal would be good. After getting Little John settled in the room, Sal headed for the kitchen. He smelled his favorite dish the minute he walked in—spaghetti and meatballs. It made him all smiles, but then he noticed there were a lot of strange faces about the place. He hoped that meant it would be a good 12-Step meeting. Back in the day, they use to call Saturday night "amateur night" because of all the people who only drank on that day of the week. Unlike Sal and his buddies—who hardly ever missed a night of drinking. He was glad he had learned the lesson not to touch that first drink before he put himself in an early grave. Sal decided that if he spoke tonight, he would talk about that. The subject of dying always got a good discussion going, because if the people were honest, none of them could say they didn't drive drunk. Many of them did 100 percent of the time. He figured they must keep all the guardian angels busy trying to keep the innocent people and the drunks safe.

Sal remembered when his A.A. group back East took a meeting to the county jail. When they finished up speaking a guy came forward and told them a story. "One Saturday morning I was still drinking since leaving work Friday night," he said. "I blindly drove up Main Street towards my house and I suddenly heard a thump. I stopped in the middle of the road to look and a big crowd gathered. I had hit a mother carrying a bag of food from McDonald's for her kids waiting in her car across the street. She was dead and I was sentenced to 30 years before I'd be eligible for parole, so please keep telling people at your meetings—'don't drink and drive.' The consequences are horrible for all."

Sal thought he'd share that story tonight about the kids growing up without a mom and a young guy growing up without a life. Booze and cars—nobody wins.

That evening's meeting was remarkable to Sal. It went on for hours because everyone had a burning desire to share a first or second-hand story. There were two people from New Jersey who knew Sal's old sponsor—Jim McC. and his wife Rosemary. They were actually very well known in the AA community. They had even helped get the first few AA meetings in New Jersey started back in the 1930's.

Since it was the end of another great day, Sal headed to his room for his evening tasks—walk and shovel Little Johns leavings, shower, and hit the sack. He couldn't help but wonder how many of his drinking buddies at Fort Huachuca would show up for the new meeting at Chaplain Cliff's chapel. Sal wanted to get his friend, Kyle, there. Even though he claimed to only drink socially, Sal remembered Kyle driving them back from Mexico and constantly going off the road, and always being at Sal's side drinking right along with him. But he recognized all he could really do was spread the message. They'll take what they want and leave the rest. Sal didn't make them drink. He couldn't make them stop.

CHAPTER 41

MOUNTAIN LION

A waking up on Sunday morning, Sal decided to let the Bonneville sit and rest for the day. He had driven it hard for a couple of weeks and it could use some time off. Sal headed for breakfast and thought he might even attend services in the chapel. He knew it never hurt to hear some good words about how to be a better person. Lord knew he never paid any attention to the nuns at St. Mary's back in elementary school. Sal had done great until the fourth grade when he turned down the opportunity to be an altar boy. He may have been the first boy to ever decline the offer, but after that, he was constantly in trouble. His mother had to beg the Mother Superior to let him back into school after they suspended him. She also had to sell extra tickets to the school plays to keep in favor.

Sal thought that maybe some people were destined to be religious and some were not. He didn't think he had much religion at all, but he had a lot of spirituality. He wanted to talk with someone about that someday. It would take someone he respected. He felt man-made religion had always been used to control and enslave people throughout the world. Children are brainwashed at a pretty young age to follow the dictates of "men of the cloth," who have been known to abuse their power all too often. They could be corrupt, even to the point where they had exterminated those who did not succumb to their wishes or beliefs.

A few months ago driving to Arizona from Pennsylvania, Sal saw a bearded guy on the side of the road holding a sign that read: "Question Authority." It was something he really contemplated as he drove. He saw the wisdom in questioning things he didn't understand instead of following blindly. A lot of things would change if that idea took hold. Rules like not eating meat on Friday, wear a tie if you're in business, or 'born a catholic-die a catholic"; it seemed never-ending. Men must be in charge of everything, women are inferior, colored people are not smart genetically, and it went on and on. As Sal talked to young people, he could tell their attitudes were changing. The kids didn't think like their parents or grandparents. They were not willing to accept that just because it's the way it's always been it must stay that way. Just because the government of old White men says we must fight and die in a war half way around the world in Viet Nam doesn't mean it has to be that way. Sal believed people would see many changes in the U.S. and around the world very soon. He hoped it was without bloodshed and rioting.

"Wonderful," thought Sal. "See what happens when a drunk doesn't stay busy? He starts to think and sometimes it gets scary." He figured that is how things would change; thousands if not millions of young people would start to discuss options in their lives instead of accepting the status quo. Sal hoped the future would be much different than it was now, perhaps because information was no longer limited to a weekly newspaper where people are told only the things the most powerful want them to know. Radio and television were everywhere; there was even satellite communication in the skies. Who knew what that would bring to the world? There were machines being built that could calculate problems quicker and better than the human mind. The future had arrived and it would bring change faster than ever before. For Sal, just getting out there and helping people was enough for him. He had no idea what was in store in the years to come.

When Sal went into the chapel he saw Brother Casper, the leader of the monastery's band of celibates, speaking to a small group. He wasn't holding a traditional mass, but a non-denominational sharing of love for each other. He spoke simply.

"Go forth, do no harm, help others, emulate Jesus," he said. "If every one would just stop and think what Jesus would do before doing anything major, we would have a much better world."

Sal pondered Brother Casper's words and decided he would try it out to see how it went. There was more genuine wisdom and love of fellow man in that humble speech than he had heard in a while. All the years of sermons he was forced to attend that said, "blah, blah, blah," talkin' loud and sayin' nothing. It seemed a waste. Sal remembered something he heard at an AA meeting. "We are right where we are supposed to be; relax and enjoy the ride." That was more real to Sal as each day passed.

Back at his room, Sal grabbed Little John for a leisurely walk. "Today we can take our time down by the river," Sal told the dog. They walked through the Sycamore and Cottonwood trees. Sal mused that only 80-100 years ago if one moseyed along like this, they better be well armed. The entire area was controlled by Cochise and/or the Geronimo bands, as well as other Apaches that wandered the area. They were looking for cattle and horses to steal, or settlers to rob and kill. It must have been fair in their minds considering the Mexicans and White men stole their land and killed them whenever they could. Sal was glad it had changed. He wanted the opportunity to help the Apache have a better life. He started hoping, again, that Johnny would agree to teach on the reservation, even if it did mean building a little church. Though Sal didn't know him yet, he felt the guy had a good heart and would do whatever he could to assist the people on the reservation.

"I guess we'll find out tomorrow, won't we?" Sal said to Little John. But the dog was too busy digging into a ground squirrel's den to pay any attention to some babbling human.

Once Sal and Little John had walked about a mile downstream, Sal stripped to his shorts. "Little John," said Sal. "This is your lucky day. If you were in your native land you'd probably be walking in a lot of snow. Maybe you would like that better cause it must get pretty hot with all that fur covering you."

Sal thought about the AA saying—"Being just where one is supposed to be." He figured it had to apply to animals, too. "Same creator for all creatures," mused Sal. It was His plan, not man's. Sal and Little John walked through the water; it was still cold—after all, it was only January—and the San Pedro River was fed from the Sierra Madre Mountains by snowmelt.

After playing around, they climbed the riverbank, where Little John suddenly started to growl. It was the first time Sal had even heard the dog make a statement. He looked around and there, about 30 feet away, was a big, male mountain lion. It was sitting on its haunches, watching them closely. Sal realized he didn't even have a knife with him, but no sooner did he think about that, then Little John rushed straight toward the puma. Thankfully, the cat jumped up and headed into the brush. Sal quickly put on his pants and boots and ran in the direction the animals went. He yelled for Little John, hoping his noise would keep the mountain lion on the run. If the cat decided to turn and face the dog, despite Little John's size, one swipe and he was likely to lose his nose. Sal could hear the dog barking just ahead of him, and when he caught up he could see the cat 20 feet up in a tree. Little John was fruitlessly jumping at the base of the trunk, growling and taunting the feline. Sal grabbed Little John's collar and kept yelling the entire time to keep the cat up the tree. He slowly dragged Little John's 200-pound mass away from the area.

"God, Little John," panted Sal. "When you pick a fight you sure pick the biggest guy in the bar. We've got to get back to the monk house while we still can."

The mile back took a lot longer as he struggled with Little John's bulk. Sal had taken off his belt and used it as a leash to keep pulling the dog down the trail. Just before he made it back to the car, he was met by a crowd of Brothers and visitors.

"What in the world went on down there?" they asked incredulously.

"We could hear you shouting and the dog barking. Is everything O.K?"

"It is now," answered Sal. "But I advise caution if you're going to walk in the woods. There's one big cat hanging out down there."

The crowd showed some relief and said they were glad it turned out O.K. for all concerned. They slowly returned to the dining hall for iced tea and lemonade. Sal returned Little John to Brother Al's room with a huge basin of water, figuring the dog might sleep for two days after all that exercise. "We'll have a great story for Brother Al on his return," Sal patted the dog on his head before he left the room.

Once Sal was seated in the dining hall and had finished off two glasses of lemonade, he told the people in the hall what had happened.

"We have never seen a cougar here," said Brother Casper. "Lots of bobcats, though."

"It definitely was a lion," said Sal. "Long tail, and at least the length of Little John—just leaner."

The group laughed at Sal's "lean lion" description, but he was sure they were glad it wasn't them who had bumped into the mountain lion. They were all mostly city folk and they thought it was best to run if they saw one. Sal was able to convince them the best thing to do was to make yourself seem as big as you can.

"If you wave your arms and yell, hopefully the cat will run off," said Sal. "That's usually the right thing to do. Their killing technique is to bite down at the base of the neck of their main prey, which is deer. If you run, the main target becomes your neck and they just might attack."

Sal told them about a kid he had read about who got killed while running on his high-school track. The mountain lion jumped the fence and killed him with one bite to his cervical spine. The bottom line was that when people were in mountain-lion territory, they had to be respectful of the danger. It was similar to taking the hunting grounds away from the Apache; if it hadn't been for the warriors working with us as scouts to hunt down the warring bands, people to this day might still have to worry about Cochise and Geronimo's descendents. If our forefathers hadn't adopted some of the Indian's fighting methods—guerrilla-warfare—we might still be ruled by the British.

"Anyway, be careful out there when you're walking," warned Sal. "Especially in the mornings and evenings; we made the cat pretty angry; he might be back."

CHAPTER 42

LOVE THOSE CEE~GARS

A fter all the excitement, Sal decided to put the rest of the day to good use and write in his journal. The first thing he needed to do was to call Mary and share his excitement if Brother Casper would let him use the phone.

When Mary answered the phone she seemed very pleased to hear Sal's voice. She had been reading law books and writing reports; talking to Sal was a welcomed change. After he explained the adventure he and Little John had, she was glad they were O.K. Sal promised her they would meet as soon as he returned from his trip to the reservation. In fact, he planned on driving to Tucson as soon as he had something to report.

Taking a big cigar from the room, Sal went to a bench by the pond to start writing in his journal. He got lost in thought for a couple of hours until he heard the dinner bell toll. Sal put away his journal, fed Little John, and promised to reward the dog since he so valiantly protected him earlier that day.

Sal had a good dinner—pot roast with potatoes and peas—and the cook saved him the bones for Little John. Before he headed out, Brother Casper gave him an old horse lead-line to use as a leash for the dog.

"If he goes after the lion again, it might not turn out so well," said Brother Casper. "Then what would we say to Brother Alex? He really loves that dog."

Sal thanked the monk and went back to walk his hero. He actually had to coax Little John to get up for a walk since the dog was exhausted. Once he smelled the bag of bones, though, he resurrected himself and followed the pied piper who promised a treat.

The 12-Step meeting that night was mellow; Sal just sat and listened since he felt he had talked enough during dinner. When he returned to his room, Little John had devoured the three bones that had been left for him. "That's some powerful jaws you got there, L.J.," said Sal. "But I still don't think you can join up with the Lee Brothers out of Tucson and start hunting lions just yet."

The last walk of the night ended with Sal flat on his back in bed and chuckling. "I think I'd rather meet up with spirits rather than with that cat we met today." And no sooner had he mumbled that to himself, Sal fell into a well-deserved sleep.

CHAPTER 43

THE WIVES

A new week was beginning for Sal. After a good night's rest and a full breakfast, he headed to the Fort to meet with the "Chaplain and his wives," which had become the minister's little joke about his entourage of helpers working to deliver food and water to the travelers. Little John was barely able to climb into the back seat, still exhausted from the previous day. Sal chuckled to himself as the dog fell instantly asleep. It all worked out well, he thought, but he shuddered to think how that could have been very different. Taking on a predator that could bring down an elk is not a good idea. They wouldn't be doing that again. Sal got serious as he thought about the Mexican families traveling across the hot desert. The desert had all sorts of day and night creatures. There were rattlesnakes, scorpions, black widow spiders, coyotes, bobcats, mountain lions and maybe even some crazy men who were known to shoot at people just for walking through the desert. Sal was glad he was able to help the travelers in his own small way.

Sal remembered an old cowboy once telling him about a pack of wild dogs he'd run into while tending cattle. It was up near Winslow where the dogs were killing off a lot of calves. He said that the foreman sent him out for the best part of that winter to hunt them down. He chased them all over that high-desert country, where he knocked off quite a few disheveled, skinny mutts. Cold, tired and hungry for some companionship, he was five miles from the main camp when he spotted the leader of the pack sitting up on top of a ridge like an antelope will do. Pulling his rifle from the scabbard he took aim and ended the reign of terror visited on those calves for the past year. He stated that he still felt bad doing that job recalling how much he loved his own boyhood dog.

Before going into the back gate of the post, Sal stopped at a café for some real coffee. He had some time before his 10 a.m. meeting with the Chaplain. When he pulled into the chapel yard, Sal could see a few cars. He was happy to see a closed van that he hoped could be used to pick up and deliver the supplies. With a van like that, it would take fewer trips to Bisbee and Douglas. Maybe he and his helpers wouldn't burn out so fast that way.

Chaplain Cliff came out to Sal's car and spoke. "I saved you a spot in the shade so your dog would be comfortable in the car. He seems like a great dog."

"Ha! I have a 'Little John' story for you when we get inside," said Sal. There were seven women waiting at the table. After the Chaplain introduced Sal, each one said her name. Their husbands were deployed overseas, mostly in Viet Nam, and two in places they weren't allowed to say.

Sal thanked them for coming and broke the ice by telling them about Little John's big adventure. When they all seemed relaxed, Sal told them what he had been doing and said he needed their help to continue. They all liked the project and were eager to participate.

"I would really be indebted to you for your assistance," said Sal. "I have a budget for gas so I can fill your cars. How would you like to begin?"

"Three of us don't have children to worry about," volunteered one gal. "So we can start immediately. We could work out a schedule with the others, arranging for childcare and such."

"That'd be great," said Sal. "So, whose van is that parked outside?"

"That's mine," said Cindy, the woman who had no children. "It's in great shape and we can use it as much as we need to."

"O.K. then," said Sal. "Why don't we use it today so I can show you the route we'll do once or twice a week?"

At that suggestion the meeting broke. The Chaplain allowed Sal to put Little John in the cool basement and they headed out. Three of the women jumped in the van with Sal and headed for Bisbee to pick up as much water as the commercial laundry could give them. En route, Sal showed them the bridge where most of the supplies were dropped off, explaining how he arranged things for the travelers and signaling them with his horn. By the time they got to the laundry, they were able to pick up 62 gallons of water and eight blankets.

The group headed to the next drop-off point with the supplies. Sal showed them where he placed the water. They put the jugs in four different spots and made sure ribbons were tied in nearby tree branches. They left one blanket at each stop since it was a limited supply.

Sal then directed the ladies over to the supermarket to pick up whatever amount of tortilla chips could be spared. Juan was glad to meet the ladies, too, and promised to do all he could for what he called 'Sal's kind conspiracy.' They hauled out five bags of tortillas and three cases of assorted beans. Juan threw in four boxes of powdered milk, which he thought would be good for the younger migrants. Everybody thanked him and then they drove away with their booty.

"Let's drive to Brewery Gulch to see if they have anything to give," said Sal. "We have room for some more."

When they arrived, Sal introduced them to Crisco. Much to his chagrin, Crisco gave Sal one of his tortuous bear hugs then laughed when he dropped him.

"I love seeing that look on your face, amigo," chuckled Crisco. "No worries, though. I haven't killed anyone—yet."

They loaded up the water bags Crisco had set aside and to Sal's surprise, Crisco slipped him $60 cash. "That's to help with the gas, man," he said real low. "I really appreciate what you're doing. Keep it up. Stop back in a month or so and I'll have more bags for you."

Sal shook Crisco's hand as hard as he could and thanked him pro-fusely. "We'll be back in a month," Sal nodded.

As they were driving, the ladies commented that Sal's "route" seemed to be well established. "We look forward to continuing it for you," one of the ladies said. "Hopefully we can expand it to more areas so we can reach more people."

"You know the manager at the base commissary lives next door to me," said Cindy, the driver of the van. "I'll talk with him to see if he can give more food. My house has a big, cool basement so we can store a lot of supplies between trips."

As they passed Bonnie and Irv's place, Sal explained what went on there and decided to stop and introduce his new crew. They dropped off a couple bags of tortillas, canned food and blankets. From there they head-ed to the San Pedro River to place the last of the goodies. At the drop site there weren't any travelers to be seen, but there was a piece of rebar stick-ing out of the ground with a rosary hanging from it. They assumed it was meant as a gracias for the food and water. Sal took it down and hung it on the rear view mirror of the van saying it would protect them all during their mission.

At the end of the first day on the job, they finished up by laughing and joking as they returned to the chapel. Cindy seemed to become the natural leader in the group.

"Do you think I should try to organize some more women?" she asked Sal. "I would be proud to do that, and once a week we could get together with or without you to organize the following week's efforts."

"That would be great," said Sal as he gave Cindy his phone number at the monastery. "Just leave a message if I'm not available and I'll call you back as soon as I can."

Sal gave Cindy the $60 Crisco had donated so they could keep the van full of gas. They hugged each other good-bye then left the chapel. Sal retrieved Little John from the basement.

CHAPTER 44

CUTACHOGI!

Just as Sal was pulling out, Chaplain Cliff appeared from around the corner. "Everything went great on the route," said Sal. "But I forgot to ask you about Johnny."

"Oh yeah," he nodded. "Johnny will come out within two weeks. He loves the idea. He mentioned he'd be willing to do whatever is helpful. He said he'd be O.K. if he can't build a mission up there. He feels that leading by example will be a big help to the people on the reservation, being there's such a long history of deceit and broken promises between the White and Red men."

Sal was elated with the news so he jumped out of the car to hug the Chaplain. "I sort of jumped the gun with my Apache contact," Sal explained. "I was already anticipating Johnny's arrival so I told him all about it. Don't know if they still do scalping today but if and when you meet my friend, Nahteste, you'll understand. He is not a man I'd want to disappoint—and never lie to. I really thought my big mouth got me into trouble again."

Sal started to leave again, but stopped in his tracks. "Uhoh...I'm doing lots of forgetting today," he mumbled to himself. "I have the coffee maker and the books for the meeting in my trunk."

"That's great," said Chaplain Cliff. "Let's take it in and set it up. I had been concerned you might not be able to get the supplies, financially or otherwise."

"Not a problem," said Sal. "We have an angel who is helping us perform our good works—whatever we need, we will have the backing for it. I've gotten the O.K. to pay Johnny and up to three other teachers on the reservation. There's also money to buy books and supplies as needed, so we are in great shape."

"Sal, someday there will be books written about you," smiled the Chaplain. "What you are accomplishing is tremendous. And you're accomplishing it as you ramble along."

After the men set up the meeting space, Sal told the Chaplain that Bud would be in touch with him to coordinate the starting date. "Two evenings a week would be best at the beginning," said Sal.

"Whatever you think will do the most good," said the Chaplain. "I am a believer now that I can see what you are capable of doing. This is all a great adjunct to my ministry. I thank you, Sal, for the opportunity to expand my service to mankind."

"I knew I wouldn't accomplish anything of value if I continued drinking," said Sal. "I totally believe my Higher Power has a hand in what I'm doing. I heard in the rooms if you're feeling down, go out and find someone to help. That will make both of you feel better."

The men shook hands and Sal headed out with Little John in tow. As one of Sal's sergeant's back at the Fort use to say, "Let's Cutachogi." The man was from down south and those hillbillies always had funny sayings. But he had been a good person. Sal was sure he had tried the man's patience several times. He began to wonder if the sergeant was still at the base. He might need to look up some of his old friends; maybe some of them would show up at the AA meetings. Sal thought he'd better find a way to get the word out on that, too; maybe the Chaplain could announce it at the Sunday service, then word of mouth would take over. Sal thought maybe Kelly would let him put a poster on the back bar—he chuckled to himself—just as soon cut my throat, he thought. I'd be taking his best customers away.

Sal looked over at Little John and told him they deserved a good dinner that evening. They headed back to St. David, arriving in time to wash up and get to the dining hall. Unfortunately, it was fish night, and Sal's spirits drooped a little. Oh well, he thought to himself, the price is right and the day turned out pretty well.

The meal turned out to be salmon that some local guys brought back from Washington State in coolers full of ice. They donated it to the monastery in trade for a room. Along with potato au gratin, peas and homemade bread, dinner was way more than he'd expected. Sal found himself sitting next to a couple that were traveling cross-country and pulling a funny little trailer they would sleep in at church parking lots. They were very appreciative to have a night in a real bed with a warm shower and good food to fill their stomachs. Life was good to them. It turned out they were both in recovery and would be attending that evening's meeting.

The couple told Sal about a funny situation that happened on their way through New Mexico. As the wife turned red, Sal began to imagine it had something to do with the Apache's Revenge. Sure enough, when they were west of Roswell, after looking for alien spaceships, they stopped to buy some cider. At the time, it had sounded so good, but a half hour later the volcano erupted. Sal let out a howl and confessed the same thing had happened to him.

"It's the worst thing that has happened on our trip so far," said the woman.

"Well," laughed Sal. "Thanks to me and my buddies, there are a few small trees to hide behind. We only had a little cactus three years ago."

They all shared a good laugh and the husband said, "We drunks must always be careful what we drink. We can get into trouble even when its not booze."

They agreed to connect at the meeting later in the evening. When Sal spotted Brother Casper near the kitchen, he said grinning, "I'll be away for a few days, can you keep the monastery under control until I get back?"

"Well, if I have a problem doing that I can always call your good friend

Sergeant Joe of the Sheriff's office," laughed Brother Casper. "I have his card right here."

Sal paled a little as he asked when the sergeant had paid him a visit.

"Oh, just this morning," answered Brother Casper. "He wanted to visit with you and said he'd be back soon. Are you in any trouble, Sal?"

"No," he answered. "I'm not in any kind of police trouble. Honestly, I have only been doing good things since I came to this monastery."

"Well," said Brother Casper. "The sergeant did say to tell you that you aren't in any trouble—he just wanted a little more information about the Mexican border. There's no need for you to call him. He said he'd find you. It sounds like you're O.K. with him; I told him you are a model boarder here—no problems. Have you ever thought of joining the monastery?"

"Uh oh," thought Sal, "I think I saw this coming," "I'm just going with the flow right now," he told the monk. "I'm way too busy to think about much more, plus there's a woman I really want to get to know better. When I practice celibacy it's not going to be by choice. So, no offense, thank you, no. I'm just not interested in being a monk. I really respect all you do, providing space for people to get their acts together, and I really thank you for all you've done for me. I can't believe it's only been a few weeks since I arrived here. I've had so many experiences in this short time; one thing is for sure, my life is not boring."

CHAPTER 45

SHARING

T he 12-Step meeting at the monastery was packed and even Bud
came over to join them. Sal was asked to chair the meeting and
after a few qualifying remarks he asked Bud and the new couple
to share their stories.

Sal was astounded at the tales he heard. Bud once owned a Chevrolet
Dealership outside of Chicago but he lost everything to his uncontrol-
lable drinking. That included a great wife, two kids and a home on Lake
Michigan. He landed in St. David on his way to Mexico to drink himself to
death. He stopped for gas at the station he now runs and ended up talking
with the previous owner. He bought the station from the guy with the last
cash he had left from his business in Chicago. That was 17 years ago and
that's also when he decided to get sober. The only AA meeting around was
in Benson where a lot of retired soldiers from the Fort and airmen from
David Monthan Air Base lived. He told them he wished he had discovered sobriety before losing everything he loved, but at that time, he loved
drinking more. There was hardly a dry eye in the place when Bud sat back
down and turned the podium over to the couple passing through.

Her story sounded similar to others Sal had heard in the rooms. She
once was a successful stockbroker in New York City where she socially
drank with occasional weekend binges. When she met her husband to

be—also a stockbroker and a drinker—they started getting together to drink after the stock market closed. Then they started slipping out at lunch to drink. They had a crazy romance—it was semi-blurry—but they decided to marry. Luckily, there were no children involved, but within a year, they were both fired for being half drunk on the job and fully drunk the rest of the time. They lived on their savings, found a bunch of meetings in Greenwich Village and got sober together. Since New York's high rent was eating up most of their savings, they decided to buy a little trailer and get out on the road to see America. They had found many good meetings as they traveled the blue highways and this was one of the best; she then thanked Sal for asking her to speak.

When the husband got up to speak, his story went back a little further than his wife's; it included when he was expelled from Yale. He lost his first wife, straightened out for a while, then landed a great job on Wall Street. He met his soul mate—his current wife—but their world collapsed around them both. He even admitted to a short battle with heroin. By luck, he and his new wife drank so much that he was unable to shoot heroin anymore, so he settled for just the booze. He might be the only junkie who kicked the habit using Wild Turkey to go cold turkey.

That story brought fits of laughter from the group, but they also realized just how powerful the addiction to booze was. They were all lucky to have found these rooms.

The husband emphasized he didn't recommend using booze to replace any addiction, whether it be food, sex, heroin or cocaine. The bottom line for them all was not to use any form of "mood-changers." Going to meetings helped him find himself. He no longer needed to be a slave to anything.

Sal thanked everyone for speaking and attending, then closed the meeting with the Lord's Prayer. The meeting after the meeting lasted for some 90 minutes longer, with newcomers crowding Bud and the couple, peppering them with questions.

Sal walked back to his room thinking the meetings were truly amazing. People get to hear exactly what they need to hear. There's never a bad meeting, some just aren't as eventful.

CHAPTER 46

REZ TRIP

The next morning, Sal awakened at 5 a.m., did his chores, and set out on the trail to the twin reservations. He knew this should be a memorable trip. The kitchen was still dark so he drove down Route 80 to Horse Ranch Road, then east toward Cochise's old, but famous, stronghold. He remembered the instructions given to him by his spirit guide. He was ready for this new adventure. Little John was sound asleep in the back seat without a care in the world. He had watched Sal load the car's trunk with supplies.

It wasn't long before Sal reached the intersection of Four Ranch Road, which would lead him up to Dragoon and over to Route 10 where he could continue his journey. Just as he turned north he saw a large Cottonwood tree at a pull off near a cattle-loading station. He decided to make a quick stop and water some cactus. He got Little John to lie down near him under the tree and proceeded to close his eyes for a bit. As past experience proved out, Sal felt a presence so he looked up. He saw the very large Indian who had visited Sal before down by the San Pedro River looking down at him. "I am Cochise," the Indian said. "This was the land that was my favorite place to live. I hated the fact that strangers entered here and killed the game that sustained my people for so many years. We never killed more than we needed, unlike the crazy Whites who came here and would shoot as many of the deer as they could. They would only take two or three of the animals and leave the rest to rot. I never understood this, as "Yusan," our "Great Spirit," provided for us while those men just killed for no reason.

"When they killed my people just like the deer, we started hunting them down to eliminate the threat to our families. They shot squaws and children at the springs that were only trying to get water. Can you explain why they would do this?"

Sal looked at Cochise wide-eyed and said softly, "I don't know. There are many bad people in the world, as there are many good. I cannot explain what I don't understand."

"I see by your eyes you are an honest man," said Cochise. "You do many honorable deeds as you go through your life. This is good. You will find that your life is short, but how you live it will determine how you will spend eternity. I know your intentions will be seen and understood by the universe of your God for this path you have chosen. Your acts of "Do good and Feel good" may sound selfish but the spirit world sees this effort as the right path, and you will be rewarded in this life as well as the following.

"Young man, you are an exception to the white men I have met, and if you continue with what you have begun your rewards and satisfaction will be great. Stay on this path and you will help many people— you and they will be much better for it. I know I am thought of as a mass murderer by the Whites, but if they would dig deeper they would see I did what I had to do to protect my people. Especially our women and children; they only wanted to live in peace in their homeland. I regret many things I did; some were very cruel and unnecessary, but I was just a man like you. I did what I had to do to protect, I tried to live in peace with your people but I was rewarded with deceit and cruelty.

"The violence I inflicted across our homeland was very little compared to what your ancestors did to my people. Consider that when they came to our land there were millions of what you call Indians and now, there are only thousands. That is proof of who was the more murderous; not only with your muskets but also with diseases you spread with the blankets you offered us. We had no protection against small pox or measles. It left only a small percentage of my people alive.

"White men killed off all our game so we had nothing to eat. They starved whole tribes. They came to us and said, "We have God on our side." What kind of God do they have who would do this to us? Can you tell me that? I believe its proof that I am allowed to spend eternity here in this land that I love, by my God, I am forgiven for what I had to do. For it was right."

Sal sat there, stunned into silence. Who could answer Cochise anyway? Having this great chief come to him twice and tell him all this would certainly change the way he looked at the Great Southwest's past. Sal did the only thing he could think of—he thanked Cochise for opening his eyes and solemnly promised to continue to do as much good for all the people that he could. He would make a special effort for those who were having the most trouble.

"Your path is good," Cochise said to him. "It needs not be a 'White path or a Red path'—stay on

whatever path guides you to help others. I know our spirits want us to follow the 'Path of Love' for one another."

Sal felt both embarrassed and ashamed of how he had lived in the past. He hung his head. When he looked up, Cochise was gone, but at his feet were two pieces of wood. When Sal picked them up he realized it was a broken arrow. He was stunned at the realization he had proof of his spiritual encounter. As he got up, he wondered if his life could get any weirder. He had once thought his spiritual encounters were elaborate dreams, but holding the broken arrow in his hand he knew the spirit world was definitely real and he was connected to it. He wasn't afraid; he realized that with God/Spirit on his side there wasn't anything to be afraid of.

Sal roused Little John and got him back into the car. He mused that he was driving a car named after a great chief—Pontiac—and he had just met another. He wondered just how much greater America would have been if everyone had lived in peace. How much could we have learned from one another, he pondered. People came to this country supposedly for religious freedom and a new beginning, escaping the persecution and mayhem of the old world. Instead, we ended up plundering the new land and it's wealth, and killing the indigenous people. Forcing our ideals on to them. Denying them their freedoms. What gave us the right to do this? Our religion? All that had been accomplished was a repeat of what the White settlers had hoped to escape.

Sal shook his head at the thought it was all done with self-proclaimed righteousness. The White man was so sure "God was on his side" that he took license to do whatever he wanted. Whew! Sal tried to shake loose from the heavy thoughts. He knew he wouldn't get any breaks when he got to the reservation since a lot of the Indians still held grudges about how they were being treated.

Sal reached around and patted Little John on the head and said, "Well, buddy, let's just enjoy the beautiful high desert for awhile and stop thinking so much." Sal didn't drive far when he pulled over onto a flat spot to feed the dog. Little John rewarded his caretaker with a big load Sal was glad he didn't have to clean up; it was just one pile amongst all the other cow pies. If a cowboy came upon Little John's load he'd surely wonder what size coyote left that deposit.

Once back in the car, the two adventurers headed through the Dragoons. There was still no place for Sal to get some coffee so he figured he might have to hold out until he got to Wilcox. It was in that very diner in the little town where he realized all the sugar and cream he put in his coffee was causing his belly to protrude. He had even met the Country-Western singer Tex Ritter in there, who just happened to be a resident of Willcox, Arizona. Maybe he should have named himself, "Ari Ritter." "Ha!" smiled good-old Salvadore Dusi.

When he hit the diner, Sal splurged on a huge breakfast with plenty of black coffee. He decided the wait had been worth it after all. A full belly always made him think more clearly. The day was going to be great—he could just tell.

Once back on the highway, Sal turned onto Route 666 and drove up to Safford where he stopped at a small super market. He loaded up his cart with canned goods—mostly baked beans, beef stew, and some sandwiches which he placed into a throwaway cooler. He decided not to mention to Little John how the Indians use to have their dogs pull their belongings on travois. When they ran low on food, they ate their dogs.

After filling up his gas tank, Sal got onto Route 70 and headed for a little town called San Carlos where he had been instructed to meet Nahteste. Following the directions, Sal went off Route 70 onto 170 and then into San Carlos where he quickly spotted the old pickup that belonged to his new Apache friend. Sal parked behind the truck and got out.

CHAPTER 47

THE REZ

"Long ride," Sal said as he stretched his legs.

"Yeah," Nahteste nodded. "We like it that way, keeps the savages out."

The men shook hands and remarked they each looked well—especially with no bullet holes in their backs. Sal let Little John out of the car and walked him until he let go a fierce spray on the pickup's tires.

"Wow," remarked Nahteste. "We could have fed half the village with that guy."

"Shhhhh!" said Sal with a grin. "I didn't tell him what you guys used to do with your dogs."

"What you mean used to, White man?" Nahteste quipped.

"Oh boy," Sal cringed. "What have I gotten us into here?"

"We are meeting at one of the Tribal Councilmen's homes for lunch," Nahteste said without missing a beat. "Let's go in your car so the dog is comfortable, O.K?"

"Sure," Sal said. He pondered whether he'd need to make a quick get-away as well.

When they arrived at the house, Sal saw seven men and four women. He was glad to see the group, thinking they must like the sound of what he and Nahteste wanted to do. After basic introductions, they sat under a shade tree where two tables were set with bowls of food. Nahteste suggested they eat first, before he and Sal shared with the Elders what they had in mind.

The food was delicious to Sal. Thankfully, there weren't any cow stomachs or eyeballs in it that Nahteste had jokingly warned him about. When everyone had satisfied himself, the chairman of the council spoke.

"Why is it you want to help us?" he pointedly asked Sal.

"I have had visions," Sal began. "I was told that to be satisfied with my life, and to help myself in the afterlife, I should follow the path of helping others. I met Nahteste and he seemed to be guided in the same direction by assisting in the education and wellbeing of the children on the reservation."

"How do you propose to accomplish this?" the council chairman asked.

Sal was taken aback by the man; he was obviously educated and the use of his vocabulary was precise. Sal asked him if he had attended college and the chairman told him he spent four years at Arizona State University. He enjoyed the education, but he didn't like being away from his people.

Sal proceeded to explain everything; how he had a benefactor, found a teacher who was also a minister, and how he thought they could bring education to the far reaches of the reservation.

"What do you need from us," one of the council members asked. "And how much will it cost us?"

"I have permission to pay four teachers," explained Sal. "Three from the reservation and the other one is Johnny. I also have money for books and supplies. I really have no idea how to reach the mothers and children throughout the reservation." I also would like to leave a phone number so that you or whoever you designate could call to discuss an offer. A Board Member of the University Medical Center may be able to arrange for the Medical Center to transfer over the packing of medical kits to the people on the rez. This would be an opportunity for a number of residents here on the reservation to make a fair living doing much good." He left the phone number with the council secretary.

The council members talked briefly amongst themselves stating that they liked the ideas, but they still needed to discuss it further. They asked Sal if he could return the next morning so they could talk again.

"Thank you," said Nahteste. "I can take Sal fishing this afternoon. We can return here in the morning."

"We want to thank you for making such a long trip," said the chairman. "We appreciate your intentions on our behalf."

Once back at the car, Nahteste told Sal they should go catch dinner. They first went to his house to pick up some fishing gear and sleeping bags then they drove into the mountains. As they drove, Sal was impressed by the quick change from rough desert terrain to Ponderosa forest. After about 40 minutes of driving, Nahteste had Sal turn down a dirt road to a small but beautiful lake. They parked under a large tree so there was shade for Little John. They pulled out the poles. Little John jumped right out of the car and dove into the lake. The dog looked like he was smiling as he splashed around with contentment.

Nahteste and Sal soon caught enough Apache trout for dinner and breakfast. Sal was actually delighted to finally fish again; he hadn't been to a watering hole with a fishing pole in years. This was something he had often done with his mom, dad and brother on Sundays when he was growing up.

Nahteste built a nice fire, heated some stones and cooked the trout. Sal fed Little John. After the fresh fish dinner, he pulled out a couple of cigars from his bag. The two men relaxed by the fire, which felt nice and comfortable considering they were fairly high in the mountains.

"The Elders seem to be pretty pleasant," Sal remarked to Nahteste. "They seem motivated and I hope everything can work out for the best for everyone."

"I could see that most of the council members are interested in what you're proposing," said Nahteste. "Tomorrow should bring a working agreement so we can all move forward."

"It's such a shame that your ancestors were put through the ordeal they were," said Sal. "Talking together would have settled so many of the problems that developed."

"Yeah," said Nahteste. "But the really severe treatment of the Apache didn't start until after the Whites had gone to war to free the Blacks. Then the government sent the Black soldiers—the buffalo soldiers of the 10th Calvary at Fort Huachuca—into the Apache homeland to subjugate the N'deh into being docile and controlled. They were mostly devious and dishonest Indian agents who put the Apache on the reservations like prisoners in their own land. Isn't it ironic the Whites could see the goodness in freeing the Black people from bondage and slavery, but because the Red man lived on land the Whites wanted to mine and raise cattle on, it was O.K. to murder some then imprison most of the Red people on the worst parts of that land? I'm sure the council will ask you some hard questions tomorrow but they seem to like and trust you. At least you won't be scalped." The men decided to enjoy the cigars and the evening under the stars. They wanted to get a good night's rest in the beautiful outdoors so they would be refreshed for the next meeting.

In the morning, Nahteste cooked the remaining fish for breakfast, gave Little John some leftovers, and then both men headed off the mountain to find some coffee. They drove to the council chairman's home, where much to Sal's delight there was a large urn of java brewing. It looked just like the pot he had purchased for the AA meetings. He wondered if he should bring up the subject of Alcoholics Anonymous and how much good it would do on the reservation. But he decided to address one thing at a time, just like he had learned in AA: first things first.

Sal chuckled to himself about how far he had come since buying tequila and hiding it outside the Army barracks when he was still a soldier so he could sneak off and pretend he was assigned to a different part of the base. He would spend the entire day sitting in someone's car drinking away his enlistment time. He was at least 100 times better than that now, actually accomplishing good things for others and himself instead of wasting his days and nights in a stupor.

CHAPTER 48

POW WOW

The coffee was high octane so it really hit the spot. The council members began to arrive. They seemed to be friendly and inquisitive. They asked Sal specific questions and he answered as specifically as he could. After they were all seated at the tables once again, the chairman began the meeting.

"O.K.," he looked across to each participant. "Let's get started. We have a busy day. Sal—Nahteste—we have had the evening to discuss your ideas and none of us have found anything that is a problem; even the most perennially negative amongst us. That being said, we do have a little problem with your main teacher being a minister and his wanting to bring his religious teachings to our people. But after much discussion, considering the gangs and drug problems we already have here, we think it will be a positive thing. We don't see that it will hurt us.

"Along that line," continued the chairman, "I want to tell a little story about where I grew up on the Mescalero Reservation in New Mexico. I was taught building skills by my father when he helped a Catholic Franciscan priest build a church on the reservation. It took 20 years to build; the priest went off to be a chaplain with the U.S. Army a couple of times. His name was Father Brown and I actually became an altar boy for him as I was growing up. I often helped work on the church—St. Joseph's Mission Church. I painted walls, varnished the pews and raked the yard. I love recalling how my dad said it was a long time before the church had a roof. One Christmas there were two totally different cultures that honored their Gods there. Father Brown had a little makeshift altar set up and was saying Mass. In the space between the church walls, the Apaches had a big bonfire going with dancers in head dresses. Over the years this was a gathering place for Mescalero and Chiricahua Apache from all over the reservation—even those that had moved away.

"My dad also spoke of how both Cochise and Geronimo's sons came and helped the priest build the church. They were two of the most feared warriors in America and now their sons were helping a Franciscan priest build a house of worship for both Red and White men. So, Sal, we all agree with allowing this missionary onto our homeland, but we do have one stipulation. If things don't work out as we all foresee, we reserve the right to have this program shut down. Along with that there is one more thing, no offense, but we want to have Nahteste supervise the project. We ask that he be paid half of what your teachers will be paid and the council will see to his expenses like gas and food when he travels. If this is agreeable, then we can give it our blessing and you can begin as soon as possible. We all know there is a great need."

Sal was delighted and said as much. They exchanged phone numbers and addresses then Sal asked Nahteste to sit awhile with him so they could plan out their next move. They both wanted Johnny to come out and stay with Nahteste to work out the logistics. Unlike the public-school situation this program would run year round with natural breaks in each season.

"Don't worry," said Nahteste. "I am really a pretty fair organizer and I can handle everything that comes up. I appreciate you putting this together and I'm happy we met when we did. I want you to know you are welcome here any time. I consider you my very best White friend. Please send up the supplies with Johnny. I will contact the native teachers who will help get this program going. I'll travel around the rez to identify all the mothers that want to take part. I think it's best to start on the San Carlos reservation. Once it is working, we'll move over to the Fort Apache reservation. By the way, there used to be a private school on Fort Apache, but it was mostly for Navajos. It's now a public school which is open to everyone; maybe they'd help with this program."

Nahteste hugged Sal and wished him a safe trip back, thanking him again for lighting the spark that would mean so much to his people. After walking Little John, Sal set out for Tucson.

CHAPTER 49

CHEESEBURGERS AND VISIONS

Nahteste had given him another short cut to try—drive through Globe then take Route 77 south to Tucson. Happy to be on the road again, Sal sang along with the radio while Little John hung his massive head out the window, dreaming of a big ham bone.

At the turn off to Route 77, Sal saw a little café. He bought two cheeseburgers for himself and two for Little John who inhaled them out of Sal's hand. He also filled Little John's bowl. The water was gone within 30 seconds. Sal couldn't help but marvel at the capacity of this dog.

Back on the road again, Sal passed two interesting turnoffs. One was "Tam O'Shanter" and he wondered if that was Irish or Apache. The second turn off was to Christmas, Arizona and he thought they probably got to postmark a lot of mail in December. Heading south to Tucson, Sal came to Hayden and Winkleman and found that this was where his old friend, the San Pedro River joined with the Gila River to travel drop by drop to Baja California. He could see his beloved San Pedro on his left, paralleling the highway. It was comforting to have such a well-known friend near by as he traveled in unfamiliar territory. He saw two large dust devils within 20 minutes of each other. The devils reminded him of the huge one he saw south of Tucson that was four feet short of a tornado. That dust devil was strong enough to shove his friends British-made, Vauxhall car off the road into a ditch one Saturday afternoon. Nature didn't seem to like that lightweight car; first the dust devil and then the flash flood.

Sal saw a turnoff that led down to the San Pedro, which he decided to take. Both he and Little John could use a foot soaking, but only carefully, as the river was a little deeper here than where it flowed through St. David. He sure didn't want a Sal soaking before he met with Mary. Little John didn't hesitate to leap from the back seat and instantly leave a deposit by the car before running straight into the river. Sal pulled off his boots and sat on a rock as he dipped his feet into the surprisingly cold water. He looked over at little John. They both let out a relaxed sigh.

"Have you ever had as much fun as you've had in the last three weeks?" Sal spoke aloud to the dog. He had to admit to himself that the past month had been more interesting and rewarding than any other time in his life. His spirit guide had been right. Helping others held the greatest reward for a person. Sal was very happy she had appeared to him and set him on a different path than the one he had been on. A month ago, Sal's big worry was where to find a job and could he stay sober. Now he had more work than he could have imagined. There was no time to get into trouble. Drinking was the furthest thing from his mind. It was really funny how the Universe guided him as long as he used his free will to follow directions.

Little John came out of the river and sat down next to Sal as he leaned against another Sycamore tree. He knew the routine by then; it was time to take a little nap. Sal had at least two hours before he needed to be in Tucson where he planned on calling Mary for an early dinner.

Like clockwork, shortly after Sal closed his eyes, he felt a presence. He looked up to see a fierce warrior decked out in war paint holding a bow with a quiver of arrows over his shoulder. He spoke to Sal in a deep voice.

"I was told to guard our sacred mountains that you call Superstition," he said. "Not so far from here to the northwest my band of warriors chased and murdered many Spanish and Mexican miners. They were trespassing and digging into the body of our mountain. I thought this was good so we killed many, then we returned the yellow rock they took from the ground. Maybe in my time I killed 200 of these men with much pleasure, until I was finally killed myself. The spirits were angry with me for what I had done. Instead of being rewarded for being a great warrior I was damned to walk these lands for eternity. This is my punishment for killing so many for nothing. I appear to you to warn you that the deeds you perform on Earth as a living, breathing man will be judged. Your eternal time will be determined accordingly. It is known you have now entered a path of righteousness. If you continue this way you will have an eternity you will enjoy forever. But I am here to warn you: if you slip back into your ways of stealing and lying drunkenness you will lose the joy and pay severely for time eternal. Continue as you now travel, I beg you."

Sal could see that the great warrior was crying. He wasn't sure if it was because of the warrior's dilemma or for what he had done in the past. But when Sal looked up, he was alone with the dog once again.

"Holy moly," Sal thought. "I am very lucky to have been given a chance to redeem myself. If I had died when Tyler and I drove through that bridge on the Colorado River near Yuma instead of being pulled out by fishermen that just happened to be on the bank that night, I would have been doomed." Sal knew he had the opportunity to make things right at the same time he helped others. He considered that maybe his message wasn't so different from the Bible thumpers when they said he was blessed. He had never found any message he wanted to hear in church or Catholic school, but he was hearing a message from an apparition who had found him along the banks of the river. It didn't escape him that this warrior was the flip side of the spirit woman.

Sal was more than ready to meet a warm and friendly spirit of this world, Mary, so he got Little John into the Pontiac and headed to Tucson. When they got to Oracle, Sal pulled into a gas station to fill up and use the phone. Mary seemed delighted to hear his voice and agreed to dinner as soon as she left work. Sal drove slowly into the Oro Valley and decided to go to the University of Arizona's campus since he had a little time to spare. He still had the long lead line for Little John so he didn't have to worry about the dog running off. He was surprised at how many cute co-eds stopped to pet the dog. He had thought only cute little poodles got that reaction. If things didn't work out with Mary, Sal thought he and Little John should have this walk again.

Sal wasn't worried about his relationship with Mary, though. He had a real good feeling about it and thought maybe this was another turning point in his life. He had always told himself he wouldn't settle down until he was at least 30 years old. But being around Mary felt so good that maybe a little cottage with a white picket fence and a couple of little Sal's and Mary's riding their tricycles might make his life complete. He realized he was putting the cart before the horse, but he also knew that's what drunks did most of the time. They had grandiose ideas that weren't well thought out. They had a tendency to just go for it without thinking about the long-term ramifications of their rushed actions. He didn't even have a real job, yet. He couldn't expect Mrs. Crane to provide for a family man. The best thing to do was just to see how things developed and live accordingly.

It didn't take long for the hero's reverie to be broken by the law. Sal was approached by a campus policeman who told him in no uncertain terms that he couldn't have a dog on campus. That was going to cost him a $25 ticket. Sal was momentarily stunned as he calculated that was approximately 100 cups of coffee. He decided he better think fast, but the guy already knew Sal wasn't blind, so he stumbled over his words as he blurted out an excuse.

"Well, officer," began Sal. "I have an appointment at Attorney Mayhew's office later today and I was just killing some time. I didn't want to leave the dog in the car. I didn't know that dogs weren't allowed on the campus."

"You were told at the student orientation, weren't you?" the officer snapped.

"Oops, sorry, officer," said Sal. "I'm not a student, but I have a meeting with Mrs. Crane and Attorney Mayhew—as in 'The Crane Family Build-ing.' Please cut me a break; I'll leave right away."

"You have a meeting with Mrs. Crane?" asked the officer incredulously.

"Yes sir," answered Sal. "We are doing philanthropic work together for the Apache reservations."

The officer's eyes lit up at this and said, "I grew up on the San Carlos reservation. Let's see how fast you can exit the campus so I don't have to write any tickets. Get going now!"

"O.K., yes sir," said Sal as he grabbed Little John's leash more tightly. "Let's vamoose, L.J."

Sal and Little John high-tailed it back to the car, both of them glad he didn't have to pay a fine. He was also glad he mentioned Mrs. Crane's name. That seemed to work well; it was nice to have important friends. He couldn't wait to tell Mary his little tale.

CHAPTER 50

BIG TROUBLE

S al found a nice park near a big hotel to walk Little John and waste
another hour. There were no co-eds to ogle at, but there were no
campus police either. There was a sign instructing people to pick up
after their dogs and Sal fully intended on complying if Little John
made a deposit. Ten minutes later Little John did as expected and Sal had
to dig through the garbage can for a couple of small boxes to clean up the
mess.

As they left the park, Sal fed and watered Little John before he headed
up to the office. Attorney Mayhew was just coming out the door when Sal
entered the building. He looked surprised as he said to Sal, "We don't have
a meeting scheduled for today, do we?"

"No, sir," Sal answered. "Mary and I are going to dinner since I was
driving through Tucson today on my way back from San Carlos."

The attorney smiled and gave Sal a wink. "You be a good boy, now,"
he said.

Sal went into the front office and saw Mary, looking radiant as usual.
She smiled when she saw Sal and said, "Hello! You're early!"

"I'll sit and wait until you're ready to go," he smiled back. "Little John
is already set in the car."

"O.K." she said. "I just need to put away a few files."

Sal held the door for her and Mary asked him if they could return to the restaurant where they had first ate together. She had a big test tomorrow and didn't want to drive too far so she could get back home early. Sal agreed. Since Little John was already in the shade and well fed, they walked over to the restaurant.

They enjoyed a nice meal together with some small talk. Sal told Mary about his trip to the reservation that day. It had been intimidating to be a sole minority on the rez, but he was treated real well. Mary talked about how hard law school was. Before the week was out she had to get up before the class and debate another student on Indian rights. The debate had to include water rights that cotton farmers want to take away to use for irrigation. But they were only offering one-tenth the value of what it was worth on the open market. Apparently, judges used to allow this in the past, but the tribe had two Yale-educated, Native-American Lawyers working for them now trying to protect their rights.

Sal jokingly asked if she was on the right side of the argument.

"Sadly, no," she replied. "I have to represent the farmer. This is really hard for me because I'm really for the Indians in this case. My professor insisted on me representing that side so I would learn that sometimes a lawyer had to work for a client whose case she didn't believe in."

"That stinks," said Sal. "I don't think I could do it."

"Well I really trust this professor," said Mary. "I believe he is teaching me the best way he can. I guess we'll see, though. I'll let you know if I get an 'A' or an 'F.'"

They both laughed, knowing that life could be trying; somehow it builds your character and that is how you become the person you want to be.

Sal finally mustered up the courage to say something personal. "Mary," he began. "I really like you and I don't even know your full name."

She laughed and stretched out her hand. "Hi. I'm Mary Mayhew."

Sal was stunned. "Uh, oh," he said. "Your dad just told me to be a good boy when I told him we were going to dinner. I thought he was kidding me, but now I realize he meant it."

Mary laughed and said, "Don't worry, Sal. He really likes you, and so do I. I hope we can see each other many more times, even if we're both busy."

Sal was happy with that idea and told her he fully intended to see her again as often as they could work it out. Mary reached across the table and took his hand as she said, "I really hope so. Not only are you funny and good looking, but also from what you are doing, I can tell you are a very good man. You're generous and kind. I'm hoping you aren't stolen away by one of those pretty senoritas or black-eyed Apache women before I can cast my own spell on you."

Sal's head was swimming. The evening was going ten times better than he could have hoped. He placed his other hand over hers and replied, "I'm pretty sure your spell has already taken hold. As busy as I have been, my brain turns right back to you whenever I stop doing anything."

"I would love to sit here all night to get to know you better," said Mary. "But I need to leave so I can study for my presentation."

They held hands as they walked back to Sal's car, and Mary reached up to kiss him. "Until next time," she smiled. "Be safe; don't do anything crazy. I'm starting to like having you around."

Mary drove away and left Sal with Little John in the parking lot. When Sal headed back to St. David he was floating on air. Things couldn't have gone better and he didn't come back down to reality until he pulled into the monastery driveway. The AA meeting was just breaking up so Sal took the dog for a walk instead. Afterward, Sal went to the main office half expecting a dozen messages. He was surprised to only find one. It was from Chaplain Cliff who wanted to hear from Sal in the morning. He said good night to the monks who were still hanging around and he took a writing pad to the pond to plan out the next few days. There was only one thing he could write on the pad and that was the name "Mary."

He knew he was in big trouble now.

CHAPTER 51

HERE'S JOHNNY

T he next morning, Chaplain Cliff told Sal that Johnny had arrived and was raring to go. They wanted to know if Sal could come over so they could work things out. Sal agreed, especially after he heard the Chaplain's wife was making a big lunch. Sal said he would be there by noon and he loaded up the dog to make a trip to Tombstone. On his way, he stopped at Bud's to pick up 20-some cans of assorted goods, crackers, and donuts.

"We're having our first AA meeting this Friday," Bud told Sal. "It would be nice if you could attend."

"I'd be proud to," said Sal. "In fact, I'm going to be there around noon today."

"Can you bring these supplies when you come over?" asked Bud. "I have a box of cups, some spoons and a box of sugar; my car is filled with folding chairs and a table. I'm planning on bringing a bunch of the books I've accumulated over my years sober." Sal loaded up the items and headed toward Tombstone. When he ran into Lu at the café, she greeted him warmly.

"You just missed our favorite deputy," said Lu. "You'll have to buy your own breakfast today."

"I'm getting luckier in every way," laughed Sal. Then he proceeded to tell Lu about Mary.

"You're a great catch, Sal," she told him. "If things weren't going so great in my love life I would have lassoed you in, myself."

"I'm just here for the coffee and any goodies you have to spare," Sal blushed.

"Don't be looking for goodies from me," teased Lu. "You go and call Mary." Sal blushed even more.

Sal pulled around back and loaded up with rolls, muffins, and three fruit pies. He decided it was probably best to go via Route 90 towards the Fort so he could drop most of the food at the bridge. When he arrived, Sal tooted his horn to alert any travelers that might be nearby. He didn't want the pies to sit out in the warm day for too long. Sal also took advantage of the stop to walk Little John. When he looked back he saw three people running out from the trees. He looked at Little John and chuckled, "Those pies won't last long will they, fella?"

Back on the road, Sal drove through Sierra Vista thinking how much busier it was now than four years ago when he first arrived. As Sal drove to the Fort, the Military Policeman stopped Sal at the gate where he proceeded to treat the do-gooder quite rudely. Sal explained he had come to meet with the Chaplain, but it made no difference to this rude soldier. He wanted to know why Sal had a giant dog in his back seat. Sal answered in like fashion that it was none of his business. Just then, the M.P.'s sergeant came over and recognized Sal.

"Hey man," he laughed. "Never thought I'd see you again. Last time I saw you was in Kelly's where you wanted to take on my whole squad. From the sounds of things you're still finding fault with my guys."

"Nope," laughed Sal as he shook the proffered hand. "I don't even drink any more. Just this Private Bozo is giving me a hard time for no good reason."

The sergeant told his M.P. to back off, indicating Sal was one of the good guys even though he was now a civilian. Besides that, the sergeant told the M.P. that Sal could probably kick his butt in any event. The sergeant waved Sal through, telling him it was good to see him again.

CHAPTER 52

BIG ADVENTURE

s Sal pulled into the Chaplain's yard, he saw Cliff walking behind the chapel with a tall man. The man had protruding ears
and was wearing overalls. This was Johnny. Sal shook hands
with him. He was pleased with his first impression of this os-
tensibly goofy-looking cus. Johnny had a firm handshake and intense
steel-blue eyes. He was the type of man you didn't easily forget. Sal figured
the man had no idea what he was in for.

"Let's walk over and sit on the patio where we can comfortably get ac-
quainted," said the Chaplain. "We have a great adventure to plan."

Sal could tell after about an hour that Johnny was the best possible
choice for a teacher. He was energetic, self-motivated, claimed to be patient and calm, but also knew a lot about building from working for his
father's construction company in the past. Sal thought the man would
probably survive this expedition into the unknown just fine.

"You'll be working with my friend, Nahteste," explained Sal. "He's an
Apache Indian on the reservation. He will be the liaison between the tribal council and you. Nahteste first said you could stay with him awhile, but
he thought better of it and decided you should rent a little place instead.
My Apache friend expects there will naturally be a few areas of friction
between mindsets. He certainly doesn't want housing to be one of them."

"I agree," said Johnny. "I can be a bit head strong, but I can also be very diplomatic when the need arises."

"Nahteste is the most intimidating man I have ever met," said Sal. "I would definitely advise you to use all the diplomacy skills you can muster."

"This sounds like it'll be the adventure of a lifetime," quipped the Chaplain. Sal and Johnny agreed. "Immeasurable good will come from this venture: education for so many more of the children on the reservation plus a religious facility that may help the teenagers before they get into gangs and drugs."

"But please be careful," cautioned Sal. "This is actually another country. It's much different in norms and values than you or I are used to."

"First of all, I will have God on my side," laughed Johnny. "What do I need to fear? And secondly, you didn't see a pot big enough to cook me in, did you?"

"You know, a great sense of humor is probably the most important thing you can take with you onto the rez," Sal said. "That, and of course, your faith will see you through."

"As a going-away present, my dad bought me a new Jeep Wagoneer," said Johnny. "It was the best four-wheel-drive vehicle available at the time, so I'm sure I can get anywhere on the reservation I need to be. I hear the roads are primitive out there. How soon can we get some books and supplies?"

"If you make a list while the Chaplain and I talk, I can arrange for someone to order the supplies and have them delivered to you as soon as possible," said Sal.

While Johnny began his task, Sal and the Chaplain went to Sal's car to remove the AA-meeting supplies. They took them down to the basement of the chapel where Sal remarked he honestly believed more good came out of chapel basements than what was accomplished upstairs.

"I won't argue with you, Sal," said the Chaplain. "In fact, I have been seeking alternative ways of reaching my soldiers. You may have shown me just the way to do it. I also believe you are being spiritually led to do all that you are doing."

"Reverend, you've been reading my mail," Sal choked in response. "That's exactly how things have been happening—in ways you or I could never have dreamed possible. All I know is that I am being guided to do the right thing. So far, its working 1,000 times better than anything I could have imagined. I feel I'm becoming someone I can respect along the way. Besides all that, I've met a woman that is close to capturing my heart."

"Well, Sal," smiled the Chaplain. "That's all wonderful. I agree you are a much-changed man since the soldier that reeked of booze who showed up occasionally at my Sunday services. Please tell me about this lucky woman; where did you meet her? I can't imagine there is a lot of opportunity for romance at the monastery."

Sal told the Chaplain the whole story of Mrs. Crane, Attorney Mayhew and Mary.

"Well that's the most amazing month of anyone's life that I've ever heard of," he said when Sal finished. "But let's speak now of my 'many wives' brigade. Their van is handling deliveries quite well. The commissary has become the best source of products—even some of the company kitchens have started saving baked goods and non-perishables for our ladies. They also worked out something with the Post laundry where they can acquire empty jugs they fill with fresh water: they place them around the Rain Valley where there's a big trail out of Mexico. You have started something that is taking on a life of its own. Someday I want you to explain to me what you meant when you said you were being guided spiritually, if you have a mind to. I would really like to hear that story. Even I need to recharge my faith every so often."

CHAPTER 53

THE REV

"Before I forget," interrupted Sal, "let me leave $50 for gas in the van. Bud told me to tell you he would be over two hours early for the meeting on Friday. He'll help set up the extra chairs, make the coffee and put the literature out."

"Sal, I'm really looking forward to this meeting," said the Chaplain. "I think it will be a big success. I wonder if we could have it two nights a week. It's Friday and Saturday that my guys tell me they get into the most trouble. There isn't much to do on the base but there's a lot of drinking off the base."

"With my short experience with AA, I have seen a couple of meeting rooms that are actually open from 5 p.m. Friday evening until 10 p.m. Sunday night," said Sal. "People come and go; whenever there are 6-8 people at a time, they start a meeting. Some people stay the whole weekend sleeping in their cars. Having tailgate picnics in the parking lots worried the heck out of the police at first. But after awhile they realized these were the same individuals who had caused them problems in the past. It's ironic, but a few of the police officers now attend some of the meetings. They drop in and grab a sandwich or a hotdog. Let's face it, these drunks were the life of the party for years; they haven't become dead, only sober."

"Reverend, you will have the time of your life with these folks," continued Sal. "Once they get comfortable with having you around as a friend—not just a judgmental authority figure—you will see. By the way, how would you feel about old retired soldiers or even civilians coming to the meetings?"

"That would be great, Sal," answered the chaplain. "We have no requirement that you must be on active duty to attend the service here. Why would we discriminate at Alcoholics Anonymous meetings?"

"Thank you so much for allowing this to come together," said Sal. "You won't be sorry, and please don't get upset if you hear loud voices or rough language. Some of those guys coming in will still be drinking—just trying to find their way—giving AA a looksee. They will argue, curse and deny they have a problem, but if they keep coming back, they will eventually see this as a better way to live their lives. This is why we share our stories, to try to teach others that if we can do it, so can they. Look at me; eight months ago I crashed my father's car into a tree. I was holding a glass of bourbon, which ended up spilled all over my head. I felt wetness run down my chest and thought it was blood. I tasted it, and when I recognized the bourbon, I imagined my blood tasted like booze—that's how snookered I was. The worst thing I drink now is monastery coffee."

"It's a pleasure to speak with you, Sal," said the Chaplain. "You have become wise beyond your years. I really appreciate all you are doing to help your fellow man. Keep it up; you actually may become Santo Sal. We don't have saints in my church, but maybe you'll become the first. Why should the Catholics have the monopoly?"

Sal and the Chaplain went back up to the patio and sat once more with Johnny. He handed Sal the list he had written and said, "I hope it's not too much to ask for. I think if we have enough books and supplies for 40 children we will be fine to start. I also found a book at the library in Ohio that is pretty instructive on home schooling. I read it and would recommend it for all the mothers who participate in this experiment. I put ten of these books on the list to start. I don't think we need to order books and supplies for the teachers, yet. I believe they should participate in the ordering. It will give me some time to feel my way around. It's going to be so much different than the public school I worked in. It had a preset curriculum. Do you think I ordered too much?"

"Not at all," said Sal as he glanced at the list. "This looks about right. It is important to start out well prepared. I wanted you to meet our 'benefactor,' but she prefers to remain behind the scenes. I think you'll get to meet her eventually, after you've proven yourself and the program starts showing results. If it's O.K. with you, Chaplain, I'd like to call these supplies in to my contact in Tucson so things can start rolling. That way there won't be much of a delay when Johnny gets up there."

The Chaplain took Sal into the kitchen and pointed at his phone. "It's all yours," he said. "I'll sit with Johnny and tell him about the experiences I've had with the Indians since I've been in Arizona. I did a two-week tour around this state as well as Mexico three years ago. We hit three different reservations. We even made it to the Tarahumara Indians in Copper Canyon down in Mexico for a very short but impressive visit."

"Great," said Sal. "Thanks! This is going very well. I'll call in and tell them to expedite the order."

CHAPTER 54

IT'S HAPPENING

S al phoned Attorney Mayhew's office to get Mary on the line. After some initial small talk, he told her what he would like her to do.

"That's fine," said Mary. "I have already been told you were going to call here with a list. I found a school-supplies company here in Tucson; the owner belongs to the same golf club as my dad. He said he had a large supply of classroom books, workbooks, tablets and pencils in stock. Just give me the list and I will order them today. I'll have him pack everything and hold the supplies until you give me the address for him to ship it to."

When Sal completed giving the list to Mary, they promised each other they would talk again, but soon. After they both hung up, Sal shook his head again at how well all these plans were working out. He walked back to the patio in time to hear Chaplain Cliff telling Johnny how excited he was to have a small part in this.

"On the contrary, sir," Sal interrupted. "You are playing a major part in everything I am doing. You put Johnny together with us; you brought your wives in; and now you are sponsoring a 12-Step meeting in your ministry. I could not have accomplished very much without all the assistance you are giving. Please don't be overly humble; you are as important as everyone else in this escapade. I really cannot thank you enough."

"I am deeply indebted to you both for allowing me to participate in this thing you have begun," interjected Johnny. "I feel in my heart that I have been shown what could become my life's work—to be able to teach children that have been forgotten, and just possibly develop a ministry amongst these people who have been so isolated from the rest of the world, always fending for themselves. I never dreamed that I would be put on a path like this. Surely God works in very mysterious ways. I will thank him and you both for the rest of my life."

Sal blushed at this and told them both he felt the same way. "Here I sit with two highly educated men who are allowing a mere high-school graduate like me to lead us into the unknown," he said. "It's been a highly rewarding experience already. If it's not God and his helping spirits that are guiding us to do this then I am the most wrong I have ever been in my life."

"No, Sal," said the Chaplain. "This is a divinely guided purpose we have been brought together for. With His help we will accomplish wonderful things. I must admit that I was somewhat apprehensive when you first approached me with your ideas, but now it's hard to contain my excitement with everything. It's all happening so quickly."

The three men stood up at the same time and hugged one another—something Sal had always been too embarrassed to do—but this moment seemed to call for it. They shook hands as the Chaplain yelled out, "Let's do it!"

Laughing, they sat back down a little embarrassed, but content with their goal. "I wonder if this is how Dr. Bob, Bill Wilson and the other founders felt back in 1935 when they started AA," pondered Sal. "We have a wealthy benefactor just as they did with John D. Rockefeller. He gave them just enough money to keep Alcoholics Anonymous going at the start. He felt if he gave them too much, being alcoholics, they might implode with grandiose ideas along with personality and power struggles. So that is something I would like to ask both of you to do. Keep an eye on me so I don't get out of control. Sometimes I think I may be moving way too quickly without thinking everything out. There really isn't a template on how to do what we are doing. So again, please speak up if you see I am go-ing off track or overreaching what we can realistically accomplish."

They all agreed to remain vigilant, but encouraged Sal to keep explor-ing his wonderful ideas. He hadn't done any harm to any one so far; still they were willing to keep their eyes open and express any doubts or offer advice with the best of intentions.

"Thanks," said Sal. "So when do you think you'll travel up to the reser-vation, Johnny?"

"I'm real excited to begin," he answered. "I thought maybe tomorrow would be the right time to drive up and meet Nahteste to get things moving."

"Great," beamed Sal. "I will create a map for you to Nahteste's place. He's at his mom's right now, but I can get you close enough that he can show you the rest of the way. I'll also write down the name and address of the person to call for additional supplies. Once you have an address, our benefactor will have a place to send your salary. Please keep in mind that until the Apache really trust what you're doing, you will be under their ever-vigilant eye. Things you say and do could be misinterpreted; it's a very different culture up there. However, they want you to succeed so they will try to guide you along the way. From what I can tell it's important that you aren't too pushy. Keep in mind you are only a guest. They have a long history of being lied to and abused by the White man, unfortunantly. Once you show them your heart is pure and you only mean to help their children, I think they will do everything they can to help this program succeed."

Sal hesitated a moment, then added, "I don't think they scalp their enemies any longer; and no, I did not see a pot big enough to cook you in."

They hoped that what they were attempting to do would make up for some of the wrongs that had been visited upon the Apache and that a certain level of trust could be established. Sal wrote out his directions, and included a list of things that might be helpful to Johnny. He added Mary's office number as well as the phone number the tribal council chair-man had given him. The chairman was very interested in their success.

Sal impressed on Johnny that Nahteste could make his transition onto the reservation easy or hard, depending on John's intentions and actions.

Johnny told Sal he had some money saved and was willing to use it if he saw a real need, even if it wasn't part of the educational process. He had the determination to make this endeavor successful and was going to do everything within his power to make it work. The way they were going about it just might be the humble beginnings that would be needed to succeed.

Sal got ready to leave as the Chaplain and Johnny decided to take a tour around the base. Johnny had seen neither the artifacts and photos of the Buffalo Soldiers, nor the timeline of when the Fort transitioned from Calvary to the latest in electronic warfare.

"Two things I should mention: One, I think its wise if you don't mention the Buffalo Soldiers up there; and two: Are you a fisherman?" Sal asked Johnny before he got in his car.

"After God's work, that is my number two love," he answered. "I brought my fly rod hoping there would be some good fishing in the mountains."

"There is great fishing," said Sal. "Me and Nahteste caught both a great dinner and breakfast the last time we were up there. Apache trout is a separate species of trout that you'll be catching up in their mountain streams and lakes."

"That would be great," said Johnny "and it might help cement our friendship. I promise to keep mum about the Buffalo Soldiers."

With that, Sal shook both men's hands then headed out. He couldn't believe it was nearly 5 p.m. and it was high time he got back to the monastery if he was going to make it for dinner. When he arrived in St. David, there was a phone message awaiting him that said, "Ninety percent of the school supplies are in; will be delivered in three days."

CHAPTER 55

SPONSORSHIP

"When the right power is on your side things just flat go right," Sal said to himself. After walking Little John, Sal put the dog in Brother Alex's room then headed over to the dining hall. He had a big surprise when he walked in. Sitting at one of the tables was Sergeant Jake Billet with his wife, Catherine. He said hello to them and the Billets indicated they had decided to attend the 12-Step meeting that evening. They had been hoping to catch Sal first to have dinner with him. Sal was delighted to see them. They started to talk.

"Catherine told me what a changed man you were when she saw you," said Jake. "And that you had stopped drinking. She has convinced me I should try to do the same. I've been letting it get out of control and maybe attending AA is the way to make a change."

"This pretty much saved my life," said Sal. "And if you let it, it could save yours."

Sal went into a delightful description of his recent adventures. He offered Jake all the help he might need then waited for an answer. "Going to meetings sounds a little funny," remarked Jake. "But so many people we know swear by them. We went to our Bisbee minister for counseling, but I just kept drinking. I tried cold-turkey but that was also a disaster. I ended up storming out of the house then went on a three-day bender. I got a DUI arrest to add to our problems so if you can stop drinking by going to these meetings, maybe I can do the same."

"Nothing is guaranteed," said Sal. "But I can promise you, when you hear the stories and realize these people are now sober, if nothing else it will take the fun out of your drinking. Maybe that's how it works. All I know is I've been sober for over six months. If I read the big book of AA, go to meetings and pay attention, I no longer feel like drinking. I have no intention of drinking booze again, either. But it's one day at a time."

"No promises," said Jake. "But we'll be there tonight. I love to drink but it's affecting my marriage, my being a good father and I'm lucky I haven't experienced a court martial yet."

After they finished their meal, Sal took them out by the pond to catch up on old times. Sal was amazed to hear about the guys who had re-enlisted.

"Two of your friends were discharged, but couldn't find work," said Jake. "So they're back. One of them is at Fort Huachuca in the same company doing the same work. The other was sent to Viet Nam along with half the Battalion for another year. I lucked out. They didn't send me to Nam. Catherine's dad is a manager at a grocery chain in upstate New York; he's promised to get me into the Union as a butcher if we move back there. So, that's our plan right now. I only have about three months left until discharge, if I can stay sober, we can have a nice life back in Catherine's and my home area."

Sal noticed that Catherine had started to cry. "If Jake doesn't stop drinking I'm taking our daughter and going back without him," she said softly.

"I'll do everything I can to help you," said Sal. "But honestly, AA can only work if you want it to. You have to surrender to the fact that drinking is ruining your life, that your life has become unmanageable. It's really up to you alone."

Sal looked at his watch and said, "The meeting starts in 30 minutes, so let me tell you a little of my story. I know how obstinate you are, Jake; we've been together since basic training. Do you recall when you were drunk and you picked that fight with a big Texan? He pulled a gun on you, but for some reason I was only half drunk, so I was able to take it away from him. That makes me a little responsible for you. You are responsible to me at least enough to listen to what I have to say. I'm 100 percent better off sober so I'm a believer."

Sal looked earnestly at Jake before continuing. "When I got back to Pennsylvania on the Fourth of July, I was drunk and acting crazy. My dad told me to shape up or ship back out. I decided to try AA where I ran into some luck. By the third or fourth meeting there was this guy dressed in a nice suit who proceeded to tell everyone at the meeting he had lost everything he had to drinking. He lost his business, his home, his wife and family, and woke up behind a bar in New Jersey next to a dumpster. He had wet himself, he had a long beard, and he was starving. He looked down at his beard and saw food stuck in it that he had vomited up during the night. He reached into his beard, pulled it out and ate it—that's when he realized he had truly hit bottom. The story stuck like a knife in my heart. I could easily see myself as that man and, from that point on, I knew what was in store for me if I kept on that self-destructive path.

"The man said he couldn't even walk, so he called out for help. The dishwasher from the bar came out to help him. The dishwasher called the Salvation Army who came and picked him up. He spent three months in the Salvation Army Detoxification and Rehabilitation Unit in Patterson, New Jersey. He now has two years sober, and had his wife and business back. He plans on staying sober from now on. He said drinking had been a lot of fun until it wasn't, and he never intended to be there again. I was so affected by that man's story that I got a good sponsor, decided I wouldn't drink again and went to every meeting I could. I made peace with my folks and lived with them until I drove out here. So here I am; do you like me better sober or drunk?"

"I'm glad it has worked out for you," said Jake. "You do look a whole lot better sober than the last time we saw you."

"Jake, please try it," said Sal earnestly. "I will happily be your temporary sponsor and I'll do my best to help you through the first 90 days. By then you'll be on your way back to New York where you can pick a different sponsor, someone back there you can identify with."

It was time to go into the meeting so the three old friends headed towards the hall. Sal told Catherine the 12-Step meetings were always open to family members. "Let's face it," said Sal. "You have suffered with alcoholism, too. Hopefully, you'll both hear what you need to and realize it's for you."

As they entered the meeting hall, Sal, Jake and Catherine could see it was packed. Sal turned down the offer to lead indicating he just wanted to be a listener that evening. It turned out there were three very good speakers and the Billets listened attentively. After the meeting was over, Sal and the Billets sat by the pond to talk.

"I would really like to give it a try," said Jake as he pensively thought about the things he had heard. "What do I have to do?"

"The first thing you have already done," said Sal. "You have become willing and that is one of the hardest things to do. You have shown up so that means you want to change your life. Admitting you have a problem and wanting to change it is the first big step. Are you working tomorrow?"

"Yes," said Jake. "I'll be home around 4 p.m."

"O.K.; I'll come to your house and we can make a plan," offered Sal. "Let me get my big book and you can read a little of it tonight. I also have an Al-Anon book for you, Catherine. It happens that I'm involved in setting up a couple of meetings and have some other literature that I can bring tomorrow. I know this is an intense evening for you both, so go home and get some rest. I'll see you around 4:30 p.m. at your house."

Catherine gave Sal a hug while Jake shook his hand goodnight. "It's a wonder we both have survived this, huh?" Jake said.

"Yeah," answered Sal. "Try not to drink tonight, O.K? We'll talk tomorrow. Have a safe trip home."

We haven't survived it yet my friend, he thought, knowing how difficult the path ahead could be as he walked L.J. then hit the sack.

CHAPTER 56

LOVE THAT SUNSHINE

When morning came it was once again bright and sunny. That was why Sal loved Arizona so much; there weren't that many gloomy-skied days. It made him feel happy and positive with the blue sky over his head and the sunshine on his face. Sal walked Little John then cleaned up before making it to the dining hall. As he finished a hearty breakfast, Brother Casper sat down next to him and spoke.

"Sal, I heard from Brother Alex. He said he would be back within three days. I told him you have been a great dog watcher and that Little John was smiling all the time. I also told him it was our pleasure that you had been with us this month. I wanted to tell you that if you'd like to stay with us, we would always have a room for you. We can let you stay here for $15 a week, which would include some meals. All I ask is that if we need a hand you will help us with whatever comes up. Things like setting up for our bi-monthly open houses then the cleanup afterwards, and maybe moving furniture or painting occasionally. If that's acceptable to you I can offer you a home for as long as you need it. Only thing is there can't be any entertaining of women in your room. That would upset our monk way of life."

"Thanks Brother Casper," smiled Sal. "I am 90 percent sure I would love to do that, but give me a few days to think it over, O.K?"

Brother Casper agreed with Sal, shook his hand and left. "Hmmmm," Sal said to himself. "I need to think this out. Never once in my life did I dream of living in a monastery. It's a lot to think about. This has been such a wild month but in all that time I haven't done one thing I am ashamed of and plenty that I'm proud of." Sal figured he would take the next three days to thoroughly think over Brother Casper's offer.

Sal knew he was a different man than what he had been last year. The AA philosophy had really worked for him and it still was working. Now that he was being given a chance to assist an old buddy, he was committed. Jake Billet had been with him during many of his insanely drunk moments. He was the one to drive them around most of the time while they were in uniform, just as drunk as Sal was. It brought to mind how while Jake was by his side, Sal had chased the new Lieutenant around a baseball field with a bat. But in Sal's defense the Lieutenant picked up the bat first and swung it at Sal, which Sal then took away from him. All this because the Lieutenant took issue with Sal relieving himself behind a car in the lot. That episode came the closest to landing Sal in the hoosecow.

As for other matters, it made sense to Sal to encourage Bud about the meeting he was going to lead in the church basement. Sal thought Bud would probably be surprised that Chaplain Cliff wanted a weekend-long meeting, which would be very cool. So many guys from the Fort could benefit from that, even though the girls in Mexico might be heart broken.

Sal loaded up Little John and some food supplies from the kitchen and headed over to Bud's Texaco. When he arrived, he could see that one of the donation boxes was heaping full with Ramen Noodles. Sal chuckled to himself and wondered how the travelers were going to eat that? Maybe they could put water in the pack and set it in the sun. Sal knew there had been times when he was extraordinarily hungry and he'd been willing to eat a lot of weird things in order to eat.

When Bud saw Sal, he wiped his hands on a rag and came over to give him a hug. "Well, it's almost show time," he said to Sal. "Think we'll be O.K?"

"Sure," nodded Sal. "You've been to more meetings than I have; just stay calm, provide the coffee and everything else will work itself out. I need to tell you what Chaplin Cliff told me yesterday. If the meetings go well once a week, he'd like to turn it into a weekend-long meeting. How do you feel about that?"

"Oh, boy," said a surprised Bud. "That's always been kind of a dream of mine. How is he going to conduct church services with us there?"

"Well," said Sal. "How about if we start Friday evening at 5 p.m., go through Saturday night, then at 8 a.m. Sunday morning we take a break? Everyone can go out to the Sierra Vista Diner for a big brunch then reconvene the meeting at noon. Better yet, if the Sunday school runs from 10:30 to 11:30 a.m., let's start back at 1 p.m."

"Yeah," agreed Bud. "Maybe we could do something like play volleyball, touch football or softball after breakfast. Some of the guys may want to attend the service, too. I trust that it will all work out; we just need to do the right thing and everything will be fine."

"O.K., Bud," said Sal. "If you think it'll work I'm willing to give it my best shot. Actually, it sounds like a great idea, but I think we should start out just having meetings once or twice a week at first. We can identify a few capable leaders for the group then move the number of meetings up. I won't be able to be there all the time but I'll look forward to a marathon meeting. I've read about them but never experienced one. I even heard somewhere they hold AA dances every Saturday night. We can't get grandiose though; it's one step at a time."

"The U.S.O. might be able to help us with that," offered Bud. Then he added, "You know, it's been real quiet this morning. Let me put your car up on the rack and change the oil and filters for you. I'll grease it and check things out." "Great! Lord knows I've been driving a lot. Thank you and everyone else in this escapade. I really cannot thank you enough."

CHAPTER 57

SURE THERE'S A FREE LUNCH

A fter giving Sal's Pontiac a thorough checkup, Bud found no immediate problems. The service was gratis, so Sal packed up the food supplies then drove down to Tombstone. Along the way he wondered out loud to Little John how many of the white crosses on the side of the road were caused by drunks. So many times he and other soldiers had driven their cars totally hammered; yet insisted on making it back to the base in time for Reveille. It had been rough when they had the Green Beret trainers putting the soldiers through two-hour physical-training sessions starting at 0500 hours, especially when they were just getting back from Mexico at three or four in the morning.

Sal could still remember the low crawl across the parade grounds when all he wanted to do was lay his head down to sleep. But he had survived it, and he felt he was a better man for it. At that admittance, Sal decided to pull onto Middlemarch Rd. where he could let Little John romp around. Just as they turned the corner, a diamondback rattler began to cross in front of the car. He looked like he was over six feet long. Sal mused that he wouldn't want to have met this guy eye–to-eye during the war games they played by the airport, crawling in the dark. The .44 magnum had been more than enough excitement that night. Sal found a decent place to pull over, check for snakes, and unload the dog. They both walked around a little, with Little John sniffing every bush and cactus, though not too close. The dog had obviously learned that painful lesson long before the two had met.

As Sal watered the dog, Little John watered the bushes. He looked around at the scenery with all its beauty. The rocks, the saguaro, and the mountains that surrounded him were just magnificent. "Thank you God for bringing me back here and allowing me to find a way to pay you back," Sal spoke aloud. They then loaded back into the Pontiac and headed to the Muffin Café where his friend Lu would be.

As Sal pulled into Tombstone he thought about how ironic it was that the reason the surrounding mines had shut down was because the water underground had flooded them out. One wouldn't know it looking at the dry desert. He figured that Mother Nature had a very strange sense of humor. When Sal arrived at the Muffin Café's parking lot, he was a bit dismayed to see two Cochise County police cars already there, with officers sitting in them.

"I wonder which desperado they're hoping to find?" Sal mumbled to himself. "Could it be yours truly?" Sal figured he would find out soon enough, and better yet, maybe he could get them to pick up the tab for lunch.

As Sal slowly made his way to the front door of the Café, Deputy Larry got out of his car and invited Sal to sit with him and Sergeant Joe in one of their patrol cars.

"Well, howdy gentleman," Sal said in reply. "Is everything safe and sound in Cochise County today?"

Both officers actually looked happy to see Sal, which Sal wasn't entirely sure he trusted as a good sign. Once Sal sat down, Sergeant Joe spoke up. "We took your advice. We decided to set up a road block on Route 92 at Hereford Road. Sure enough, we caught three vehicles loaded with drugs hoping to drive through. One was all heroin—18 kilos—plus we were able to catch three guys in the van that bailed out when they saw us pulling cars over. The second car made a U-turn and Deputy Larry here chased it down. He used a technique he had just learned at a Highway-Patrol training seminar. He clipped the left rear bumper and spun the car right into a ditch. The third was a pick-up with a tarp that covered seven huge knapsacks of marijuana with a street value of nearly $40,000. It was a record-breaking night for the guys in white hats. It was fun for a change but it only happened because you put us to the wise to where a lot of smuggling was going on."

Both the Sergeant and the deputy had big grins on their faces as he continued. "We called the monastery two hours ago and they said you were coming this way. We hoped to catch up to you and give you the good news. Lets go in and we'll buy you lunch; it's the least we can do considering how you've made us look good with the Sheriff."

"Well, I really appreciate the fact that you took me seriously," said Sal. "And I am starved so let's order lunch!" Sal chuckled to himself that no one at home would ever believe the month he was having. Just then, Sal saw Lu wave them over to her section.

"Well if it isn't the 'Good, the Bad and the Ugly,'" she grinned. "You guys sort that out amongst yourselves while I grab you a fresh pot of coffee."

As they laughed, Sargeant Joe jabbed at the deputy. "Larry, you could be all three easy," he said.

"Now you have to buy lunch for all three of us for being such a wise guy," the deputy replied.

Sal laughed at the ribbing because he didn't care who bought lunch as long as it wasn't him.

"We told the Sheriff how much you helped us out," said Joe. "He wants you to stop by the next time you're in Bisbee to meet him. He said he has something special for you. You should do it quick while you're in his good graces. He can be a little hot and cold, what some might refer to as moody, about his opinions of people."

"O.K.," said Sal looking a little leery. "I need to go to Bisbee later today anyway. I'll stop in this afternoon if that's O.K."

"Hang on," said Deputy Larry. "I'll radio in to make sure he'll be there." With that, the deputy went out to his car to make the call. He returned after a few moments with some information. "The Sheriff will be in the office all day," said Larry as he sat back down. "We brought him lots of paper work to do, but he's feeling real good about doing it. This is the biggest bust in Arizona history. You're a regular hero with our guys now."

The officers were looking for some promotions to land at their end of the table. As they continued talking, Lu came over with fresh coffee and a pad to take their order. To their surprise, Sal ordered a huge amount of food; he added an all-meat plate for Little John to go. Since he was the co-pilot to a lot of Sal's adventures the two officers agreed that picking up Little John's lunch was the fair thing to do.

According to Deputy Larry, the department was instituting a new program for a roving roadblock team that would cover the county, and would only concern themselves with drug busts. They weren't interested in stopping the travelers from coming through the county as long as they weren't smuggling.

"Yeah," said Sal as he began to show his sympathies. "Those poor families are only trying to make a better life for themselves. We would probably do the same if we were born on the wrong side of the border."

"That's probably true," said the sergeant. "We have a lot more problems with the soldiers driving drunk than we do with any of those immigrants. They try to stay out of our sight and just make it to Tucson or Phoenix."

"I may have some good news on that front," explained Sal. "A couple of us guys from St. David have started an open AA meeting at the Post chapel. If one or two evenings a week works out, Chaplain Cliff wants to turn it into a weekend-long meeting with picnicking, tailgating, sports and on-going gatherings from Friday night to Sunday. That should cut down on the drunk drivers coming back from Naco, Nogales and Aqua

Prieta. How's that sound to you guys?"

"That would be great," Sgt. Joe agreed. "Can we refer any civilians to the meetings? We know a couple of guys who want to get sober but don't know where or how to do it."

"I definitely have some recruits for you," added the deputy. "That would include my brother-in-law; my sister's about to toss him out of the house."

"That's no problem," said Sal. "Chaplain Cliff told me the more the merrier. He's hoping to pull a few of the attendees into the church and save their souls after AA helps to save their butts."

"O.K.," the sergeant said. "You sure are a busy guy for an unemployed drifter. We had you pegged all wrong; expected lots of trouble from you before we ran you out of Cochise County. Turns out you're helping plenty of us; I for one, appreciate all you are doing. I'll keep an eye out for that Bonneville of yours and help you out whenever I can."

"By the way," interjected Deputy Larry. "You sure seem to drive around a lot. What are you doing on the road so much?"

"Well, I love to drive," answered Sal. "I have friends all around the county. I keep making new ones. It just seems like it's my job right now. Doesn't pay much, so I sure appreciate you guys buying lunch. I am having a lot of fun doing what I'm doing; may even take up residence at the monastery."

"You're going to be a monk?" asked the sergeant incredulously. "C'mon, Sal; I see how the waitress and some of the women customers look at you. You're a regular lady-killer. How could you ever become a celibate monk?"

"No, no, no, no," Sal shook his head vigorously. "Not a monk; Brother Casper invited me to stay there for awhile. I would pay my way as well as help out with chores there, too. Speaking of women, I met a wonderful lady in Tucson. She has really shaken me up. I never planned on even considering settling down until I was at least 30. She's got me thinking about that little cottage with the white picket fence. I'm in trouble, guys, but I love it."

"Well, we're both married," said the sergeant. "It has its ups and downs but it's sure great to come home to someone that's glad to see you no matter how late you are. It's nice to have someone listen to how your day has gone. The way I look at it, most guys who divorce end up getting married again pretty quickly. So they must believe it's better to be with someone than to be alone. What do you think, Larry?"

"Yeah, I married right out of high school," he replied. "Now two kids later sometimes my wife and I feel like two old fuddy duddies, but hey, who cares? We're both happy and satisfied with the way our lives are going so don't be afraid of committing to someone and spending your life with her. If you're glad to be with one another, you'll be fine. It doesn't always work out, but if you don't try, it will never work out."

"I never knew you were such a philosopher," gibed the sergeant.

"Well I don't know if you two are just part of a 'misery-loves-company conspiracy' or not," laughed Sal. "Or maybe you genuinely love being married. I know I never once heard my mom and dad fight. They even hold hands on the couch when they watch T.V. so I know it can work out. I'm willing to give it a shot when the time is right. Thanks for the lunch, guys. I have to head over to see the minister's wife to see if we can get an AA meeting started in Tombstone."

"Whoa! What the hell are you going to do next month?" laughed the sergeant. "Run for governor? No moss is growing under your feet is it? Sure glad you decided to come back to Cochise County. We can use a lot more citizens like you. Please let us know if there's anything we can do to help. This all makes our jobs easier. Be sure to tell the Sheriff what you're doing because he may have some ideas to assist you. See you soon—when we do, the meals are on us."

Sal pulled out of the parking lot shaking his head in wonder. Things had developed in such unexpected ways this last month. He was happier now than he had ever been.

CHAPTER 58

JENN

———✦———

When Sal pulled into the church driveway, he could see that Jenn was home. Once again, Lady Luck was with Sal, so he went up to the door and knocked.

"Well, hey, Mr. Sal." Jenn answered the door with a smile. "How are you doing? I was just thinking about you. Come on in and sit down so we can talk about how to make this new meeting a success. Would you care for some coffee or lemonade? How about a sandwich?"

"Lemonade would be great," said Sal as he went inside. "Just finished a big lunch made even greater because the Sheriff's boys paid for it."

Sal started to tell Jenn what had happened to earn him a free lunch. She laughed after hearing the story then commented, "Sal, you lead a charmed life, you know that? I believe it's because you sincerely love helping others and for that your guardian angel takes extra special care of you."

Together they went over everything that had to be done before their first AA meeting. Jenn planned on starting it in three weeks. She had tables and chairs, plus the books, literature and coffee maker that Sal had delivered.

"Every AA meeting is supposed to be self-sufficient, declining outside contributions," explained Sal. "Every meeting pays for itself sending only extra money that can be spared to 'General Services,' the home office of

AA. We've never received monetary help from anywhere but from our own members. Everyone pays a dollar if he or she can afford it, or spare change if that's all they have. No one is ever turned away for being too crazy, broke or unwashed; even if they come drunk or are still drinking. One of our sayings is 'If you are still out there, your showing up here helps the rest of us keep our memory green.' In other words, until someone comes back to the rooms and tells how much better it is to be out there drinking than in here working on staying sober, we as members will continue to work on not drinking or drugging. All it takes to be a member is to say you are. Another saying of ours is, 'One day at a time.' Sometimes it's 'One hour at a time.' Whatever it takes to make it through the night and day without picking up a drink."

Sal continued his spiel as Jenn listened intently. "Just think about this," Sal said. "Since Dr. Bob and Bill W., the founders of AA, started this program to save their own necks, literally millions have come into the rooms and gotten sober, leading much better, more satisfying lives. When you consider the effect this has had on their families and friends you can now multiply the benefits that occur when the drunk surrenders to the fact that his life has become unmanageable, but he needs help to change it. For some it doesn't happen immediately, but if they keep coming to the meetings and don't drink, we can promise their situation will improve. Their families may return if they've left. They'll be able to hold a job again. For me, it was well worth the price of admission just to be able to wake up every morning and not be terrified about not remembering what I had done the night before when I got drunk."

Sal looked at Jenn sheepishly when he realized he had been carrying on for some time. "I'm sorry," he shook his head. "I didn't mean to get on my soap box, but I feel very strongly about the program. It surely saved my life."

At this point Jenn hugged Sal to assure him everything was all right. "I'm a believer, too," she said. "It wasn't easy for me to stop from crawling into a bottle when my life was falling apart. If I had had the benefit of an

AA meeting and the support of a sponsor it would have been much easier to deal with my problems. Luckily, I found my hero in the Reverend. With his counsel and love I made it through. Now I have a burning desire to help others find the way as well. So thanks Sal, for giving me the opportunity to share my love for my fellow man as well as help show him the way."

"Well, aren't we a couple of do-gooders?" laughed Sal. "But this is how it works. We are saved from more misery and we get to pay it forward and help the next one suffering. You know, it feels a hell of a lot better than drinking ever did. I grew up working in my parents' hotel with a restaurant and tavern. At eight years old I saw a lot of men who could no longer live at home with their families. Fathers of kids I knew from school would waste their paycheck sitting on the bar stools I had to scrub every Saturday morning. It never dawned on me as I snuck drinks from the glasses that were half full that I could easily become like them. By the time I went to high school I worked out ways I could get drunk a couple of times a week. I'm so lucky I didn't kill anyone or myself driving drunk. I guess you're right about my guardian angel working over time for me."

Jenn told Sal that a couple who had been in recovery for six years had agreed to help get the meetings started. They thought that having the meetings twice a week on Monday and Saturday would work well. It would probably end up being mostly locals on Mondays, but they expected a few tourists too. Sal applauded the fact she had arranged assistance. AA had developed a successful template for its organization: chairman, secretary and financial "trusted servants." The chairman arranged for the speakers and kept the agenda alive; they also organized volunteers to come early and get the coffee made. Neither Jenn nor Sal thought spreading the word would be hard. The Reverend could announce it at Sunday service plus they could put it on the church marquee. Word of mouth would do the rest. Sal intended to let Sargeant Joe and Deputy Larry know when the meeting times were so they could pass it along as well.

"If you have any questions you can call me at the monastery and leave a message," Sal concluded. "I think I'll be staying there for awhile. Right now, I need to drive over to Bisbee. I have an appointment with the Sheriff, believe it or not—and it's supposed to be a good one. Then I'll be talking to a prospect about starting to work the AA program. An old Army friend of mine could use some help."

Jenn gave Sal another hug and told him she was glad he was back in town. She liked him a lot better now than in his "helldorado days."

"Adios, Jenn," Sal waved as he left. "Time to get into gear and do God's work."

"I'll let you know what day we're having our first meeting so you can be there, Sal," Jenn called out. "Good luck with everything."

CHAPTER 59

THE SHERIFF

As the "Lone Ranger" drove away with his trusty sidekick, Little John, Sal thought about the town's history, which had some good parts and some bad. He figured he was lucky to start adding to the good parts. He decided to make a quick stop at the bridge to drop off the supplies he had gathered then give the "big boy" a walk. "Then we'll go see the Sheriff of Nottingham," Sal said aloud to Little John, your namesake's stomping grounds.

Once Sal made it to the Sheriff's office he found a shady side of the building so he could safely leave Little John in the car. Sal approached the secretary's desk and indicated to her the Sheriff was expecting him. The secretary nodded and told Sal to go to the door marked "Private." As he did so, she buzzed him through the door and notified the Sheriff Sal was on his way in. It was different being on the other end of the counter, mused Sal. He easily could have been the jail keeper's primary guest in his less-enlightened times.

The Sheriff came out of his office and shook Sal's hand fiercely. The man was big and brawny and Sal had a flashback of Nahteste's nephews.

"Well, well," said the Sheriff with a grin. "Salvadore Dusi. Good to finally meet you in person. I've heard a lot of stories about you, first questionable, but lately all good. I ran a little check on you with your hometown Chief of Police. He told me how he chased you out of town when you were in the Army Recruiter's car after a night of mischief. Seems you blew away the porch light of your least favorite teacher and threw cherry bombs into the houses of the runner-ups. He did say he was glad to have you join the Army and get out of his town, but when you returned you didn't get into any more trouble. I told him you were responsible for helping us pull off the largest drug bust in Arizona history. He told me you would be welcome back there anytime. In fact, there is an opening on his force if you're interested."

"Well those are words I never thought I would hear," Sal grinned. "Honestly Sheriff, I love it here in Arizona. That's why I returned. I'm looking forward to making a life for myself out here."

"Well, c'mon," nudged the Sheriff. "Let's get some good coffee and sit down. Call me Eldon, please. How do you like your coffee, son?"

"Just black, sir," said Sal. He quietly reminisced that in the past, lawmen called him son, too, but that was only the first part of the phrase. "I guess I've come a long way," Sal thought to himself.

The Sheriff returned with two large mugs of coffee and handed Sal one as he said, "You can keep that mug when you're through," smiled the Sheriff. "The number on it rings right through to my secretary. She can reach me anytime day or night. If you think it's advantageous to speak with me, you can even call collect. I'm very pleased with what you have done for us already. I have to believe that if you stick around, we'll be hearing from you again. I also want you to have this old badge of mine. It doesn't have a badge number, of course, but you can show it to any of my deputies or the State Patrol and tell them to call me before they begin writing any tickets or causing you any grief. We consider you on our team now, and as you know, we take care of our own. Along the line of what your Chief back in Pennsylvania was saying, if you decide you need a good job I'm pretty sure I could hire you as a special deputy. I can give references to the county stakeholders. It wouldn't be a problem—even for a guy from Pennsylvania like you."

The Sheriff let out a big guffaw at his own joke and continued. "I mean it, Sal. We really appreciate it when a citizen does what he can to help us out. This isn't an easy job to do, especially for an understaffed, tight-budgeted Sheriff. We are the first line of defense on this side of this international border that we have to contend with."

"I don't even know what to say, sir," Sal finally got a word in. "I really appreciate all you are doing for me. I'm really just happy I could help out a little. My plate is pretty full right now. I'm involved in starting a couple of AA meetings. If you can help get the word out I would appreciate that."

"You just talk to Barbara, my secretary," said the Sheriff. "She'll make sure everyone in this office is aware of the where's and when's. We can sure use some help in that area. In fact, would it be O.K. if some of my deputies attended? There's lots of stress in this job. A few of them may be getting themselves into some trouble using booze to relax."

"Sure," said Sal. "Just don't let them show up in uniform. That might empty out the room before we get started."

They both laughed as the Sheriff began to dismiss his visitor. "Sal, it's been a pleasure to meet with you," he said. "Anything we can do for you, just ask; my door is open. And if you ever want to talk about a career path, come back in and we'll discuss it. Need to break this up now; you wouldn't believe how much this job entails. I'll be working until midnight trying to catch up. I hate paper work—that's the hardest part of this job."

"Thank you very much Sher—Eldon," Sal caught himself. "I'm glad your people were able to pull all that poison out of the pipeline. It messes up and kills a lot of young people before they even have a chance to find themselves."

The Sheriff started walking Sal out as he continued talking. "Please tell all your deputies that I appreciate their service to us civilians. I shudder to think how it would be out there without their dedication and willingness to work long, hard hours guarding us all. I have quite a few law-enforcement people in my family and I have to admit, most of them have told me it's a love/hate vocation. Their families pay the price, too. Please pass on the schedule for the AA meetings; that's a big focus of mine right now. I have many good ideas; hopefully I can implement a few, you know, bring them to fruition."

Sal and the Sheriff shook hands and he went to Barbara's desk to give her the information he had. As he pulled away from the Sheriff's office he checked his watch and found it was after 4 o'clock. It was time to head to Jake and Catherine's house and do whatever he could to help Jake get back onto the right path for the good of himself and his family. Sal found a large pullout that the truckers used so he could unload Little John for a few moments. The dog unloaded a large deposit too, which was better there than at his friend's. Sal brought out the folding shovel he had lifted from the Army post and threw Little John's offering into the Ocotillo cactus. Sal didn't want any of the trucker's stepping into that mess—he believed in karma and didn't want to be paid back in spades.

CHAPTER 60

STEP ONE

S al surprised himself when he remembered the turnoff from the highway to get to the Billetts' house. He didn't think he had ever visited them when he was sober. "But I am now," Sal mumbled to himself. "Who would ever believe that I'd be the one to help out old Jake? I bet I'd win the wager on that from every guy in the Company at Fort Huachuca if they were asked. I sure was a screwup for the duration of my Army career and everyone there knew it."

Sal thought he was really lucky he never came close to hurting or killing anyone because of his reckless drinking. He remembered that one time he took a backpack and four bottles of tequila into the hills south of Nogales, Mexico one weekend. He headed to where some loco locals somehow had hauled railroad cars up onto the hillside for homes, probably by mule. He found a group of crazies like himself, between his broken Spanish and their broken English and with the tequila as an interpreter, they drank all night laughing and telling stories they each understood at least in their own minds. He ate their tortillas filled with who-knew-what and slept under the railroad cars. After a very bizarre weekend he hitchhiked back to the Fort in time for Monday morning's roll call. He was picked up by one of the guys he knew who drove a laundry truck and was bringing a load of clean uniforms back to the Fort from a laundry in Nogales, Arizona.

"Who says the Army isn't fun?" Sal reminisced to himself. He was now convinced that all of life was what you made it. He also began to remember the first time he hitched a ride into Naco, Mexico. As he walked around, a pretty senorita spoke to him and invited him home for dinner with her family. It was the first time he ever ate burro meat. The girl's father had shot it that morning as it wandered in the desert. It turned out to be a very pleasant evening, though. When they had finished, the girl told him she had to go to work, and much to Sal's surprise, they walked a mile into the red-light district. She pointed Sal to the safest bars and told him to make sure he arranged a ride back to the Fort. Then she kissed him on the cheek and left; Sal only saw her two or three more times in the next couple of years, when he wandered around that crazy area. Once when he witnessed that man being shot in the head and again at a New Year's Eve party in a Holiday Inn restaurant in Sierra Vista, Arizona. A couple of other wacko soldiers had snuck her across the border in the trunk of their car just for the weekend fiesta. Sal had no part in that, though. Nevertheless, Sal was pretty sure he wasn't the only crazy soldier out there.

As Sal pulled up to his friend's house, Catherine, Jake and a cute two-year-old girl came out to greet him. Catherine was the first to speak, "Why don't you two sit out here and visit while I see about dinner," she said. "Hope you like lasagna; it's Jake's favorite. He told me you liked it, too."

"It's my favorite also," Sal salivated as he spoke. "I haven't had home-made in a long time. Thank you so much."

"Well, I read some of that book you gave me instead of drinking," Jake started. "I thought it would be all sermon-like and goody-two-shoes, but man, these guys went through the same stuff that I am going through now."

"Yep," nodded Sal. "That book is just a big meeting written down. It's what I turned to not so long ago whenever I started to get squirrelly. Even now, I try to read a few pages every day. There is so much wisdom written there in a form I can understand. The guys that started this thing were either brilliant or divinely inspired."

"O.K., Sal; I told Catherine and now I'm telling you. I intend to get off the booze habit as quick as I can. What do I have to do?" Jake looked at Sal expectantly.

"After dinner, why don't we pour all that booze that's in the house down the drain," said Sal. "Even the beer; and I want you to do it. For every ounce that goes down the drain, you tell it, 'I don't need you anymore; I have a Higher Power and it's no longer you.' It may sound silly, but it worked for me and a lot of others that I've met."

"All right, Sal," said Jake. "I can do that. Seeing you now and remembering how bad you were inspires me, and makes me believe I can beat this problem, too. Will you help me through the beginning of my staying sober?"

"Absolutely," swore Sal. "This is how it works; one drunk helping another. They say whenever there are two recovering drunks together, that's a meeting."

"I wish there was a meeting here in Bisbee," said Jake. "Maybe we can try to find one?"

"There are two new meetings starting in a couple of weeks," said Sal. "And we also have one every evening at the monastery. I feel strongly that you should attend a meeting for the first 30 days, or we'll have to get together and talk for a while. Once you meet some of the guys at the Fort meeting maybe you can hang out with them over coffee. Don't worry about it, though. I'll stick with you; it helps me as much as it'll help you. I'm actually pretty new at this myself. I need all the reinforcing I can get."

Just then, Catherine stuck her head out the door. "The best lasagna in Bisbee is getting cold, guys," she smiled. "Come on in."

The men followed her into the house and sat at the table to work on the fresh salad and Italian bread.

"I could get used to this," Sal said as he was finishing his third helping. "I've had three big meals today and all of them have been delicious. Please save the table scraps for my dog; he needs a lot of fuel to move that load on paws."

When the group retired back onto the porch, Sal continued thanking his hosts. "Thank you so much, Catherine," he said. "I know you don't feed Jake like this every night because he looks about the same as when we were at Fort Monmouth; back then he was known as 'Butterball.'"

Jake grumbled at that, "After you finish doing the dishes we can talk, so why don't you hurry up?"

Catherine laughed and told Sal not to bother. "You two can sit here and have some apple pie I just took out of the oven. I'm just now brewing some fresh coffee."

"O.K. Jake," Sal snickered. "Let's see what we can figure out together."

"If I join this group does that mean I can't ever drink again'" asked Jake as soon as they sat down.

"That's the first thing about 80-percent of the people ask when they choose to come to AA" laughed Sal.

"Well, what about it?" pushed Jake. "I need to know."

"From my limited experience, you attend meetings as you want to," Sal answered. "You don't drink and you keep going to meetings. Eventually, you will no longer want to drink. In my case, going to meetings eliminated my desire to drink, so to answer your question, someday I might be able to drink in a reasonable manner, but right now I don't want to. I don't think it's worth the chance that I could slip back into the mess I was in. It's totally up to you, though. You know what it's been like up to now. You'll have the chance every day to go back to the way you were."

Sal hesitated a moment before continuing. "I heard at a meeting once, that if you don't like sobriety, AA will cheerfully refund your misery—with interest. We need good examples of slipping backwards to keep the people trying every day. 'Keep your memory green.' I think the first thing to do is to pour out all the liquor and wine in the house, even in your car if you have some stashed there. From here on out, if I'm going to be your sponsor, I have to insist you be 100-percent honest with me or it won't work. Will you agree with that?"

"Yeah, I will," promised Jake. "I know I've been a mess for a while, if I want my family to stay intact and I also want a decent career, I need to do it without drinking. I always told myself that I wasn't hurting anyone but myself, but after hearing some of the stories the other night, it made me realize I was destroying my marriage, as well as my wife and daughter's life. I don't want to be that selfish, nor do I have the right to be. So, O.K., I'll be honest with you, let's get pouring out those bottles before Catherine serves the coffee and pie."

The men went back into the kitchen and cleared out the pantry of bottles. Sal had Jake do it while chanting like a mantra: "I don't need or want you anymore."

"Holy smoke," commented Sal as he watched Jake. "You really loved your Jose Cuervo."

"Yeah," nodded Jake. "It got me where I wanted pretty quickly and it was less than $2 a bottle down in Naco, Mexico." After 13 bottles were poured down the drain, Jake motioned Sal to the backyard where he had a small storage shed. Under the shelf of an old workbench were seven more bottles of tequila and four of 154-proof run.

"You could have opened a bar out here," laughed Sal. The men disposed of the last alcoholic beverage right when Catherine was ready to serve dessert.

"Kathleen has to go to bed soon," motioned Catherine towards their three-year-old. "And I promised her some pie. She helped me make it, you know."

"Sure," nodded Jake. "Let's do that right now." As Sal feasted on the dessert he couldn't help but ponder once again how nice this domestic deal really was.

"Are you considering settling down any time soon with a wife?" Catherine asked.

"Actually, I've met someone that has really caused me to rethink my idea of not marrying until I was over 30," said Sal. "She lives in Tucson. We have just started seeing each other. It feels right, though. AA states not to form any new or strong relationships for a year after joining, so I have a ways to go yet. I will do all I can to keep it going slow. That may be a problem, but I'm not drinking and have no intention to ever do it again. The concern is that if the relationship blows up it could lead to drinking again. A lot has happened to me to change my life in the months since I stopped drinking—especially in the last month. But, hey, I'm not here to talk about me. Over the next three months I'll try to tell you the whole story, but for now, I'd like to concentrate on Jake."

With that, Catherine took their daughter to bed and commenced clearing the kitchen.

"You've heard some of my story, Jake—hell, you've even lived part of it," Sal shook his head as he spoke. "Like when I chased that lieutenant with the baseball bat and you were driving the jeep. We both know we are qualified as very competent drunks; even card-carrying, drunk, union-journeymen boozers. This program is fairly simple. It's partially based on the K.I.S.S. principle—"Keep It Simple, Stupid!"

"I don't think there is any doubt we have done lots of stupid things," agreed Jake. "I know some of yours and you know some of mine. Remember how we planned to go AWOL our first month out here in Arizona? I wonder how that would have turned out."

"Well, what I'm trying to say is that I don't think I'm any better or worse than you," Sal told Jake. "We both let booze control us way too often and we both have a strong desire to not drink anymore. It's something that continuously messes up our lives as well as those around us. If you want my help I will do all I can for you until you move back to New York. Then you'll need to find a good sponsor there. Best to pick someone who won't put up with your crap and has had enough experience in the program to guide you along. You've taken the first step on your path to sobriety—you've poured out all the liquor you had—that's real important. If there's anymore anywhere, you need to get rid of it now. So... Is there any more?"

"Yeah," Jake looked down at his feet. "I left four bottles of tequila next door at Rob's house. You remember him, right?"

"Yes," said Sal with a pained look on his face. "I owe him and his wife a big apology for that stupid, drunken night last year. But you're not at that step, yet, where you make amends to those you have wronged. We can still go over there though. You can watch me while you pour out the booze. It's best not to just give it away; that way, if you show up over there begging for it they won't feel obliged to return it to you. I'm not saying this is going to be easy—you're probably going to want to drink again. This is just the AA way—the best way, I believe, to stop drinking and stay stopped."

"Let's go over while we're thinking about it," said Jake. "So we can get it out of the way."

"It'll remove the opportunity for you to slip with taking just a short walk," encouraged Sal.

CHAPTER 61

AMENDS

A fter Jake told Catherine where they were going, he knocked on Rob and Nelly's door. Nelly answered with a bit of a surprised look on her face. "Hey Jake!" she smiled. "What's up?"

The moment she spotted Sal, she almost let out a growl. "What are you doing here?" she demanded. "I told you to never come near me again. You've got a lot of nerve after your actions the last time you were here."

Jake started to explain but Sal stopped him. "Let me do it Jake," said Sal. "This is something I must do for my own recovery. I really want to apologize for making such an ass of myself. Plus the embarrassment I caused you and Rob—is Rob here? I need to tell you both how sorry I am."

"I'm right behind you," a stern voice sounded that swung them both around. "If you start any crap again I'll put this shovel to good use 'upside your head.' What are you doing here? I thought you went back to the East Coast?"

"I came back and am now living at a monastery in St. David," Sal explained.

"Oh my God," said Nelly incredulously. "That I do not believe! This is a story I really need to hear. Let's all sit down at the picnic table—and Rob, put down the shovel, O.K? You shouldn't threaten people like that; you could end up in trouble."

Rob sat down after putting the shovel against the house, but still in close reach. "I'm not just threatening," Rob pointed his finger at Sal. "If this guy starts any stuff again, I intend to brain him."

"Please calm down," Sal implored Rob. "All I want to do is explain what I have done since being discharged, and offer my most sincere apologies for my idiotic actions when I was here last."

Sal plunged ahead and told them a condensed version of what he'd been doing since joining AA last July in Pennsylvania. He emphatically told them how very bad and foolish he felt about putting the move on Nelly after Rob had passed out because they all had drank so much. But Sal had no excuse to give them.

"I am asking for your forgiveness," Sal said as he wrapped up his story. "I am a very changed guy and am very sorry for all the stupid things I did when I was drinking."

"You always were a nice guy, Sal," Nelly replied. "So I believe you when you say you're sorry. I accept your apology, but if you ever show up at my doorstep drinking I'll use that shovel on you myself."

"Thank you," said Sal a bit relieved. "I absolutely do not intend to ever drink again, so please don't worry about that. I have found a very comfortable place in my life where I do not ever want to do anything that will cause me to hate myself again."

"Wow," mumbled Rob. "That is something I never expected to hear from you. When I saw you after you pulled that crap on us, you just put your head down and mumbled that you were sorry. I never bought that, but this time I feel you have changed and mean it when you say it. You are welcome here any time as long as you're not drinking."

Rob shook Sal's hand and Nelly gave him a brief hug. Jake then proceeded to tell them that he was going to stop drinking, too, and that he needed to collect his bottles of tequila so he could pour them out. At that instant, both Rob and Nelly laughed out loud.

"What a day!" Rob shook his head as he looked back and forth at Sal and Jake. "Two of the biggest boozers at Fort Huachuca have stopped drinking. There's hope for anyone if you two can stop. I would have given 100-to-1 odds that neither of you would have stopped drinking before it killed you. I've got to admit it, Sal, I'm pretty impressed. I've never known anyone as self-destructive as you over the two years I knew you. So, Jake, what can we do to help you achieve your goal? Chase you away if you come over for a drink? I've never been around anyone trying to stop drinking. My family is expert at the opposite—they drink daily. I'm afraid there's only three bottles left; I finished one off in the last two weeks—sorry, but I guess that's no big deal if you plan to dump them down the drain. I helped by pouring one down my gullet. I'll go get them and I'll put them on the sink so you can do the deed."

Rob walked into his kitchen as he called out mischievously, "I wish I had a movie camera; I could probably sell the scene to 'Ripley's Believe It or Not'!"

"Come on in the kitchen," Nelly said. "I want to watch your face when you do this. I still can't believe you've both stopped drinking; it's a miracle for sure. There are a lot of Army wives that are going to be begging you for help with their crazies. If you two don't start hitting the bottle again then I will absolutely believe anyone can stop."

"O.K., Jake, start pouring," said Sal. "The sewer rats down the line will be happy tonight."

"Ha!" laughed Jake as he unscrewed the caps. He faked a few sobs as the liquor disappeared down the drain. "Sal, I was always able to blame you for getting me to drink so much, but then you were gone and I still drank too much, maybe even more. Finding that you're now responsible for helping me stop is somehow appropriate. I just never would have believed our lives would have taken this turn for the better. I guess God really does move in mysterious ways."

As the last of the liquid drained down into the sink, Jake suddenly got thoughtful. "I really do intend to not drink anymore. I've been a real jerk to Catherine and have yelled at Kathleen for no good reason."

"Oh, yeah," Nelly interjected. "We've heard some of your rants and felt real bad for both of them. I wanted to send Rob over to straighten you out but I knew that would end up badly, you having been a New York State wrestling champion at one time. I, for one, am very happy you are going to try and not drink anymore. I hope it works out for you."

Nelly turned to Sal and gave him some encouragement he hadn't expected. "If anyone can kick his butt, you can, Sal," she said. "Rob has told me about your fights at the N.C.O. Club on base."

"O.K., I've done my dirty deed," interrupted Jake. "We need to go talk on my porch now."

Sal thanked both Rob and Nelly for their forgiveness and promised to see them again soon. Once Sal and he were back at Jake's house, Catherine refilled their coffee cups.

"Do you really think I can do this?" asked Jake.

"Oh yeah," Sal nodded vigorously. "You just need to desire being sober more than you desire being drunk. What do you think? Are you ready to change your life for the better? If so, I will do all I can to help. If you change your mind I'll get out of your way. Don't worry about missing out on something because you've stopped drinking; there's plenty of misery out there to go around for all who want it. It will always be waiting to jump on you again. There's a saying in AA about people going 'back out' and doing more research. They're told to come back and let us know if their lives are better when drinking; if it is, we'll all join them. Out of the millions that have gone through the program, no one has returned to tout the great benefits of returning to drink, as far as I know."

Sal looked thoughtfully at Jake before he continued. "If you are serious about stopping I would suggest you read the Big Book of Alcoholics Anonymous cover to cover, especially if you get squirrelly and are craving a drink. All the stories in there are true, told by folks just like you and me. They found a different life by going to meetings and sharing their stories and accepting they can't have that first drink. It's not the last one that gets you drunk, it's the first. I know if I have one I have no idea what will happen or how much I'll end up drinking after that. I like to think of it as an allergy to alcohol—just stay away from it; that's what works for me. Once I stopped drinking and started attending meetings I found that working in my father's bar was not possible. It made me feel really weird to be around all that booze, which is kind of funny, considering I was released early from the Army to tend bar. I helped in other ways, though, while I stayed there. I worked in the store, drove to the wholesale market, and picked up groceries. I even carried all the beer down into the basement cooler. That's one of the reasons I wanted you to dump all your alcohol; it's too much of a temptation, especially when you're new. I'm going to leave you one of the 12-Step books, but only read about the first two steps of the AA program. In fact, read them over and over; maybe when you sit on the throne—I do my best reading there."

Sal began to gather himself up as if to leave. "We need to call it a night, Jake," he said at last. "You've actually done a lot to improve your chances at sobriety. I believe you'll be a success. Any questions before I go?"

"Well, I know this is stupid, but do you think I can just have a beer or two at night?" Jake asked hopefully.

"Nope, sorry buddy," Sal said adamantly. "Even a low-alcohol beer can kick off an allergic reaction that just makes you want more. Have Catherine make lemonade or iced tea for you and keep pouring that down your throat. You just can't drink any alcoholic beverage. I've heard of people getting into trouble by drinking apple cider just to get a buzz, like back up in New York, remember?"

"Yeah, there's a great place for that called 'Fly Creek' near my folks' place," said Jake. "O.K. then; I want to put an end to the craziness I've been causing. You've convinced me, Sal. I can change if you can change. When I think back to some of the stuff we did I'm surprised we are still alive or at least not in prison. This is an opportunity for me to change and have a real nice life upstate with Catherine and Kathleen and any other 'K' that might show up."

Jake looked a bit more resolute when he looked Sal in the eye. "Yeah, help me kick this habit. It's just getting worse. I'm ready to stop."

"I'll do all I can buddy," said Sal. "But it's really all up to you. I can show you what worked for me but you are the one who has to work the steps and go to the meetings from here on out."

Sal and Jake agreed to meet on the porch the next evening to discuss the assigned reading. With that, they hugged each other before Sal started to leave. He gave Catherine a quick "thank you," then got into his Pontiac and drove away.

CHAPTER 62

GREAT PHONE CALL

Heading back to the monastery, Sal thought his meeting with the Billetts had gone quite well. They had gotten rid of the alcohol, he was able to make amends to the Elias's next door, and Jake was really trying to get his head into the program. "Maybe I'll be a good sponsor after all," Sal said to himself.

Arriving at the monastery Sal found a note under his door saying Mary had called. He immediately went over to the office to use the phone. Mary answered after a few rings. Sal was happy to hear her voice.

"How are you doing, Sal?" she asked with interest.

"Pretty good," he answered. "Brother Al is returning so I'll be staying in my own room at the monk house."

"Oh, no!" she exclaimed. "Don't tell me you've decided to be a monk?"

"No, no, no!" exclaimed Sal. "I'll explain it when I see you. There are lots of ears around here, you know."

"I have something to ask you," Mary said as she laughed about his last remark.

"O.K.," said Sal. "What is it?"

"My father needs an important document hand-delivered to Yuma," she said. "It has to be signed in the presence of two witnesses. Would you be willing to go there with me next Monday?"

"Of course," Sal said without hesitation. "For sure. I'd love to go on a road trip with you."

"O.K., great," said Mary. "Glad you're so agreeable. It'll be fun. How about you pick me up at the office at 7 a.m. Monday?"

"No problem," agreed Sal. "I'll drive. We can make a day of it. I'll even dress a little better with my Sunday boots. I have knee-high leather and lizard ones I've been dying to show off to you. I picked them up in Nogales."

"All right, then," she giggled at the image that came into her head. "It's a date. See you Monday morning."

"Thanks for thinking of me," Sal said before she cut out.

"Oh, don't worry about that," Mary said slyly. "I think about you all the time. I'll bring my camera so I can get some pictures of you to look at when I'm not seeing you in person."

"Well, you just made my night," smiled Sal. "Bye!"

"That was one of the best phone calls I have ever had," Sal said to himself. He walked Little John but it wasn't too long before he was down and out to the world, fast asleep.

CHAPTER 63

WELCOME HOME

The next morning after Sal handled his Little John chores, he went to the dining hall and sat awhile with Brother Casper. The monk told him that Brother Alex was expected to arrive at the monastery that afternoon. After a pleasant breakfast together, Sal excused himself. He went over to brother Alex's room, retrieved L.J., then sat on the bench by the pond where he could pull out his notebook and go over things he had to do. So far, he was satisfied with the duties he had delegated to people he could trust, but he needed to get to the library in Benson and pick up whatever was in the donation boxes. Since, sadly, Little John might not be riding with him after this, Sal wanted to bring him along for one last adventure.

When Sal and Little John arrived in Benson, they found an over-flowing donation box. Nicole then took Sal to a spare room in the library that had six more blankets and at least 75 cans of food. To his delight there were also two-dozen coloring books with crayons. She told Sal the ladies had purchased them for Sal to give out to the children.

Sal could barely fit all the loot into his car around Little John's body. He thanked Nicole profusely then went back to St. David. At the monastery Sal sought out Brother Casper to see if he could move into his own room earlier than expected. Brother Casper showed him a little cottage near the path to the river where Sal could reside. Two other monks would be sharing the living quarters with Sal, each with his own bedroom and a shared bath. There was an unfinished patio at the rear of the cottage. Sal decided he would work on it over the weekend while he waited for his trip with Mary.

Fortunately, there was ample parking space to put the Pontiac into because the other two monks did not have vehicles. Sal unloaded his library booty, went to the dining hall to have lunch, walked Little John then began working on the patio. There were plenty of flat rocks and river rocks on the ground, so Sal worked up a good sweat trying to clear the area. He had never done a job like this before, so he needed to figure out how it was supposed to be done. Little John laid in the shade watching Sal labor in the sun, "as is usual with dogs." Sal laughed to himself thinking, "If a flying saucer came down to check out Earth and the leader asked the first scout who their leaders were, the answer could be: 'Well, I first thought it was the beings standing upright in the fabric skin but then I saw those creatures picking up the defecation of the four- legged, furry creatures, also serving them bowls of food, so I would surmise it must be that the furry creatures are the leaders?"

"If you laugh I'll find a wagon to hitch you to and you'll pull the stones for me," he glared at the dog. But Little John didn't laugh out loud; he just panted in the afternoon heat and looked, what appeared to be, aimlessly ahead.

It seemed like Sal had just gotten started when he heard a big booming voice calling in the distance. "Where's my Little John?" said Brother Alex as he came around the corner of the cottage. Little John moved faster than Sal had seen him move all month. He jumped into Alex's open arms and knocked him flat on his back. Sal nearly wet his pants laughing at the sight. The two rolled around the ground laughing and barking like it was the best reunion ever.

Getting up and brushing himself off, Brother Alex approached Sal with an open hand. "Wow, he sure didn't stop eating due to lonesomeness while I was gone, did he?" Brother Alex shook Sal's hand vigorously.

"No, he tried to eat his weight every day," said Sal. "He nearly succeeded, too."

The two men sat down to tell each other how their month had gone. Brother Alex was happy with all he had been able to accomplish for his folks. Sal told him a little about his life in the last month as well. Brother Alex was amazed at what Sal had been doing and told him how glad he was that he was staying at the monastery.

"You know you seem to fit in real well here," said Brother Alex. "And hang on here; I have something for you that I left in the car." The monk took off down the trail with Little John close on his heels. When he returned he was carrying a bag that contained two boxes of Cuban cigars. Sal couldn't believe his eyes.

"The doctor insisted that my dad stop smoking," explained Brother Alex. "So he gave me all of his cigars to get rid of."

Sal was unquestionably delighted with the gift. He thanked him profusely and asked if they could meet that evening so he could try one out. It would also give each of them the opportunity to get into more detail about their respective adventures.

"Well, I'll take Little John now and let you work in peace," said Brother Alex. "I need to get resettled into my room, which I have missed terribly."

Sal went back to his attempt at patio making, which was beginning to turn out better than he first thought. He realized quickly that the secret was in taking one's time with setting the stones. Burying the river rock half way into the ground, Sal placed them carefully between the flat stones. He decided to place an outline of a Sycamore leaf shape in the center of the stones to commemorate how the tree played such an important role in the path he had chosen.

By the afternoon, Sal had made good headway on the patio but it was now time to wash up for dinner. He made plans to finish it the next day, when he'd have plenty of time. At the dining hall, it was like having a Family Thanksgiving Day dinner with everyone welcoming back Brother Alex.

As they laughed and joked, Sal suddenly remembered that he needed to call Jake so he asked Brother Casper if he could make the call.

When Sal reached Jake, he apologized for not showing up on his porch to talk. "Brother Alex returned and in the excitement I forgot about getting together."

"No problem," Jake told him. "It's funny, but Rob came over and I haven't even eaten dinner yet, myself. He wanted to talk about his drinking and wondered if there was a book he could borrow from me to read about AA. If it's O.K. with you, can I give him your Big Book for a couple of days?"

"Wow, didn't see that coming," said Sal. "Sure, let him have it. You can read the 12-Step book I gave you until we meet again. I'll get another Big Book for him. So, it's O.K. if I don't come back over tonight?"

"Yep, I feel good," said Jake. "I was a little shaky driving home from the Fort today, but I'm feeling proud about what I'm doing. I'll be fine. How about tomorrow night? I can come up there for awhile and then we can go to the meeting?"

"Good thinking," said Sal. "Bring Rob if he wants. It should be a good one. There are a dozen or more people that have checked in for the weekend so there should be some good stories to hear. I'll be here all day; I'm working on building a patio. My new room is in a cottage down towards the river. Look for my car out front. See you then—and just fill up on lemonade, nothing else, right?"

"Yes sir," said Jake. "I hear you. I really want to do this. I'll see you tomorrow. Thanks."

No longer responsible for Little John and his monster "cow pies," Sal relaxed with a mug of unleaded coffee and walked into that night's meeting. It was crowded with visitors including 11 monks that he recognized. Sal sat in the back just wanting to listen. He had been carrying the message enough for this week.

As it turned out, it was a good meeting with plenty of stories about sobriety. One speaker told the crowd how he had tried heroin and his life totally collapsed in a matter of two months. At the end the group got up and held hands to say the Lord's Prayer together. Sal slipped out afterwards and hit the pillow on his new bed without dreaming. He was glad to see that Brother Alex was too tied up with other people to come down to his cottage and talk.

In the morning, the weather had changed to a comfortable cool. It was just right for wrestling rocks. The patio was taking shape and was nearly finished by the time Jake and Rob showed up. They appraised Sal's handiwork and told him he should come to Bisbee to make patios for them. "Nah! That's part of the package you get to do on your own," said Sal.

CHAPTER 64

FRIENDS

To Sal's delight, Jake had brought a cooler with leftover lasagna, pepperoni and cheese, and two gallons of lemonade. "Give me a chance to clean up and we'll sit down by the river to eat and talk," Sal said. "We have a little time before our meeting."

As Sal sat under his familiar Sycamore tree with his two friends, he smiled to himself as he thought about the spiritual visits he had experienced before this. He didn't know how Jake and Rob would take to a sudden apparition, but the men had too many questions to sit still.

"How did you decide to go to AA?" Rob inquired. "Was it a really hard thing to do?"

"You have to remember I'm pretty new at this, too," Sal said modestly. "I think I should pass most your questions onto those who have more time in the rooms than I do. Let's walk up and listen to a few of them. The meeting starts in about twenty minutes."

As luck had it there were three really good speakers who were all alcoholics, who indicated they had some serious time in the program. After the meeting ended, Sal advised Rob and Jake to speak with them in order to just get comfortable being in the rooms of AA. Sal knew it would pay off over time. Forty-five minutes later, the room was cleared and Sal walked with his buddies back to his cottage.

Rob was stunned by what he had heard that night, as was Jake. "I sure don't want me or my family to get to that point," said Jake. "Living in a refrigerator box in winter is definitely not my idea of a good time."

"Our lives are less than perfect right now," said Rob. "What with being broke and all, but once we leave the Army and have good jobs all that will change. We can provide well for our wives and children. There's no need to get drunk every night or every week. It doesn't really help anything and obviously causes a lot of problems. I'm sure glad you popped back in our lives, Sal. This time around you're very welcome, not like before. So if you can change as much as you have, I don't see why we can't. Thank you for allowing us to come to the meeting and for talking to us openly and honestly. Maybe we're all finally growing up."

With that said, Rob and Jake drove off, agreeing to come up at least three evenings a week to a meeting. They also agreed to attend some of the new meetings and, hopefully, Sal would make it down to Bisbee to hang out, just to keep them both from getting too squirrelly.

CHAPTER 65

LEARNING TO JOURNEY

N ow that he was alone with his thoughts, Sal mused about his busy day. It was time to sleep but he kind of missed Little John, and wondered how his old sidekick was doing.

In the morning, Sal went through his usual routine then headed back to his patio. He wanted to finish it by noon. As he sat down to admire his work, Brother Alex and Little John showed up. Brother Alex was extremely impressed with Sal's improvements, especially with the river-rock outlines. Now he wanted one, too.

"Oh well," Sal smirked. "If things don't work out with my do-gooder stuff, I can always build patios for a living."

"Or you can become a monk," laughed Brother Alex.

"Nope," Sal answered immediately. "I couldn't handle that celibacy deal. I met a great woman while you were away. In fact, early tomorrow morning she and I are going on a road trip to Yuma."

"Well congratulations," said Brother Alex. "I hope things work out for you. You seem to be pretty easy to get along with. I'm sure she's impressed with you. Good men are few and far between it seems. Most here have a lot of baggage: ex-wives, kids, issues of all sorts. Now that you've gotten into AA with both feet, you've changed into a good catch for any woman."

"Thanks for your vote of confidence," said Sal. "I'm hoping she continues to see it that way. By the way, I need to get up real early. I'm picking her up at 7 a.m. You wouldn't have an alarm clock I could borrow, would you?"

"Sure, no problem," said Brother Alex. "But what would be even better is Brother Cal gets up early because he does some of the breakfast cooking. You've met him, right?"

"Yes," Sal nodded. "He's a good guy."

"Well the door right around the side of this cottage goes into his bedroom," explained Brother Alex. "He is in the kitchen by 4:30 every morning. Let's talk to him. He can pound on your door and get you moving, O.K?"

"Sure," said Sal. "That'll work. No hangover and I don't even have to do any physical training in the dark. Ha!"

Brother Al then asked Sal if he was interested in participating in a drumming circle scheduled for that afternoon with a few of the other monks.

"I have no idea what that is," said Sal. "I have never played a drum."

"Well, actually, it's not a musical thing," explained the monk. "We all tap an animal-skin drum at the same steady beat while a few of the Brothers lie down to experience journeys. Sort of like what you told me you experienced over by the Huachuca Mountains. It's called Percussion-Driven Journeying. Would you be interested in trying it? I picked it up in California and I've been teaching all the receptive guys here for a few years. In fact, there's a book in the reading room that I brought in written by the man who taught me the Shamanic journey techniques I've been passing on."

"Oh, hey, I have that book in my room," said Sal. "All I've read so far is how he went down to the Amazon to live with the head hunters and took the Ayahuasca herb to experience an out-of-body episode."

"Yes, that's the one," Brother Alex nodded. "After traveling the world as an anthropologist, he focused on different Shamanic methods practiced in various cultures. He learned that drumming and rattling repeatedly in a monotonous fashion induced a state of semi-altered consciousness which allowed one to travel to different worlds/dimensions, such as the lower world, the upper world, and the one I tend to stay away from—the middle world. It's where souls that haven't gone into the light wander aimlessly. Dr. Harner calls that 'the land of the great unemployed.' I went there one time during my training and it scared me silly. I do not want to go there again. My favorite seems to be the lower world. I find animal spirits there that have helped me to help and heal others. I've even acquired an animal spirit helper for myself. A trained Shaman cannot ask the compassionate spirits for help for themselves—only to help others. In fact, the word Shaman means vessel in an ancient Siberian language. Artifacts found in Siberia date to nearly 30,000 years old. Please join us; you will be amazed when you learn how to do this on demand, rather than the haphazard way you've been contacted by your spirit guides."

"O.K., I'm game," agreed Sal. "It's been way beyond interesting, so far. I'd like to learn more. But isn't this against your Benedictine Order rules?"

"Not at all," said Brother Alex. "Contacting compassionate spirits to aid and heal is a lot like praying. It just involves a different technique that isn't too far removed from meditation. I've always wondered if Jesus didn't practice some Shamanic art; especially when he went into the desert for 40 days and nights. I also find it interesting how the Native Americans go out to be alone on a Vision Quest when they are young. It seems that all human cultures are somewhat connected and enjoy similar techniques for contacting the spirit world. In fact, I recall Dr. Harner telling us during his classes the Jivaro Indians and the Australian Aborigines used very similar methods for their journeys and dreamtime. Their medicine men sure didn't phone each other up and discuss their techniques over the phone, did they? It seems so many cultures have similar practices and celebrations to worship their God or Saints to intercede on our behalf. Anyway, come over to my room; we'll fit you in and you will definitely enjoy your afternoon."

"O.K., you said two o'clock?" asked Sal and Brother Alex nodded. "Then I'll see you at two.

Sal took the time he had to go over his limited wardrobe and try to decide what he should wear for his big day with Mary. He took out his liz-ard boots and his freshly washed bell-bottom jeans that fit easily over the boots. He didn't want to tuck the pants into his boots like he did when he was in Mexico—he had been showing them off like the old-time vagueros did. Sal chose a nice cowboy shirt he had purchased in Tombstone during the Helldorado Days celebration. Knowing he sometimes messed up his shirts by spilling coffee as he drove, Sal packed extra clothes in his gym bag just in case of an accident.

After that chore was finished, Sal cleaned out the car and washed the windows. He wanted it super-clean for Mary, even though there really wasn't much to see on Route 8 to Yuma. In his opinion, it was the least scenic and most desolate part of Arizona. He then went over to see Brother Cal and arrange a wake-up call at 4:15 a.m. He also begged a couple of ham sandwiches then decided to take a stroll down by the river. Sal sat on his favorite boulder on the bank of the river and put his bare feet into the wa-ter. He looked around cautiously, hoping the cougar that had showed up a week ago had moved on.

When Sal finished his lunch, he moved under a big Sycamore to think about Mary and his upcoming week. He had at least two hours before the drumming circle so he figured he had time to take a quick nap. As soon as Sal began to relax he sensed a presence nearby. His favorite spirit began speaking to him, encouraging him once again that he was on the right path by helping and inspiring others. This was a very good thing.

"I am happy you have accepted the inspiration I offered you," Tearlisa, his Guiding Spirit, said. "In so doing, you have altered others' lives in a very beneficial way. As you walk forward in life, many paths will be offered to you but you alone must decide which one to take. Hopefully you have realized through the deep satisfaction you feel by assisting others that this is the path to walk. You must continue to make the right choices so that you are ensured a good afterlife."

Sal half-consciously agreed, but when he looked up, no one was there. No one in Pennsylvania would ever believe him if he told them about these experiences. They would be sure he was hitting the sauce again. He wondered if he could contact these spirits when he wanted to once he learned how to journey on demand. That would really be something, choosing which spirits to speak to. It would be fantastic. Sal slipped back into his nap and spent the rest of the time in peaceful, yet uneventful rest.

When Sal awoke, he checked his watch. It was 1:30 and time to head to Brother Alex's. When he arrived there, Sal met four other monks, three whom he had spoken to before at the meetings. Once everyone found a comfortable space, they began to instruct Sal to lie on the floor and cover his eyes with a bandana. He was told to relax and picture a spot where water goes down into a hole. This visualization would help him slip down into the earth and metaphorically travel to the lower world. The monks told him that was where he might see different animal spirits and possibly communicate with a few.

Sal told the men he was ready to begin. He had a strong desire to learn this journeying technique. The monks started drumming, and as Sal relaxed, he pictured a spot in the river where the water flowed under a large rock. He saw himself slide down into the dark shadow. Suddenly he was moving at great speed—down, down, deep into the earth itself. The next thing he knew, his descent slowed to a crawl and he found himself in a glen of unusual ferns surrounded by lush tropical plants and trees. The light was different from anything he had ever seen, but he was not afraid. In fact, it relaxed him and made him comfortable with his surroundings. As he looked around, Sal noticed animals moving through the foliage. As he turned from side to side he became aware of a doe near by.

Sal wondered to himself whether the deer had a message for him. Without actual words being heard aloud, he received a thought from her.

"Continue on your chosen path," Sal could hear her say. "You will be aided along the way to help others. In so doing, your way through life will be made easier, because you are becoming a means for compassionate spirits to help others. This type of human is what these spirits seek; it allows them to intercede and assist the less fortunate."

Sal did not feel any apprehension as she spoke. It actually felt normal in a strange sort of way. As he looked around there were rays of light in colors he could not describe. It was like nothing he had ever seen before. It was beautiful.

Sal instinctively felt a change in the tempo of the drumming. The change drew him back to consciousness. He could easily see the tunnel that had led him to the lower-earth realm, so he moved into it and rapidly returned through the hole under the river rock. He slowly removed the bandana that draped his eyes and looked around at the monks in Brother Alex's room. All eyes were on him, but no one spoke. As Sal emerged fully back to waking consciousness, he said, "Did I do O.K?"

"You have journeyed for nearly two hours," said Brother Alex. "We are glad you finally returned because we were beginning to get fatigued from so much drumming. You don't need to explain to us what you saw on your journey, but if you have any questions we would be happy to try and answer them."

"Is it O.K. to tell you what I saw?" asked Sal.

"Of course," replied Brother Alex. "It's good for you to ask advice of us since we have all done this before and it's safe to to talk with us about your trip. But don't talk to just anyone about it. From past experience we have found that others who haven't done it look upon us as very odd."

"Well, thanks for that advice," said Sal after he gave them a brief recap of his journey. "And thanks for drumming so long. I had no idea that so much time had passed."

"Out-of-the-body experiences are not limited by earth-bound time or distance," explained Brother Alex. "What you've done here is exceptional for it being your first journey. You have achieved what most of us have taken quite awhile to realize; that's probably because you are so open and receptive."

Even though Sal was still lying on the floor, he was tremendously tired.

"That's your body reacting normally," explained Brother Alex. "You had no fear or apprehension even though it was your initial journey, but your body is programmed to sleep whenever you lay down. You'll feel more exhilarated when you get up and move around."

Sal stood up and actually did feel rested. He asked that next time they do this they teach him to drum so that others could go on their journeys. They agreed to teach him and thanked him for his unselfish attitude. They explained to him this was one of the reasons they had joined the monastery—to learn to share and be kind to others. They knew this was the right thing to do, but coming from a mean and increasingly selfish, "Me First" world, it had taken them a long time to achieve what Sal seemed to already know. Sal was actually a good example for them.

At that moment, the group hugged in a circle, much like the huddles experienced in high school basketball after a game well played. Sal could feel the genuine feelings that each of the men felt for each other in spite of their diverse backgrounds. Sal briefly wondered if this would be a good life for him after all, but the moment passed quickly. He knew that a family life with someone like Mary was much more to his liking. Aside from that minor difference, Sal felt these monks had a good thing going without a lot of stress and anxiety. Not needing or expecting anything in return was a good way to be accepted by your peers. He felt as if he was their equal.

CHAPTER 66

INTROSPECTION

T hinking back to the few times Sal had experienced this camaraderie with his fellow soldiers and teammates, he realized how few and far between it had been. Whether it had been a particularly intense game or exercise, he could count on one hand how many times he had felt this equality among his peers. Once again, he saw how getting drunk and obnoxious was such a waste of time and energy. Seeking out the feeling of exhilaration without personal gain was something so much better.

Sal recalled how, on a lesser scale, there were AA meetings he had participated in where he had felt similar feelings. When someone had a major breakthrough by admitting he needed help offered by the group, there was a realization that no one in the room expected or desired anything in return. It was enlightening. One could feel the mutual goodness of each person shining through. In the first few meetings he had attended, Sal had found himself crying as they joined hands and recited the Lord's Prayer. He felt lucky. He had been given a chance to resurrect himself from a life of humiliation and despair. He began to understand what Chaplin Cliff had said about being blessed. Recognizing one's Higher Power and serving Him in whatever way one found was a better way to travel through life.

The only axiom Sal had ever taken issue with during the AA meetings was the one that said, "Better to give resentments than to get them." But he realized he was fairly new to AA and hoped he would understand that better later on. At the present time, though, he could not see that giving resentment would do anything but cause him harm. He recalled how the son of a man who owned a gas station up in Utah knew an undocumented Mexican couple that were being taken advantage of by a polygamist rancher. Because they were undocumented, and the rancher could get away with it, they were given a run down cabin to live in that had dirt floors and no heat. They were required to work seven days a week on this man's ranch. The wages he paid barely let them survive. The rancher threatened to report them to the immigration authorities should they try to complain. The man who owned the gas station took pity on the Mexican couple and purchased for them an old, but sturdy house trailer, which he moved them into. He bought them groceries, found better jobs for both of them and even found an old, reliable pickup truck for them to drive.

Sal now understood that the gas-station owner had done it because it made him feel good to help fellow human beings during hard times. Sal thought that if Mormons could actually become saints, this guy really fit the bill.

Back at his newly completed patio, Sal sat in his chair and remembered the years he attended St. Mary's Parochial school he had been taught that God was a demanding, vengeful being who controlled people through fear of punishment. He had believed he must do the right thing or he'd go to hell or at the very least purgatory where he would bake for a while. His lessons from AA were entirely different. That program had been designed by two falling-down drunks who demonstrated that 'taking right actions' could change one's life for the better. Sal felt he was serving God in a much better fashion by taking right actions than being afraid of all his sins. Confessing his sins to another man and reciting a few prayers by rote didn't really work for him. Maybe it did for others, but Sal knew too many mean and selfish men who would spend one hour at Sunday mass, then speed out of the parking lot at church, cursing people that got in their way, continuing to be the same obnoxious hombres they were when they entered the church. On the other hand, there were people like Mother Theresa who spent their entire lives among the poorest souls in the world, aiding them as best she could. She never knew where her next meal was coming from, but her faith carried her through and allowed her to serve all she came in contact with. Someone once told Sal that hers were actions of selfishness; that she got great satisfaction from what she did. If so, that was the most favorable of all selfish tendencies he had ever heard of. Sal was sure that if Jesus came to walk the earth again, he would embrace what she was doing and look unfavorably upon the actions of those who worship one day and then practice deceit and cunning in the quest for power and money the rest of the time.

Sal thought he was probably lucky to be aware of this at a relatively young age. He knew by his work others could gain by his example, but he had to guard against grandiosity. He knew that in reality he was but a humble servant and he was being given a gift from his Higher Power.

With a sigh, Sal got up to head to dinner and prepare for the next AA meeting. It had been another incredible day filled with new and exciting experiences. He was looking forward to the camaraderie of the dinner-table guests. He was content to listen to the speakers at the meeting. When he returned to the cottage after dinner and the meeting he threw his bag into the trunk of the Pontiac and prepared for his trip. He added two gallons of water to cross the desert and went to bed. Four fifteen in the morning would come quickly.

CHAPTER 67

THE TRIP

Awakened by a thump on his door, Sal got up to shower. He then put on his best outfit and headed for Tucson. He stopped in Benson for some real coffee and by 6:45 a.m. he was pulling into the parking lot of attorney Mayhew's office. Mary pulled up next to him within seconds of his arrival. They hugged good morning as Sal tried to contain his excitement. She was dressed for business in a long skirt and high heels, but she told Sal she had jeans and hiking boots in a bag just in case they went somewhere that required more rugged attire. Sal showed her the knee high, very ornate cowboy boots he wore under his jeans. She could barely suppress a giggle at that sight.

"This is my kind of woman," Sal thought to himself. They drove up Route 10 toward Casa Grande to the intersection of Route 8 West.

"You know, one time I hitchhiked from the Army base in Yuma," Sal made conversation. "It was a very hot June day and I kept catching up to a boy who was riding on a rail car on the tracks next to the highway. We would wave to each other as we passed. I used to be quite a drinker, you know. I stopped at a bar in Eloy and had a few beers. The next ride I got I fell asleep and woke up to find out I had missed my turnoff to Sierra Vista by 25 miles. I had to hitchhike back to the exit. The whole trip took me 15 hours."

Sal took a deep breath and plunged forward. "Mary, I spent most of my time in the Army either getting drunk or recovering from a bad hang-over," Sal confessed. "I need you to know what I was like. Last July, I was led to an AA meeting. It was that or I would be kicked out of my home in Pennsylvania. I haven't had a drink since then and never again intend to drink. Mary looked at Sal, but didn't say anything for a long time. Sal's heart stopped in anticipation of what she might say.

"I only know the man you are now," she finally said. "If you continue to be this man I believe we will be the very best of friends. Have I said too much?"

"No," Sal shook his head. "What you are saying is all I could ever hope to hear. I intend to live up to your expectations. I would be a fool to disap-point you. I've been given a wonderful opportunity to redeem myself and having you come into my life is a blessing I could never have dreamed of. This road trip is such a perfect chance for us to get to know each other. Just tell me to be quiet if I talk too much. I'm very nervous when I'm with you and I don't want to blow it."

"No, Sal," Mary answered. "I appreciate your honesty. I never would have guessed anything about your past if you hadn't told me. I must admit I've lived a very sheltered life; I'm told I am very naïve. I've never had a serious boyfriend, but saying that, I know what I want and so far, you are just the man I pictured. I am looking forward to you letting me into your life and letting me know everything about you. If I didn't think you were an honorable man, I never would have asked you to drive me across the state. I've been so intent on getting an education and becoming a lawyer, I have not had the time or the inclination to socialize. I don't know where our relationship is going, but so far, you are the knight in shining armor that I want to get to know. Please don't let your expectations get too high; I must spend most of my time studying and working towards my law de-gree. I won't have much time to spend with you. I find the university takes a lot of effort on my part. Even the professors aren't all that enamored with a woman wanting to practice law. Sometimes I have to do twice as much as some of the men in my class just to stay even. If you want a full-time girlfriend, I may not be the one for you."

"Oh no!" interrupted Sal. "I understand. I know I just popped into your life out of the blue and I appreciate whatever time I can have with you. If I get too pushy you need to tell me. I have never had a real girlfriend before either."

Mary laughed at that and said. "I thought as good looking as you are you would have had many girlfriends. I told you I'm naïve." Mary hesitated for a moment before continuing. "Let's just go slow. If it's meant to be it will be. Right now, let's enjoy this day; I'm very happy to be sitting next to you. Tell me all you know about this land we're driving through."

"O.K," nodded Sal with great satisfaction. "That lone peak sticking up on your left is Picacho Peak. It's the site of the only real battle fought in Arizona during the Civil War. It's too early but that cafe on the right has the best soft ice cream in the state."

"Ha!" exclaimed Mary. "I have a real tour guide for my first trip to Yuma."

As they continued to drive along, Mary told Sal a little about how her classes were going, and before they knew it they had turned onto Route 8.

"I see what you mean about this being desert land out here," commented Mary as she looked out the window. "I can just imagine how hard the people traveling by horse and wagon had it. Is there any water before the Colorado River?"

"Well actually, the old trail goes a little north of here along the Gila River," said Sal. "So they had some water. We'll pass through Gila Bend and you'll see. A few years back I was part of an Army basketball team from Fort Huachuca that was playing for the championship amongst all the military bases in the state and we drove through here on our way to Yuma. We stopped at a diner in Gila Bend, but our coach and two of our players were colored and so they wouldn't serve them. We all went hungry because we left after making a few choice comments to the owner regarding his ancestry. That was the first time I experienced prejudice like that. I still get mad when I think about it. It was O.K. for these men to go and fight and die but not O.K. to eat a lousy cheeseburger in that crummy diner.

Sal looked around as he recognized where he was. "Let's stop at that gas station," he pointed. "I'll fill up and get some coffee. It looks pretty clean and the next stop is a long ways away so we better make use of the facilities."

When they got back on the road, Sal mentioned that the next stretch of road was the loneliest he had ever traveled. After a little chitchat, Sal got a grin on his face and said, "I have a treat for you. This place coming up next is called 'Dateland'. They have a date milkshake that is better than anything I have ever drank. I should have stuck to drinking them and I would have been a lot better off."

True to his word, Sal introduced Mary to the best shake she had ever tasted. "This is wonderful," she said. "If nothing else good happens this makes the trip a success."

"Ha," Sal laughed. "I have another surprise in store for you after we finish in Yuma."

"I can't wait," said Mary. "I hope it's just as delicious."

Since Yuma was laid out in a grid they had no problem finding the office and getting the forms signed.

"You know I've never been to California," commented Mary. "At least now I have been close."

"Oh no," Sal grinned. "We are going over to Winterhaven which is just over the bridge in California. That way you can say you've been there."

As they passed through the inspection station, Mary commented on the size of the town. "I expected much more out of California than three bars and two gas stations," she said. They turned back around and headed to Yuma, which had 15 bars, 10 gas stations and a really tough jail. Sal gassed up, again, and headed up Route 95. After traveling for about a half hour, Sal turned onto a sandy road.

"Where are you taking me?" Mary inquired curiously.

"You'll see, "Sal, answered slyly. "This is the surprise I was talking about earlier. This is just so you'll know I really know my way around this state."

Sal navigated the car towards the nearby mountain range. "That hunk of rock is called Castle Dome," he said. "It's all part of the Kofa Range, which is named after the mining company that still operates around here,' King of Arizona'. On the east side they mine for gold; on this side they mine for silver."

As the washboard road they drove along crested a hill they came upon a big, run down ghost town, "Whoa!" Mary said, "didn't expect this." Sal was glad to see this part of the surprise had the desired effect. Mary's eyes were wide open in amazement.

"Used to be thousands of miners living here," he said to a smiling Mary. "And it gets hot out here—hotter than Tucson, by far. I slept in a tent and at night it would be well over 100 degrees. On the way back, remind me to point out something else."

Mary was glad she had changed into her casual jeans at the last gas station. She wanted to walk around and do some exploring, taking pic-

tures with the camera she brought. As they walked a path between two shacks, she marveled at how the buildings were still standing considering how hard the wind blew in this area. Seeing a photo opportunity, Sal pointed to a doorway.

"Take my picture inside of this building without the door," he said. Sal hadn't gotten four feet into it when the floor gave way. It sent Sal nearly five feet into a dark, dugout crawl space. Mary screamed at Sals sudden collapse through the floor. He yelped as he heard a menacing buzz around him. He realized he had fallen into a snake pit and the rattlers were none too happy about it.

"Sal, what can I do?" Mary called frantically.

"That buzzing is the sound of a bunch of rattlers," Sal called out. "They are all around me. Oh, my God, I can feel them hitting my legs. I don't know how I'm getting out of here cause the floor is too rotten to lift myself up."

"Oh Sal, I am really scared," cried Mary.

"O.K," Sal said trying to think. "Go back the way we came and look for a heavy, old board I saw near where we parked. See if you can drag it over here. I can't move or the snakes will get riled up again."

Mary was gone only a few minutes when she came back crying. "Sal, I can't believe God would be so cruel to bring someone as wonderful as you into my life and then have you die from snake bites right in front of my eyes."

Mary was clearly starting to panic.

"I won't die if I can help it," said Sal trying to soothe her nerves as well as his own. "See if you can slide the board across the floor near my head. Rest it carefully and don't step onto the boards yourself' cause it won't hold you. I think the beams on the sides will hold my weight—at least they better."

With great effort Mary slid the board across the rotted floor. Once it appeared stable, Sal reached up and put both his hands on it. He pulled himself straight up and crawled across it to the dirt outside.

"Whew! It worked," Sal panted as Mary hugged him so tightly she nearly suffocated him. She looked down at his legs and was astonished to see streaks of venom dripping down his pants. Sal couldn't believe what he saw, either. He almost fainted right then and there.

"I laughed to myself when you showed me those silly boots that went up to your knees," Mary confessed. "But I think they saved your life."

"I don't want to touch these pants," Sal laughed a little. "Please go to the trunk of the car where my gym bag is. Bring it back and I'll cut off these Levi's with my buck knife."

When Mary came back from the car Sal was sitting on the ground in his boots and boxers. Even the boots still had traces of venom dripping down. She couldn't help but laugh at the sight.

"Sal, forgive me, but I must take a picture of this," she giggled.

Sal laughed too—almost hysterically, considering he would have surely died without the boots he wore. He stood up and posed with his boots to his knees and no pants. He removed his wallet and change out of the jeans and left them on the ground. Sal found a big rock and used it to wedge his heel to pull off his boots without touching them. Once that was done he put his other jeans on.

"I know we should throw the boots into that shack and drive away, but they saved my life," said Sal. "I really want to save them now."

"O.K.," Mary agreed. "How about I get one of those jugs of water and you can wash them off?"

"Yeah, that would be great," Sal said. "I think there's one of those old, wooden dynamite boxes back by the car. We can put them in the trunk."

Mary retrieved the box and the water and brought them to Sal. He moved the boots from side to side on a stick as Mary flushed them with water. Sal pushed the boots into the box with the stick once they were rinsed off. As they walked back to the car together, Mary decided to take a photo of the floor in the shack.

"Please be careful," Sal called after her. "Don't get too close to the floor boards. We've had way more excitement than we needed today."

The path back to the car made Sal yelp and jump as he continuously stepped on burrs and cactus needles in his stocking feet. Mary giggled at Sal's constant cursing, relieved about what had almost ruined their day and most likely Sal's life. Once the boots were in the trunk, they headed down the bumpy road. Both Mary and Sal kept laughing when they'd catch each other's eye.

"You wanted me to remind you of something else I should see?" Mary asked, as they drove down the road. "Ha! Haven't I showed you enough for today?" Sal laughed out loud. Then he said.

"Oh, yeah, a while ago the Army stuck a bunch of us out here while they developed something I can't talk about. So for four or five days at a time, about ten of us brave soldiers faced down coyotes, scorpions, coral snakes and stink bugs in 120-degree heat. We had this one guy from Brooklyn who acted like a mafia tough guy and was a real hard-ass, to cover the fact that he was deathly afraid of bugs.

"I was driving in a jeep one night and hit a jack rabbit on this road. I thought I killed it because it was so still. I put it in the back of the jeep and when we got back to the tent that guy was asleep in his sleeping bag. I unzipped it quietly and placed the rabbit in his bag so that he'd wake up with a dead rabbit in his bag. About 20 minutes later there were these horrible screams from the tent and this guy comes flying out covered in blood, then suddenly, the rabbit comes running out between his legs. Seems the rabbit had only been knocked out but bleeding badly from the jeep hitting it. So when it came to, it tried to kick its way out of the sleeping bag. This poor guy was awakened by this freaking rabbit breaking through the zipper of his sleeping bag. I was laughing so hard it was difficult to run away, but I made it to the jeep before the guy made it to his carbine. I took off into the desert with no lights and before long; I swear I heard bullets crackling over my head. He denied that, but I'm pretty sure he was shooting at me. I came back the next day and he never spoke to me again. I've always wondered if there was something to the whole karma thing, but after today I'm sure of it."

"Oh Sal, you really were an awful person before," said Mary. "You weren't exaggerating when you told me that. You better never do anything like that again, and absolutely never play any tricks on me. I would die right there on you."

"I promise," said Sal. "This is the new and improved Sal. Actually, there's a little more to the saga of that hard-ass guy in the desert. Not two weeks later we were out here again. Locust hit when that guy was miles from camp. He was in an open jeep and by the time he made it back to the tent, the jeep was half filled with grasshoppers. This guy was crying hysterically. I had to run and hide I was laughing so hard. I thought this time he would surely blow me away, but all he did was jump into the tent and cry. I guess you never know how tough a guy is until the chips are down. He never acted like a tough guy again; his spirit was broken by the grasshoppers. No more stories about Yuma for now. Let's get back to civilization, O.K?"

"Yepper, for sure," nodded Mary. "Do we have to drive all the way back into Yuma before we can get on to Route 8 towards Tucson?"

"Just about all the way to Yuma, I'm Afraid," Sal replied. "The shortcuts that I know are terrible. They're all powdery alkali dust and I don't think the Bonneville could make it through that. Considering how the day has gone so far I really think we should stay on the hard top roads. But to make it up to you I'll spring for another supersize 'date shake' when we get to Dateland, O.K?"

"You, bet; I love those," said Mary as she scooted across the wide front seat to be closer to Sal. "I'm glad you don't have bucket seats in here. I'm going to like sitting close to you while you tell me your stories."

"Is your Dad going to be all right with me when you tell him what happened after we left Yuma?" asked Sal with a little concern in his voice.

"Oh, I think so," Mary smiled. "He really likes you. He even said you were very mature for your age. He thinks you are destined for great things. He'll be glad you are O.K. and that you never put me in any danger. But let's get off that subject for now. Can you sing?"

"Oh, God no," Sal about choked. "I couldn't do that to you. I really can't carry a tune but I'd love to hear you."

"O.K." Mary said. "I'll sing some Kingston Trio songs I learned in college, I think you'll like them. Why don't you sing along the best you can?"

"All right," shrugged Sal. "Consider yourself warned."

Mary started out with the song "Tom Dooley" which Sal knew most of the words to, soon they were singing their hearts out.

"You're not nearly as bad as I expected," Mary grinned. "Just tone it down a bit and we can try to harmonize."

"O.K., I'll try," said Sal. "The only times I ever sang besides the choir in parochial school were on the trips back and forth to Mexico. Half drunk or full drunk, no one cared how we sounded just as long as it was loud."

Before either one realized it, Sal and Mary were pulling into the Dateland Cafe. Mary headed to the restrooms while Sal, in his socks, filled the car with gas. When he finished, Sal went into the cafe and special-ordered a huge milkshake. The clerk put it into a half-gallon container while Sal gathered two straws, which he doubled up so they would reach the bottom. As he handed this grand drink to Mary, she cracked up laughing.

"Uh oh," she giggled. "We're going to have to stop again soon after drinking this. And thank you; this is just what I needed."

Back on the road, Sal and Mary slurped and sang all the way to Gila Bend. They made a necessary stop and got back on the road to Tucson.

"So tell me something about your life," insisted Sal.

"Well today has been more exciting than nearly the total of all my years growing up," laughed Mary. "I won't say it was boring, but looking back I just went from school to soccer or field hockey, Glee Club, swimming classes, and so on. By plain, old good luck nothing dramatic happened during all my years of schooling. In fact, until today the most exciting experience I had was when some anti-war hippie shot down a National Guard helicopter just beyond the soccer field. No one was seriously hurt, but it badly scared all of us."

"Wow, I remember hearing about that," exclaimed Sal. "I'm glad it didn't come down on your field."

"Yes, we were all O.K.," Mary continued. "We were just a bunch of shook up college girls. Tell me some more stories; maybe about Tucson if you have one."

"I actually do," said Sal. "But this time I was only an observer to what happened. A group of us soldiers came up to Davis Monthan Air Force Base to stay at the transient barracks so we didn't have to pay for a motel room. One of the guys with us was a Jewish orphan from Hungary. His parents had been killed by the Nazis during World War II. As luck had it, there were three German Luftwafte pilots checking in at the same time we were. I assumed they were there for some training. So our guy, Saul, was a Korean karate fanatic and had studied this martial art since he was a young boy. He also spoke fluent German and he asked the pilots about World War II, one of them foolishly answered that sadly, they felt it was a failure because the mighty Germans weren't able to kill all of the Jews. Saul instantly attacked all three of them before the rest of us knew what was happening. By the time we could get in between them two were unconscious on the floor and the third was trying to climb over the admission counter to get away. They were bloody, missing teeth and it was all we could do to hold Saul back from committing more mayhem.

"A squad of Air Police showed up and separated everybody until they could sort out what happened. After interviewing my buddies and me, the A.P.'s let us all go except Saul. The Sergeant-in-charge pulled me aside and told me to pull our car around back in 10 minutes. We did as directed, the back door of the barracks opened. Saul was escorted out by two A.P.'s. Sergeant Goldstein told us if we promised to leave Tucson right then, he would turn Saul loose instead of sticking him in the brig. We happily agreed as we grabbed Saul and headed for Nogales. Our Tucson weekend was over but we were free to go, you see, trouble wasn't always caused by me. I didn't speak German and had no idea what was being said, but I sure couldn't fault Saul once he translated the pilots' words for us."

"You sure find yourself in hot water a lot," said Mary, smiling, "Do you think this was just a stage in your life or are you with me because you think you'll need a good lawyer throughout your life?"

"Well, I don't know about the lawyer part," said Sal. "But I'm believing that having you in my life has become very important. Besides, you saved my life today so now you're responsible for me, you know."

"Uh oh, I think we just went from crazy story to serious time in ten seconds," said Mary. "I have to admit I may be more frightened by the feelings I've become aware of than I was with the snakes. A month ago I was a single law student, concentrating on my studies with no time or inclination for a relationship. Then along comes 'The Sal Man' and my whole world is flipped upside down."

"Mary, I will always be totally honest with you," said Sal. "And I need to admit that my idea of settling down was not going to happen until I hit 30. Then I would look around for someone who wanted to build a life with me. I never dreamed I would be knocked off my feet like this. So don't look to me for advice; I'm just as confused as you are, but I will say it sure does feel right."

"Yes, Sal, I would agree it does feel right," nodded Mary, "and staying with this thought, rather than have you drive to St. David tonight, do you think it would be O.K. if you stayed over at my apartment?"

"Whoa!" said a surprised Sal as he almost drove off the road. "Of course it would be O.K., thank you!"

Mary squeezed over a little closer to Sal and smiled. Sal felt like he was floating on a cloud. It had been an incredible few months, and it kept getting better for him. They decided to pick up some Chinese food and take it to Mary's place, once there, they sat out on the patio, which Sal studied carefully.

"I could expand this out a bit if you wanted me to," he said. "I just finished one at the monastery and decided if my do-gooder stuff doesn't pan out I can become a patio man."

Moo-shu pork never tasted so good. After a glorious night Sal re-

luctantly kissed Mary good-bye, promising to call her that evening. She thanked him for a wonderful road trip and the crazy date saying she would be waiting for his call.

As Sal drove down Route I-10 to the Benson turnoff, he kept shaking his head at how great his life was turning out. Learning to love others, love life as well as himself, was an amazing lesson he was glad he was learning. Now he could reap the benefits of this accomplishment, especially since he wasted so much time pursuing selfish interests, getting drunk, chasing women, and stealing. He never found any satisfaction beyond the moment doing that. Now that he had surrendered to the fact that he was an alcoholic who could never drink another ounce of booze, who was also being guided by a spirit, he was astounded that life could be so good. From this day forward, Sal promised himself that he would pass on the things he learned to the other suffering alcoholics & non-alcoholics to the best of his ability. He knew beyond a shadow of a doubt that he had been granted the "Courage to Change." Now he was beginning to understand "the Wisdom to Know the Difference."

CHAPTER 68

JERSEY

P ulling into the monastery, Sal was surprised to see a Harley motorcycle parked under a tree. It looked familiar. He parked his car near the cottage, ran in, changed his clothes, found his sneakers and headed over to the dining hall to see if his buddy, Jersey, was hanging out there. Sure enough, as Sal looked over at one of the tables, he saw Jersey visiting with two of the monks.

"Well, hi there! Sal," smiled Jersey. "I was hoping you were still here. How are you doing?"

"Just great," Sal reached out and shook his friend's hand. "I'm surprised to see you back here."

"Just passing through," said Jersey. "Do you think it's O.K. to stop here?"

"Sure it is," laughed Sal. "Let me grab a coffee and we'll catch up. I've scored two great 'Cubans' so let's go out to the pond."

Once outside on the bench Sal explained to Jersey that the Sheriff's Office was very pleased to have nailed a bunch of drug runners near the border by using the information that Sal had given them. The deputies had said nothing more about the shooting incident he and the soldiers had been a part of, near Nahteste's house.

"That's great," said Jersey. "Don't need any hassles. Let me tell you what me, Big John and Minx have been up to. After we left here we were heading to New Orleans. As we were crossing through New Mexico we found a great roadhouse near Carriozo. We were able to camp there— of course, we didn't drink, not surprisingly, our not drinking was kind of funny to the other bikers that hung out there, but we stayed sober and met some good guys. We started talking with a couple of Mescalero Apaches. They knew Nahteste. We told them a little about our exploits down by the border, and they told us what a big problem heroin was on their reservation. They said it was killing off the young guys. We went up to the rez and they introduced us to their "Warrior Society." Once we got comfortable with each other, we opened up completely about what had happened in Arizona. They thought that was a great idea, so 'Mr. Feel-Good Man' be proud that you've started a movement that is picking up followers all over the Southwest."

Sal wasn't sure he was happy to hear these words, but he didn't interrupt Jersey as he continued talking.

"One thing led to another and now Minx is in love with a widow on the rez. Her husband O.D.'d from heroin. The whole "Warrior Society" has committed itself to stopping the flow of drugs onto the rez."

Jersey hesitated a few moments while Sal took in the information.

"I've only gone out with them one time," he said. "But they are a powerful force to contend with. Three are marines and two are Special Forces guys recently back from Nam. With the training they are providing the other members they are developing a small army, around 50 strong. They know most of the drug traffic comes up through El Paso from Juarez. The night I went out with them they found four vans hidden in the brush north of El Paso off Route 54 near Alamagordo. The vans weren't guarded so one of the Green Berets, who is an explosive expert, fashioned four charges under the axles. After the drug runners filled the vans with the drugs and started to drive north he remotely detonated them. Needless to say, nobody walked away. The funny thing is, there hasn't been a word in the newspaper about any of this. I don't know if the reporters have been warned not to write anything about drug smuggling or if anyone even knows the whole story. I do know that when these shipments don't show up at their scheduled drop offs, the drug bosses in Mexico will come looking."

Sal was dumbfounded as he listened intently to Jersey's tale. He knew one thing, he didn't have any desire to know a thing about cold blooded murder, but he was hearing it anyway.

"We decided to leave behind an old backpack with a week old newspaper from Tijuana in it," said Jersey. "It also had some blasting caps and some bean burritos. Hopefully they'll think it was a rival gang messing with their route. The Warrior group has gotten word out to a lot of Apaches on the rez and off it to tell us about any activity they know of down that way so we'll know when and where they're moving the drugs. We know we won't stop all the deliveries, but if we can make a dent it will be a big help. With a shortage of drugs on the rez the Warriors are concentrating on users getting shaky without their daily fix. Once they know which ones are the users, they'll start what amounts to an intervention program. You can't believe how intimidating a group of Apache can be when they pull you out of your house in the middle of the night and stick you in a building to go cold turkey. We're all hoping to clean these guys up and slow down the drug use on the rez. Having ex-users on our team will give us intelligence about the dealers. That's who we're concentrating on to shut down. It's a helluva program. Another good thing is that some of the warriors are Tribal Police so we have some protection. The marines and soldiers know others along the border they are contacting to see if they want to start similar deterrent programs in their areas. It may not be the most orthodox way to deal with the drug situation but I have to tell you, I couldn't be prouder of what we've accomplished already."

Sal was absolutely stunned to hear all this news. "I'm proud of you too," he said. "But please don't tell me any more. I don't have any need to know. We are all doing what we can in the best way we are able. I'm glad you guys are safe, so try to stay that way, O.K? You're dealing with some very bad men and they are going to be very upset with their losses. There's no telling what might happen if they figure out how this is going down. I've been offered a position as a special deputy with the law here in Arizona. I really don't want or need to know any more."

"Hey, this is one great ceegar," laughed Jersey as he nodded his understanding. "Thanks! So what's been happening with you?"

Sal told Jersey about Mary and included his recent snake episode.

"Well, that's pretty exciting," smiled Jersey knowingly. "So now you have a woman who's responsible for your life. Good move, my friend. And good luck with it all. I am going to have to head out so I can take care of some business in Camp Verde. Then I'm going to ride back to New Mexico. If you ever need me or any of the guys, just give a shout out to the Mescalero Reservation. We're known over there by most of the men."

Jersey gave Sal a warm hug. Sal could only think that these giants like Jersey and Crisco sure like to hug hard. Jersey then fired up his Harley, waved and headed north.

"Well, that was unexpected," Sal thought as he went into his cottage. Seems I'm not the only one having exciting experiences in sobriety. With that, Sal committed to a peaceful nap so he could rest up before he planned the rest of his week.

CHAPTER 69

A SLIP

S al awakened near dinnertime, which was his cue to rise. He figured
he must have needed the sleep if he slept this long without inter-
ruption. He felt lucky not to have a nine to five job that took up
his time. He figured he would eat, go to a meeting and work on
his schedule afterward. He wasn't going to forget his evening call to Mary,
either.

When all was said and done, Sal ran into Brother Casper. "You had a
call while you were gone," Casper said. "A 'Catherine' called and asked that
you call her back as soon as you could. Here's the number."

Uh, oh, Sal thought to himself. That didn't sound promising. As soon
as Sal connected with Catherine, his worst fears were confirmed. Jake had
gone to the fort on Monday morning, but didn't return until 3 a.m.—and
then with a snootful. Catherine was upset and wanted to know if this
meant there was no chance for Jake to achieve sobriety.

"No," consoled Sal. "Half the drunks that come into the program slip
before grasping it. Where is Jake now?"

"He's sitting on the porch drinking coffee with Rob," Catherine answered. "He's pretty dejected and full of apologies, and I'm very upset with
him."

"I'll come down tomorrow afternoon to talk with them," said Sal.

"Then I'll make dinner for everyone," Catherine said somewhat re-lieved. "I really appreciate your support. Do you think he can do it? Get sober, I mean."

"Oh yeah," said Sal. "I know he can. Stay close to him tonight and I'll see you tomorrow."

Sal sighed heavily as he hung up the phone. A few doubts began to rise inside him as he thought about the task ahead. "Man, I hope I have enough knowledge to do this." He thought to himself. "I wish I had my sponsor, Jim McC., to guide me. I think it will serve me well to do some Big Book reading tonight."

Sal thought about how many things there were on God's green earth that humans used to feel better, yet ended up making themselves miser-able instead. He was thankful there were programs developed to help peo-ple avoid the pitfalls. With enough time, people were able to work through their tough times, without chemical crutches. He knew from experience that when you tried to use external fixes to alter your internal problems; it often ended up making things worse. As Jim McC. had told him, "when-ever someone goes out and uses, you need to take a lesson from it and not do the same thing. The lesson is: we don't have to repeat their mistakes. Instead, we can take what they have done, apply it to our own lives and recognize what a mess it makes of theirs and would make of ours."

One of the best lessons Sal had learned was he had better be success-ful in his own sobriety. Because substances would always be available if he decided to drink or use again. The program promised to refund his misery if he so chose. Jake's screw-up just made Sal's determination that much stronger. Everyone had free will and needed to find his own way. Luckily, there were plenty of others who had gone through that very experience and were happy to show what worked for them. The drunks always say, "'I'm not hurting anyone but myself." But they didn't give any consider-ation to the wives, children or parents.

Sal took out his Big Book and started to read. The thing he loved about this book was that no matter where he opened it up, the stories seemed to be applicable. There were so many similar experiences people had that you couldn't help but get the advice you needed if you were just open to it. The program had already helped millions of people.

Sal figured that if he had skipped algebra in high school and substituted classes on the 12-Step program, he would have accomplished so much more. Of course, Sal knew how he had skipped most classes to grab a couple of pulls from the vodka bottle he kept in his car, so he probably would have skipped those classes, too.

When Sal opened the Big Book he came to the chapter called "Working With Others". He read that he should not be pushy. Teaching by example was the best way to pass on the message of sobriety. The person still drinking had to want sobriety, only then could he be helped. From that point on, Sal decided he would ask Jake if he wanted Sal to return and talk more about AA He wouldn't attempt to force anything.

Before going to sleep, Sal walked over to the office and called Mary. He was happy to hear her voice. She told him about her day and thanked him, again, for the memorable trip. Sal told her he would remember those 24 hours forever. After promising to call again in a few days, Sal went back to his room. There would be plenty of challenges for him to face tomorrow.

CHAPTER 70

DUTY CALLS

T he next morning, Sal got up early and went over to Brother Alex's room to see if he could walk Little John. He missed the big lug and thought they could spend a little quality time together.

"Go right ahead," said a yawning Brother Alex. "Just put him back in the room afterwards. He's already had breakfast so be prepared."

"I totally understand the system," smiled Sal. "I'll carry a shovel and a bag with me."

The two old friends took off toward the river. It was a little nippy this morning, but Little John was still anxious to jump into the water. Sal had just sat on the bank's edge when 200 pounds of wet, shaggy dog shook himself less than two feet away.

"Yuk! You still smell like a skunk," laughed Sal. He was absolutely sure Little John was chuckling along with him. They headed back to the monastery and began to dry off almost immediately. That was one of the nice things about Arizona—the weather promoted dryness. Sal could remember his old barracks in Yuma, where you could wash your jeans, put them on wet, walk out the front door, and by the time you came in the back door the jeans were dry.

After Sal deposited Little John in Brother Alex's room, he went to the dining hall to grab a weak cup of java. He needed to sit by the pond and plan out his day. It began to formulate as quickly as he began to write: Benson, Bud, Tombstone (lunch), Chaplin Cliff, Bisbee. With the agenda set, Sal drove off to tend to his tasks. His first stop brought him to the Benson library where he filled his car with goodies from the donation boxes. He briefly spoke to Nicole and her ladies before he stopped to see Bud at the Texaco. Bud filled the Bonneville with gas for free and Sal crammed all the donations he could from the overflowing box.

"We've decided to have three meetings a week, the first two have been packed," Bud updated Sal, "If all goes well we're going to start the weekend-long marathon meetings."

"That's fantastic," said Sal. "I'm so glad to hear that. Thank you for the gas, the donations and all your assistance. I have to get to Tombstone, now, so I'll keep in touch."

When Sal checked in at the rectory he found that Jenn was still extraordinarily enthused over the meetings soon to be held at the church. She told Sal they were starting this week.

"Can you join me for lunch at the Muffin Cafe?" asked Sal.

"That would be nice," agreed Jenn. "Let me tell the Reverend our plans."

Lu greeted Sal and Jenn. Lu had also been attending Jenn's husbands' church for the past few years. Once settled in, they began discussing the upcoming events.

"Since the meetings are open to everyone I have to warn you they could get a little sketchy," said Sal. "There hasn't been this kind of meeting in this area so you never know how it will go."

"I'm not worried," smiled Jenn. "The Reverend has agreed to attend all of the meetings in the begginning as an observer to make sure everything gets off on the right track. Once it all settles down into some kind of routine I'll lead an Al-Anon meeting concurrent with the AA meeting. That way family members can be there, but be in another room nearby."

"That's a great idea," said Sal. He realized that if he just got out of the way most things worked themselves out. Having spent so much of his time conniving ways to reach his desires—mostly to drink—he still had to learn that he didn't have to be the controller of everything. He explained this to Jenn, who just laughed.

"You're the one with the good ideas," she said. "And the one who gets the ball rolling. As for the rest, we can take it from here. I'm lucky to have the Reverend helping me on this. When it comes to discussions with one's Higher Power he has the doctorate degree."

They both chuckled and Lu came over to their table to see what they were doing.

"What's so funny with you two?" she inquired.

"We're starting an AA meeting at the church this week," Jenn answered.

"That's great!" Lu said. "This town could certainly use that kind of service. I'm not a bartender, but you'd be amazed at how many people tell me their problems. At least half are alcohol based, either they are drinking too much or a family member is. Now that I know about the meeting, I'll spread the word; just give me the schedule."

"That's great," smiled Jenn. "Looks like we won't be sitting there just staring at each other."

After their meal, Sal dropped Jenn off at the church promising to be there for the first meeting on Thursday evening. He secretly hoped he would have two AA candidates with him when he got there.

Sal also needed to return to the cafe and pick up the donated food that Lu had told him was ready to go. Sal filled the Bonneville to the brim and made a drop at the bridge on Route 90 before heading to Chaplain Cliff's. But when he got to the bridge he was surprised to see that someone had already dropped off assorted foods, blankets and a few coloring books. He had to squeeze his bounty into the drop because there wasn't any extra room. Before leaving, Sal blew his horn a few times to alert any travelers who might be within earshot.

When Sal arrived at the church he was excited to see three of the volunteer Army wives talking with the chaplain. They instantly surrounded his car and began talking at once. Sal got out and shook hands all around in greeting. The good news was that the Commissary was coming through with a substantial amount of supplies. They had also connected with seven establishments in Sierra Vista that agreed to give them their day-old products. One of the grocery stores was saving dented canned goods, ripped bags, and boxes for them to pick up once a week. They were still grateful for Sal allowing them to get involved with the project. It was turning out to be a very gratifying experience for each of them.

After the ladies drove off, Sal and the chaplain headed to the patio where a bottomless pitcher of lemonade sat waiting for them.

"You know Reverend," laughed Sal, "if you had kept me full of lemonade when I was drinking maybe I wouldn't have gotten into so much trouble. Perhaps you have come up with a new program to keep the soldiers sober?"

Sal went on to inform the chaplain of everything that had happened so far, including the episode with the snakes.

"There you go," nodded the chaplain. "Your guardian angel is always protecting you. He even had you wear those big boots."

The chaplain went on to fill Sal in on how Johnny was doing on the reservation. He was fitting in well and had already identified two teachers who would start teaching on the rez full time once the regular school year was over. They were currently teaching in Morenci, but could begin teaching on the rez in May.

"Johnny has promised to check in once a week," said the chaplain. "He'll be calling your friend in Tucson for whatever he needs. It seems all your programs are going well. I absolutely believe you are being guided by a divine spirit."

"Well Reverend, you won't get any argument from me," said Sal. "I honestly cannot believe how things are falling into place. Thank you so much for your assistance on all of this."

"Oh you've given me an opportunity to do hands-on ministry work," smiled the chaplain. "Together we are accomplishing plenty of good for many people. If just a few like-minded folk can do this, just think what would happen if thousands of good-hearted people out there were to work together without concern of a reward. A lot would be achieved. I recall during my training I had the occasion to sit in a hospital administrator's office in Goshen, New York. The administrator, Gerry Flynn, had a sign on his wall that said: 'Think what could be accomplished if no one worried about who got the credit.' I think about that little sign many a day. It guides my actions for I truly believe the good we do is recorded by a power much more important than our peers.

"When I think of that I often wonder if that is a selfish act by us humans. As you have said to me in the past, 'There is no such thing as an unselfish act.' If that's what it takes to motivate us mere mortals to do good then let's go with it."

"Yep," laughed Sal. "I guess I've progressed from doing things strictly for my own satisfaction to helping others—which is also for my own satisfaction, except the difference is now my actions help instead of hurt."

"I must tell you Sal, you have achieved a level of maturity and growth at a young age that most people never attain at any age," said the chaplain. "I truly feel blessed that you have come into my life again. It may not only help me in my ministry, but also help me immensely in my own life."

"Well Chaplain," blushed Sal. "I have to laugh at the thought we are the founding members of the Fort Huachuca Mutual Admiration Society. I recall how much I hated being sent out here to such isolation and how its turned 180-degrees to becoming the center of my life. As a soldier I counted the days until I could leave this behind me. Now that I'm free to go anywhere I please, I have decided to make my life in this region. Maybe it all comes down to an 'attitude of gratitude' as they say in AA"

"I have no arguments with anything you say, Sal," said the chaplain. "Whatever your inspiration, it's very welcome and there is obviously a great number of people being affected positively because of it. So—is everything set for our meeting here? It's very exciting to see all this falling into place. Is Bud as excited as I am?"

"Oh, yes," nodded Sal. "It's put a big sparkle in his eyes. He's ready, willing and able to make the meetings a big success. Thanks for letting us use your space and for all your help. Is there anything you need from me at this point?"

"No," the chaplain shook his head. "Just show up occasionally to check us out and make sure we are on the right path."

"No problem there, Reverend," said Sal. "Remember, I need these meetings, too. I never want to stumble backwards into the life I had before. I can't believe how great my life is going now, but I'm aware enough to know I'm only one drink away from losing all I have gained. I could easily fall back into being as miserable and self-centered as I was before becoming sober. I still don't know for sure whether I have an allergy to alcohol, a disease of intolerance or a mental disorder that is devastatingly disruptive when fueled by alcohol. What I do know, is that if I don't take that first drink, things stay much better for me. If that's selfish, it's O.K!"

Sal got up and stretched his limbs before making his good-byes. "Well, Chaplain, I need to head down to Bisbee. I have an old friend and drinking buddy who has decided to change his life. You'll be meeting him soon at one of the meetings here. Plus, his wife, Catherine, is a heck of a good cook and she promised me a fine dinner. I don't want to be late, so thanks for everything. I'll be seeing you again, soon."

As Sal headed for his car, Chaplain Cliff called him back to give him some food donations. Sal loaded four cases from the basement and dropped the food off at Irv and Bonnie's. They in turn promised to drop a case of food off at their water tank each day. Then he headed over to Jake's in anticipation of a great dinner.

CHAPTER 71

CARRYING THE MESSAGE

When Sal arrived, Catherine and Rob's wife were sitting on the front porch. They waved him over and offered him "the beverage of his choice"—lemonade or coffee.

"I may be about to O.D. on citric acid," smiled Sal. "I better go with the coffee."

By the time Sal finished his java, Jake pulled in with Rob riding shotgun. They shook hands all around, though Jake was looking chagrined instead of his usual pugnacious self. The women excused themselves and the three men sat down to talk.

"Well, I guess you've very disappointed with me," Jake began.

"No," said Sal. "It's a very lucky fellow who could go cold turkey on his first try. My job is not to judge anyone. Just because I got the message loud and clear the first time I sat in a meeting doesn't mean I'm any better or worse than the next guy. As we sit here we are all one drink away from making a mess of our lives. So don't be so hard on yourself; you help me recognize how powerful alcohol is. Tomorrow it could just as easily be me sitting in the hot seat wondering what happened. For the first six months I felt like there was a little devil sitting on my shoulder telling me it was

O.K. to have one or two drinks. No one would know. Especially when I was off driving on my own. All I can do is share my story of how it was, what happened and how it is now."

Sal took a drink of his coffee as he allowed his words to sink in. "Because you both know me it's easier to explain since you've seen me at my worst," Sal continued. "You can see how I've changed. All I can do is tell you what worked for me. It's totally up to you to decide what is best for you."

"Alright, what do I need to do now?" asked Jake.

"I don't want to leave Rob out of this," gestured Sal. "So Rob, you've had the chance to experience my craziness first hand—and Jake's too, for that matter. Have you decided to stop drinking?"

"Yes, I have," said Rob. "I haven't lost anything yet, because of drinking, but it's obvious if I continue on the path I've been on chances are good I will lose it all. I feel I've been given a great opportunity to change before the 'proverbial' hits the fan. So if you don't mind, I'd like to listen to what you have to say. I intend to take whatever steps I can to stop myself from going from social drinker to problem drinker."

"You're certainly welcome as far as I'm concerned," said Sal. "It's up to Jake since it's his porch and his drinking that we're discussing."

"Oh, it's fine with me," said Jake. "Stay, listen and learn. No reason not to learn from our mistakes. I know I'm not far from losing my family if I keep this up; having a friend next door to confide in and help watch over me is a good thing."

"O.K., Jake," said Sal. "What made you get drunk the other night? Any idea?"

"Nope," Jake shook his head. "Other than the fact that I'm obstinate by nature and couldn't believe I wasn't stronger or more powerful than anything in a bottle."

"Well, being you are a state champion wrestler and have certainly fought against opponents who were known as the toughest guys in New York State—and still a little liquor kicks your butt—are you willing to admit you have a problem?" Sal grinned, as he looked Jake intently in the eyes. "I know this might sound backwards, but I've been taught that until you surrender you can't win the battle with booze—and I believe it. Quite honestly, this may be the toughest opponent you've ever fought."

"O.K.," said Jake. "Even when I don't want to drink I end up doing it. I know I'm not weak, but I don't know what makes me do it?"

"Ah, that's the $64-million dollar question," said Sal. "I don't have that answer, but for me, I would decide I could have one or two drinks and then wake up the next morning in a puddle of puke wondering what happened. I have admitted to myself that alcohol is far more powerful than my will power, so the only way I can stay sober is to not allow myself that first drink. I don't believe I'm especially weak or strong but just had the good fortune to go to some AA meetings. It's mostly because of my Dad's urging, who, in his years behind the bar has seen firsthand the damage alcohol can do. I've learned that as long as I don't have that first one, I'll never have that second or tenth one and sure enough, I haven't been drunk again. That's become extremely important to me. My sponsor had over 20 years sobriety and he was quick to point out he was only one drink away from throwing it all away. This came from a man who's had the D.T.'s, was made to drink paraldehyde, and was close to being subjected to a frontal lobotomy for being crazy. Are there different degrees of alcoholics? I guess so. But really, I'd much rather stop now than lose my family, my self-worth and finally, my life. All that being said, what do you plan on doing, Jake?"

"I think I agree that no matter how tough I am, that first drink will lead me to ruin," he answered. "When I look at what booze has given me, I don't see any real benefits, it's made me miserable, it's made Catherine miserable and eventually it'll make my children the same. While I still have a chance I would like to stop and stay stopped. What do you suggest I do going forward?"

"I can only pass on what has worked for me," said Sal. "Go to meetings, don't have that first drink, change your attitude and friends that still drink, at least until you are strong enough in sobriety to be able to be around alcohol without being tempted. If you're serious, there's a new meeting in Tombstone and another at Fort Huachuca. Tombstone is starting this week; the Forts meetings are brand new too. If you can, go to both, and the nights that you don't go come up to St. David to one of our meetings. If you surround yourself with others who are trying to stay sober, it's your best chance at also being successful. I remember when I asked my sponsor how long I had to attend meetings, he said, 'Until you want to.' He also asked me 'how long I drank' to make his point. Even when you no longer have a burning desire to drink, go to the meetings and pass on what you have learned to the new guys—and there will always be new guys. Show them no matter how big and tough you are alcohol will win the fight unless you admit your weakness and surrender to the fact that you just can't have that first drink. This is true for most addictions, drugs, for instance. If both of you go to meetings every night I believe you have a really good chance of succeeding."

Sal took a drink of his coffee and continued. "Nothing else that has been tried seems to work as well," said Sal. "Some people have been successful using religion, and others have quit drinking on their own. There is such a thing as a dry drunk. It's someone who doesn't drink, but is still miserable. I've even met a few in AA who are extremely angry that they can't drink. Overall, the groups are made up of folks who used to be the life of the party, so we still have a good time but without the hangovers. If you both agree to go I'll write down the times of the meetings and the locations. After that it's up to you to get there. No one will force you to speak at the meetings, but if you're like me you will want to. It's something like a public confession. It's an exciting adventure; at least for me it is. I look forward to seeing you guys at the meetings. We shared enough pre-sobriety craziness so we'll be able to look at each other and identify with the speakers. I can honestly say I enjoy the meetings more than I ever liked sitting in a bar."

With all that said, it was as if a cue was given when Catherine came out onto the porch to let the men know dinner was ready. Sal thought the guys had it made with home-cooked meals every night. This one was as memorable as the others. Pot roast, mashed potatoes, salad, corn on the cob and to top it off, blueberry cobbler for dessert.

"Wow, no wonder Jake is turning into even a bigger butterball," grinned Sal, patting his own full belly.

"Why don't you join me on the lawn so we can work off some of the meal ?" retorted Jake. "We could do a little wrestling."

"Oh no," said Sal. "I've seen you in action. I want no part of that. Go ahead and take Rob."

"Nope, not me," sighed Rob in the contented fashion that a full meal can provide. "I was with Jake at the Copper Queen hotel when three miners started getting a little argumentative. Before I could jump in all three were flat on the floor begging for mercy. I swore then whatever nasty thing Jake did to me I would just quietly walk away with my tail between my legs."

"Yeah, but my toughest opponent is the one Sal is helping me fight," said Jake. "This is one fight I really intend to win."

Catherine wrapped her arms around Jake and kissed him. "I sure hope so," she said. "Because your trophy is already in the oven. I went to the doctor today and we're pregnant again."

"Woohoo!" yelled Jake. "That's even more of a reason for me to shape up—out of the Army soon and another child! I am going to do this. Give the man another piece of cobbler."

"Hey! They never promised that in the Big Book," smiled Sal. "But I'll take it."

Everyone laughed at the banter, happy to have the mood turn light.

Since Jake and Rob needed to be at the Fort by 5 a.m. the group decided to break up for the evening. There were 'thanks' all around and Sal headed north.

CHAPTER 72

BY THE GRACE OF

As he drove, he wondered how many of the little white crosses on the side of the road were the result of drunken drivers. He figured at least half. Then there was a car full of high school teenagers celebrating their first drunk and they hit a bridge killing all of them. It didn't make sense to him. His sponsor used to wonder why he himself was saved; a broken-down drunk who couldn't man his own station on the battleship he was on in WW II while fighting the Japs. He would drink the hootch made from aftershave lotion and bread and be falling down drunk.

Back at the monastery, all seemed very quiet when Sal pulled in. He parked his car and sat down on his new patio. He began to marvel at how many more stars he could see here than in Pennsylvania, Here there weren't any disruptive lights or pollution. Sal silently hoped it would stay that way, especially since he figured kids in Pennsylvania probably didn't see a star clearly until they left. Sal chuckled to himself as he thought about how he's also seeing things more clearly now being his eyes aren't glazed with alcohol. How could anyone doubt that we are creatures put here by a magnificent, all powerful being? Maybe we are part of a great experiment or great plan? Sal wondered how many others were out there on similar planets looking out at their stars and pondering the same thing.

Figuring it had been another great day, Sal got himself ready to hit the sack. He thought about organizing another trip to Tucson to spend some time with Mary if she could spare the time. He wanted to send her flowers, but he thought that might cause her some problems. With those pleasant thoughts to ponder, Sal turned out the light. His last thought was how he didn't have a lot of material things to offer her, but he could make sure Mary was never bored.

CHAPTER 73

DOCTORS

T he next morning at breakfast Sal sat at a table with two new visitors from New Jersey. Both of them were doctors who had met each other in the service. As luck had it, they had recently retired with healthy pensions so they never had to work again. They told Sal they had always loved the Southwest and were looking for someplace to use their medical expertise.

"Would you consider going to an Indian Reservation to train people in hygiene and to handle emergencies?" Sal asked.

"That's just the sort of thing we're looking for," Dr. Tanner said. "Any ideas?"

Sal laughed knowingly, "If you need ideas, say Hello! to Professor Salvadore."

Sal proceeded to tell them all he had been up. He explained there was a great need for medical assistance in the far reaches of the reservations. He described the new educational program just starting for the children on the San Carlos Apache Reservation. That it could always use additional help.

"We would love to get involved in something like that," they said.

"If you're really serious I can introduce you to Chaplain Cliff at Fort Huachuca," said Sal. "He's the one who got Johnny here to Arizona from the Midwest. Johnny is a fully degreed teacher and an ordained minister.

Now he is living up on the San Carlos reservation teaching the mothers there how to home school their children ." "Johnny will also be hiring two or three teachers to assist him with these programs. They intend to start a brick and mortar school there." "Wouldn't it be a great idea if you two doctors could piggyback onto this program and teach the mothers personal hygiene techniques along with basic first aid skills. Especially the ones that are so isolated on the farther reaches of the rez?"

"Oh, we're definitely serious," they said. "Let's meet the man and see what can be worked out."

"I'll give him a call and see if we can go over now," said Sal. With a quick trip to the office phone, Sal got hold of the chaplain, who told them to come right over. Ever the host, the chaplain promised a big picture of lemonade would be waiting for them.

Sal drove to Fort Huachuca with the two doctors and sat with the chaplain to discuss the possibilities. The chaplain felt it was a great idea to have the expertise of doctors on the rez, so he quickly agreed to give Johnny a call to set things into motion. When the call connected to the council office, the woman who answered said both Johnny and Nahteste were expected for a meeting that morning with the council president. As soon as they arrived, she would have them call the chaplain.

After considerable lemonade, Dr. Tanner spoke up. "How far is it to the base hospital?"

"Only about three miles," said Sal. "Why? Too much lemonade?"

"No, no, no," laughed the doctor. "I served with a Lieutenant Colonel Johnson who was transferred here a year ago. It would be nice to say hello if it's convenient."

"Sure," said the chaplain. "Let's have Sal drive you over. If Johnny calls, I'll explain and have them check with the council. Then we'll call them back when you return."

"Sounds like a good idea," said the other Dr. Tanner.

The doctors were lucky. Dr. Johnson was in his office when they arrived. He was very surprised and pleased to see them so they spent a little

time swapping war stories. Turns out they had served on several dangerous missions together, including a M.A.S.H. Unit in Korea that was almost
overrun three different times. Sal sat quietly for a change and just listened
to them reminisce. He was developing a new respect for Army doctors
and the extreme conditions they operated in. He was thinking about how
many lives they had saved instead of making the big bucks in private practice. After agreeing to return for a meal at the Officer's Club, they said
their good-byes and headed back to the chaplain's house.

"Ah, you just missed their call," said the Reverend as they all made
themselves comfortable again. "They were very excited, especially Nahteste, who said to tell Sal that his being picked up by him near the San
Pedro river may have been the most important ride he ever had."

Sal quickly explained his and Nahteste's first meeting and how he
feared he might be scalped. The doctors called the reservation-council
office and spoke with the head of the council. They made arrangements
to drive up to the rez and finalize their plans. When they were done, Nahteste spoke with Sal, thanking him for his efforts.

"Johnny is working out great," Nahteste told Sal. "I take back everything bad I said earlier. In fact, when we meet again, I intend to slice open
your hand and become blood brothers with you."

"Better my hand than my throat," laughed Sal. When they finished
laughing with one another, Sal asked to speak to Johnny. "Is the fishing as
good as I promised?" he asked.

"It's better than anything I have ever experienced," replied Johnny. "I
am so glad to be here, Sal, there is so much need. Considering we have
only just begun once we polish up the program we intend to start another
one on the White Mountain Rez. I just may have found my life's work and
ministry. By the way, Nahteste's bark is much worse than his bite. He's a
good man and is a pleasure to work with. That Mary is just an angel. She
gets everything I need instantly. I wonder if she's married?"

"Oh, I know for a fact she's spoken for," said Sal. With that, they hung
up and continued with the chaplain.

"Well this has been another great development," the chaplain said to Sal. "Thank you for thinking of it. It sure holds true with what we spoke of yesterday, doesn't it?"

"I'll say," agreed Sal. "I can't wait for next week."

Sal turned to the Tanners and asked if they were interested in seeing the Post Museum. "Maybe see how Army medicine was handled back when?" Sal offered. They agreed to go, but the chaplain stayed behind.

The Tanners thoroughly enjoyed the museum, especially the 10th Army Division and the Buffalo Soldiers section.

"When we joined the Army it was segregated," said Dr. Tanner. "We rarely worked with any of the colored soldiers because most were relegated to being cooks and mechanics. Looking at how the Buffalo soldiers fought bravely against Poncho Villa's rebel army and all the Apache warriors it seems so absurd today. Now that we get to help the Apache, whose ancestors were the very ones who fought the soldiers, shows the absurdity of war. Look at the debacle of Viet Nam. This is the reason we left the service; we wanted to use our talents for more peaceful purposes."

The three had lunch at the Military Inn and Sal told them he wanted to show them the famous "Battle of the Bulls" site.

"We haven't heard of that one," said the Tanners.

"Well, I have had firsthand experience with it," said Sal. "I even saw a re-enactment."

Really?"

"Yes, I'll tell you the story on the way over. You may not believe me—I barely believe it myself—but it happened." Sal proceeded to tell the Tanners about the strange "other worldly" experience he had on his return to the Huachuca Mountains at Miller Peak Road. Sal spoke more about the battle the closer they got to the spot.

"I swear everything I'm telling you is true," said Sal. "But I can understand if you don't believe me." Sal suddenly wondered if he had said too much, considering it only took two physicians to agree on his mental state—or lack thereof—to have him committed. He spoke quickly before he was on a free trip to join Winnie Ruth Judd, who killed 2 women, dismembered their bodies, put them into luggage and shipped them from Phoenix to California, at the State Hospital for the Insane in Phoenix. "Relax, Sal," said Dr. Tanner. "We have both experienced similar things and realize that sometimes there are situations we all encounter that are beyond the norm and make us question our own sanity. Be assured we understand and are not judging you. What you have seen is probably similar to what any one can access if they are open-minded and accept the fact the spirit world is all around us. We are both of the mind there is much more ahead of us all, and we believe that living on earth is just one step on our eternal ride. Maybe we are all here to learn and develop our love for each other."

"Wow, it feels good to have highly educated people concur with what I have seen and felt," said Sal, somewhat relieved. "I must admit that a few times I started to think I may be losing my marbles."

"Oh, no," they both laughed. "There is a whole lot more going on around us than what we all have been indoctrinated to believe from our schools and churches. Consider yourself very blessed to have been allowed to see beyond the veil at such a young age without having to endure severe trauma, like the near-death experience."

As the car pulled next to a historical marker (which Sal had begun to call his hysterical marker) Sal spoke, "I can't promise you will see what I did, but I'll do my best to be a good tour guide and explain the historical truth exactly as I saw it."

They spent about 20 minutes walking around as Sal explained the battleground. The Tanners laughed at that, telling Sal this was the least lethal battleground they had ever been to. As they drove back to St. David through the north of Tombstone they explained to Sal how they believed that many of the Bible stories may have been caused by mass hallucinations from moldy bread, which was a staple of the diet back then. Conversely, what Sal experienced could actually have been a visitation by spirits. It would not be believed by the masses.

"Well, doctors," said Sal. "I'm not that well educated, but I do know and believe what I have seen and if you will join me on a hike down by the river back at the Monastery after lunch I would like to show you where I had a revelation that completely transformed my life."

"O.K., let's do that hike this afternoon," they said. "We are open and receptive people and would love to see where and how you became such a generous, kind person."

During lunch, Sal received a note from a monk saying a Sergeant at the Sheriff's station wanted a return call. Sal excused himself and called Sergeant Joe at the "cop shop." He asked Sal if they could meet somewhere in the near future. Sal agreed to meet him at the Muffin Cafe on Thursday around 5 p.m. Sal needed to go to Tombstone at that time anyway, so it fit nicely into his schedule. He couldn't help but feel a little trepidation at what the sergeant might want.

Sal gathered the two doctors and they headed down the path to the river. He told them about Little John and the mountain lion they had encountered the month prior. Surprisingly, neither doctor seemed the least afraid.

"You don't seem to be worried about bumping into a lion on the trail," said Sal.

"Oh, Sal, if you had seen what we have during our Army careers you would realize that not much can scare us," Dr. Tanner replied. "We've both seen way too much of man's inhumanity to man to be worried about nature. Besides, we're sure the lion would be more afraid of us than vice verse. Let's just enjoy the trees and beautiful flowers. Nature can be harsh, but it's always beautiful in its own way."

When they reached the big Sycamore tree where Sal had experienced his life-changing encounter, he had the doctors sit down under the tree. He began to tell them his story.

"I have to start back a few years," said Sal. "Back when I was on the path of drunkenness and couldn't be trusted, even by my own family, I wasn't worth much as a man. Then I got sober through AA and came back to Arizona to seek my fortune. Under this very tree a 'Squaw Spirit' appeared to me. She explained how important it was for me to change my selfish ways. She told me I needed to do as much good for my fellow man as I could. The difference it would make for my future, even for eternity. This is what changed me from a self-absorbed, semi-greedy guy into a man determined to do well and assist others who are in need. It allowed me to open up to the possibility of love."

"It is so refreshing for us to have met you, Sal," said Dr. Tanner. "Your goodness shines through your youthfulness. Look at what you have done to change our lives in the short time we have known you. It seems to me that what you have spoken about—being a true Shaman—shows how the spirits can work through you to assist others. It's happened with us. We feel guided to the Indian reservation to do what we can to help. This is all happening because of what you've told us."

"Don't doubt the power that has been given to you," said the other Dr. Tanner. "Use it wisely; your possibilities are boundless if you continue to do good. We both were guided at a young age to endure medical school with the same altruistic attitude that you have. Even after serving our residencies, we chose to enlist instead of going into private practice. It's where we thought we could accomplish more good. We did it for the satisfaction and fulfillment that comes from helping our fighting men. We don't have any regrets for our choices; we still correspond with some of the doctors we trained with prior to the Army. They chose private practice and gained a lot of fortune, and in some cases, fame, but many of them are on their second and third marriages. They've admitted their dissatisfaction with the path they chose. Some have even admitted to a dependency on drugs and alcohol. So we definitely understand what you are doing. Your path is a much better way to live. You've reinforced our belief to continue to help others for as long as we are able. Thank you for trusting us with your story, Please Sal, for your own sake and also those you are helping, 'STICK TO IT'!"

Surprisingly, the couple gave Sal long hugs and told him if he were their son, they could not have been prouder. Just then, a bald eagle flew past them with the elegance that only an eagle can project.

"Well, it looks as though the spirits concur," agreed the Tanners.

CHAPTER 74

RIGHT ACTION

T hat evening, as Sal sat down to dinner with the Tanners, he
looked up in time to see Jake and Rob walk in the door.

"Hey there," said Jake. "We decided to come over for tonight's meeting."

"Why don't you eat dinner with us, too?" offered Sal.

Rob and Jake sat down as Sal made introductions. Sal explained how the
Tanners were formerly Army surgeons and were now onto other projects.

"If you want to know anything about the person I was before," said Sal,
"these two know me at my worst."

With that, Jake and Rob told the doctors about some of Sal's exploits,
leaving out the juiciest stories, but saying enough to validate what Sal had
told them. They all agreed they were glad to be Sal's friends now. They really enjoyed the new, improved version.

When meeting time came around, the Tanners asked to participate. It
would be their first 12-Step meeting even though they had counseled in-
numerable soldiers over the years. There was somewhere between 20 and
30 attendees along with some of the monks. This was one of those meetings where Sal decided to sit and listen, rather than talk. The leader asked
a few of the visitors to share, and though their stories were different, there
was a familiar ring to them all.

They had started partying at a young age and soon became solitary drinkers; they experimented with drugs, but most slipped back into boozing; some lost their jobs, some their families and eventually they were introduced to the program. When they decided to quit, some were able to do it immediately, while others did it after many tries.

All in all, it was a typical meeting, but the Tanners were greatly impressed. They were glad to now have an insight into the mindset of drinkers, since their premed and medical training hadn't provided that.

"Most people that don't have a drinking affliction find it easy to judge," said Sal. "But it takes a lot to break free of the overwhelming need to drink or use drugs. In most cases, when drunks come out the other side they are stronger, better citizens ready to help others. When I think of the millions who've found a new way of life, I believe it has to make America a better place. This message is now being carried around the world. It came from very humble beginnings, just a few drunks helping each other."

Rob and Jake shook hands all around and left, promising to be at the inaugural Tombstone meeting Thursday night. The Tanners gave their good-byes, indicating they would see Sal at breakfast. Sal went home to his cottage, happy at how the day had progressed, marveling at yet another opportunity to serve and initiate good deeds.

At breakfast, the Tanners asked directions to a good store in Tucson so they could load up on supplies for their move to San Carlos. Their intention was to get there by the weekend.

CHAPTER 75

NEW IDEA

S al sat by the pond with his journal to plan out future moves. He
was wondering, again, what was to become of his meeting with the
sergeant. Brother Alex walked by with Little John. Sal asked if he
could take the dog swimming after lunch. Of course, Brother Alex
told Sal he could take Little John any time he wanted.

By the afternoon, Sal was headed to his and Little John's favorite
swimming hole. Sal sat under his favorite tree hoping to have a vision or a
unique visit from a spirit. It wasn't long before his Indian spirit appeared
once again.

"I am pleased by all you are doing," she told Sal. "Stay on this path, but
don't forget your family for they were the ones who gave you important
roots."

Sal realized he hadn't written or called his parents in quite a while.
When he looked up, only Little John was there. Sal took off his boots and
soaked his feet in the river. He watched the dog play around with some
tadpoles and once again shook his head at what his life had turned into.

Sal and Little John walked back to the cottage to get ready for the
rest of the day. After he dropped Little John off at Brother Alex's room,
Sal showered and changed into the last of his clean clothes. I better remember to do some laundry, he thought to himself. Or I'm going to start

smelling like Little John.

A clean-shaven Sal headed to Tombstone after he made one quick stop at the Texaco station. Bud showed him all the donations he had stored in the back room that were ready for distribution. Sal promised to pick them up within the next few days so he could get them to the travelers.

"I'm really excited to get the meetings at the Fort started," said Bud. "I'll be seeing you at Jenn's meeting tonight, too." They shook hands and Sal headed on his way.

Sal stepped into the Muffin Cafe and Lu gave him a big smile. It had only been a couple months since he first stumbled in here, Sal reminded himself. So much had happened and Sal had to admit none of it had been bad. In the old days, he never had two consecutive months where he hadn't experienced at least five disasters. One of the promises they speak about in the AA meetings is about turning one's life around. He had done just that.

Lu sat Sal in a booth at the far end of the cafe after Sal told her he was meeting Sergeant Joe.

"Uh oh, Sal" teased Lu. "Now what did you do?"

"Nothing bad that I know of," Sal grinned. "I guess I'll find out soon, though. Here he comes through the door."

The sergeant shook Sal's hand and sat down across from him in the booth. "What have you been up to," he said with a friendly smile. "Anything you can't tell me?"

"No sir," Sal said honestly. "I've been busy with only good things. Have you made Cochise County safe for everybody?"

"Doing our best," the sergeant replied. "Order whatever you would like; this dinner is on the county."

Once Irene took their orders the sergeant got down to business. "I do have something to ask you, Sal," he began. "What do you know about glass bottles out in the desert?"

"Well, I've been known to place some water out there to keep people from dying in the desert," Sal said solemnly. "Why do you ask that?"

"One of the old time ranchers who controls over 25,000 acres has been asking our office why his men are finding a lot of empty jugs on his range" the sergeant explained. "He's wondering about them, afraid they might start grass fires from the sun magnifying through them. I really don't know if that's possible, but he wants us to check it out. It's just started in the last couple of months. One of his ranch hands saw an orange Pontiac driving the back roads."

"I've been placing water under some trees for the travelers," admitted Sal. "Really didn't know that I was causing any problems."

"I don't know that it is a problem, Sal," said the sergeant. "I just needed to try and figure it out. At least now I can tell Luke Cantrell, the rancher, the reason. He's a good guy; hates to find bodies out on his range. Over the years he and his workers have discovered over two dozen dead travelers—especially in the summer time. Any thoughts about what you could do differently? I agree with you that anything that can be done to prevent these poor folks from dying out there must be done. I've had to pick up over 100 corpses in my years; it's a real shame, especially when it's a kid. I can't help but think of my own children out there in that heat."

"Well, I might have an idea," said Sal. "If this Cantrell is a good guy like you say, do you think he'd be O.K. with some of those Army water trailers? If I could buy some, and had some canvas bags to place with them, do you think his cowboys would keep them filled? They would need to tow them out to different spots on his range."

"I believe he would," said the sergeant. "That would save a bunch of those folks from dying of thirst, but how in the world could you afford to do that? Did you find a gold mine in your ramblings?"

"Yeah, maybe I did," said Sal cryptically. "Give me a week to try and put that together. There'll be no more glass jugs lying around. The travelers can carry the bags filled with water, then even when they're empty they can hold on to them until they get to the next water source, seems like a decent solution, don't you think?"

"I like it, but the county can't afford to do it," said the sergeant. "You would have to fund the trailer and the bags. I'll talk to Mr. Cantrell and ask if he would be willing to fill and haul them if you provide them. I like you, Sal, you're a real dreamer, but you do seem to be able to get things done."

Sal finished his huge steak and ordered two pieces of pie with ice cream. "Good thing the Sheriff likes you," said the sergeant as he looked at Sal's clean plate. "He'll get a kick out of your water jug deal, but he'll be happier if you can make Cantrell happy. He controls a lot of the votes and the Sheriff lives or dies by elections."

"O.K., Joe," said Sal. "I will do my best to put this together. I'm pretty sure I can pull it off."

"You know, Sal, there must be over 100 ranchers large and small that have found bodies bleaching in the sun on their land," said the sergeant. "If you can change that, I can sell them on working with you. Can't wait to tell the Sheriff what you have in mind. I never thought we would get a handle on the dead immigrant problem, so good luck."

Joe picked up the check and shook Sal's hand. "See you next Thursday, same place, same time," he said. "Bring your appetite."

"Well, I've never seen him smile so much," said Lu as she watched the sergeant leave. "You are a miracle worker, Sal. Ever think about running for Governor?"

"Naw, I can't," smiled Sal. "I'm not crooked enough for this state."

CHAPTER 76

HELLDORADOS FIRST MEETING

"B y the way," said Lu. "Jenn left me a bunch of schedules for that meeting at her church. I already gave out half of them so you should have a full house. I also have a lot of food stacked up for you. I hit up a couple of the sales guys from our suppliers and they've been throwing extra cases of canned goods on the delivery truck for you."

"I promise I'll pick them up tomorrow morning, O.K?" said Sal.

"That'll be fine," she said. "Have a good meeting. See you later."

Sal headed over to the church to see a near empty parking lot. He knew it was early, so he went in to talk with Jenn.

"Glad to see you," she gave Sal a quick hug. "I put the coffee on but it hasn't perked yet, and it's been a half hour."

"It's O.K.," said Sal. "I forgot to tell you those big pots take awhile. It'll be fine."

Sal looked around the room and saw the table full of literature. There was even a sign that said "Welcome!"

"That's a nice touch," smiled Sal.

"Yeah, it came from our summer Bible school," said Jenn. "I thought it wouldn't hurt to hang it up."

It was 45 minutes before the start of the scheduled meeting and people started coming in one and two at a time. There were even families with
a couple of kids.

"Well, Jenn, I think before long you'll have to open up the other room
for your Al-Anon meeting," said Sal.

Just then the Reverend came in and shook Sal's hand. "Looks like you
were right about the need for this," he said to Sal. "Glad to be a part of it.
More than half the counseling I do has to do with drinking. Its mostly the
wives trying to decide what to do."

"It can only help, Rev," said Sal. "Thanks for allowing it to be here."

Sal noticed that Rob and Jake moseyed in, followed by Bud. Sal introduced them to each other, including Jenn and the Reverend. When Sal
looked the room over at least three-quarters of the seats were filled.

"What do we do to get started?" asked Jenn.

"First we'll welcome everyone, then you can introduce me," said Sal.
"I'll identify a few speakers and that should take care of the evening.
Drunks mostly like to tell their stories. Let them know it's a 'no smoking'
meeting and no swearing is allowed. There are families in attendance."

With that Jenn opened the first ever Tombstone AA meeting, explaining she was new to all this. Hopefully it was the start of something that
changed lives for the better. Everyone cheered and clapped—there had
to be over 50 people in the room by the time the meeting commenced.
Sal found two guys who had over four years sobriety that were willing to
speak. Once Jenn introduced Sal, he shared for a short while before hand-
ing it over to the first speaker. The man had a good story. He was glad
there was finally a meeting in Tombstone because he had been driving to
Tucson every week. After the second speaker finished, Sal introduced Bud
to give meeting times for the new group at Fort Huachuca. The meeting
closed as they said the 'Lord's Prayer' but a lot of people stood around and
talked for at least an hour. It was definitely what Sal, Jenn and the Reverend considered a success. They started calling themselves the "AA Corral"

group, saying the "O.K. Corral" took lives; the "AA Corral" saved them.

After everyone left, Sal helped Jenn clean up. The Reverend was smiling broadly when Sal asked if he would mind being the treasurer.

"No problem," he said. "I can handle that."

"Jenn, you should designate a leader, soon." said Sal. "That way you don't have to be here all the time, especially if you want to get the Al-Anon meeting going."

"I agree," she answered. "I'll see about that right away."

CHAPTER 77

BETTER OFFER

Sal left and headed back to the monastery nearly running over a herd of javelina on the way. Once back, he phoned Mary and told her how well the first AA meeting went. He also asked her if she could schedule a meeting for him with her dad and Mrs. Crane for either Friday afternoon or Saturday morning.

"Why don't you come over tomorrow afternoon and stay until Sunday," Mary offered. "I'll need to study by Sunday so you'll have to leave by noon."

"That'd be great," smiled Sal. "I'll be there for sure by 3 p.m."

Sal hung up and excitedly began to plan his trip. He needed to pick up food donations from Bud and Lu and drop them off at the needed locations. He also wanted to get to Tucson as soon as he could. Everything was looking bright in Sal's world until he remembered his laundry. He took his overstuffed laundry bag and some detergent and ran quickly over to the laundry room, which was deserted at this time of night. He stuffed two machines full and decided he could hang it all on his patio in the morning. Once it was dry he could pack what he needed and head out.

Sal felt he had had a good week. Now he needed a good night's rest.

In the morning, Sal hung up his clothes and headed over to Bud's. With his change of plans, he needed to explain to Bud why he couldn't attend the Fort's first AA meeting. Bud completely understood that he had received a better offer.

Sal swung by the Muffin Cafe and picked up a real cup of coffee, then loaded Lu's food stash into his car. There was no room left for any more donations. Sal was glad he no longer toted around Little John, he thought briefly. As he needed all the room he could get, but he still missed the big lug, smelly as he was.

After Sal unloaded the food at the bridge, he realized he hadn't eaten yet today. As he drove through Tombstone, he stopped and picked up a couple of cheeseburgers-to-go at the Muffin Cafe, where Lu was surprised to see him again.

"You know, Sal," said Lu. "If I weren't mistaken, you look like you have a glow about you."

"Well I'm on my way to Tucson to spend some quality time with Mary," Sal said.

"Aha!" smiled Lu. "That's it! Well, don't go bothering any snakes with her this time. You might scare the poor girl off."

Lu laughed, as Sal turned crimson with embarrassment. He waved Lu a good-bye and hit the road. As he drove past the church he saw Jenn outside trimming some shrubs. He tooted his horn and Jenn gave him a thumbs up as he passed. Things are going well for a lot of us do-gooders for a change, Sal thought to himself. He certainly felt he was now an integral part of the community, in a very short period of time. He remembered his favorite axiom that said, 'Do Good—Feel Good', and he truly believed it worked. His conscience hadn't had to work overtime since he embarked on this path.

Once back at the monk house, Sal took down his clothes from the line and packed his bags. He was now presentable to go to his Tucson meeting. He loaded his bags into the Bonneville and jumped into the shower. Once dressed, he left his big, life-saving boots in the closet because he wasn't going to tempt fate again. He knew his guardian angel had protected him the first time around and he was grateful.

Sal suddenly realized he hadn't heard from Mary. He jogged over to the office to use the phone when a monk called out, "Hey, I have a message for you; a Mary called an hour ago and said "Tell Sal be here by 2:30 for a meeting."

CHAPTER 78

WOW!

Sal glanced at his watch and gasped. "Oh brother, I have to leave right now! It's already 20 minutes after one."

Sal jumped into his car and raced off down the highway. Because he pushed past the speed limit all the way, he arrived in Tucson with ten minutes to spare. Mary greeted him with a big, warm smile. "Hey Sal, sit out here for now; Mrs. Crane hasn't arrived yet, and my Dad's on the phone."

"It's so good to see you again," Sal said to Mary. "I miss you more every day."

"I feel the same way," Mary beamed in reply. "If I wasn't so jammed with class work, I would have driven to St. David to see you."

"Well, I must admit I'm really glad to hear you say that," smiled Sal. "It would stink if only I felt this way. Maybe once you are out of law school we can work it out to get together for dinner on a regular basis."

"I've been thinking the same thing," Mary said. "I'm sure we can work something out. I can't wait to give you a big hug; better wait until we are away from the office, though."

They both giggled like a couple of school kids just as Mrs. Crane came through the door. When she saw Sal, she lit up like a spotlight.

"Oh, Sal, I hear you've been doing marvelous things!" she said with a tone of pride in her voice. "Please tell me all about it, and I'll tell you how pleased I am you have let me join your little band of do-gooders." Attorney Mayhew guided both Sal and Mrs. Crane into the conference room. He shook Sal's hand as he asked, "Please give us a rundown of what you've been up to young man—and I need not know about any encounters with snakes. I couldn't sleep for three nights after Mary told me about that experience." Oh, I'd like to hear that story," said Mrs. Crane. "I'm dreadfully afraid of snakes but I love hearing about them."

Sal smiled as he thought about what he was going to ask her to fund. He was hoping she would still be as enthused after that. When Attorney Mayhew walked in Sal filled them in about the two AA groups, which had started up this week. He explained how successful the Tombstone meeting had been. Sal was hoping the Fort Huachuca meeting was just as popular. He should know how popular by next week. He was especially excited about telling them both about the two physicians he met, how they were going to work on the reservation to teach some badly needed skills, also provide healthcare where needed.

"I am so delighted to hear that," said Mrs. Crane. "These endeavors are so beyond my initial expectations. I must tell you I am one hundred percent behind whatever you dream up as long as it helps the unfortunate get through their struggles." Sal filled his two benefactors in as best he could. "Well what will be the next adventure?" asked the attorney

"Let me start with the less costly of the two," said Sal. "The two doctors will need a variety of equipment and supplies, which I believe we should take care of. They have agreed to work there for free, and pay their own expenses as far as food and lodging go. I think we should reimburse them for car expenses. They will be traveling a good deal around a very large reservation and eventually that will extend to two."

"I agree," nodded Mrs. Crane. "That sounds like a wonderful service for the people on the reservation. I will be more than pleased to take care of whatever expenses come up."

"Yes, it sounds very worthwhile," said Attorney Mayhew. "Have them coordinate their needs through Mary and we will procure whatever they need."

Attorney Mayhew waited a beat before he addressed Sal on his second proposal. "You say this is the least expensive of your two ideas; I can't wait to hear what else you've come up with."

"O.K.," said Sal. "I've gotten a little bit of grief from the Sheriff's office about glass jugs being discarded along the trails on the ranches between the border and Tucson. I was totally honest. I explained to the sergeant I was placing water in the desert for the thirsty travelers. He told me he was very upset with his office having to go out and recover bodies from these same ranches because the travelers succumbed to the elements. He applauded what I was doing but would prefer I did it without using glass bottles. I think I have a good solution, especially if the ranchers are willing to help refill water tankers every couple days."

Sal took a sip of the water Mary had brought in while he was talking. "I have a friend in Bisbee who manufactures canvas water bags," Sal continued. "I'm sure I could get a great deal with him to purchase a large supply. The big problem, though, is the water tanks. Any type that is enclosed will work; I believe there are plenty of government auctions where we can purchase a few. They will be pricey, so I really need to leave this part up to you. I'm just the monkey in the middle, but if you want to go for it, we can start out slow, like with five or six tanks. We can test those out and see what works best."

"Why don't you let Mrs. Crane and me discuss this privately?" said Attorney Mayhew. "Do you think you could spend about ten minutes talking with Mary while we discuss this?"

As Sal left the conference room, Attorney Mayhew winked at Sal, which caused him to blush.

"What's wrong?" Mary asked Sal as he came up to her desk.

"I think I've been found out," stammered Sal.

"About us?" Mary smiled.

"Yes," nodded Sal.

"Oh don't worry about that," she said. "I've always told my Dad everything. He thinks you're a fine young man and he recognizes I'm a grown woman, who is soon to become a lawyer. He's fine about us, since I've scared him with a few stories about other boyfriends who were nothing like you."

"Wow, you'll be a great liar—I mean lawyer," laughed Sal. He genuinely felt relieved he had passed her Dad's test, but most importantly—hers.

After a few moments, Attorney Mayhew opened the conference-room door and asked Sal to come back in.

"We've talked it over and Mrs. Crane would like to start with 20 water tanks," he told Sal. "And as many water bags as you think we'll need to order."

"I can't tolerate the idea of people perishing out there in this way," said Mrs. Crane. "I'm proud to be in a position to alleviate some of their suffering."

"We both agree there should be an initial test," the attorney added. "That way you can work out any logistical problems. Once the bugs are worked out we'll make the funds available to provide water on all the ranches and properties that the travelers cross."

"I have to tell you I am overwhelmed with your generosity," said Sal. "This could make a huge difference in eliminating deaths in the desert, particularly during the summer."

"I must say I never felt as alive as when I'm in your presence, Sal," said Mrs. Crane. "Sharing your ideas enlivens me. If I were a few years younger I believe I would give you quite a chase. I may have a fight on my hands from someone just on the other side of this door, though. Now, I've made plans for the four of us to have dinner at my home this evening so please say you will attend."

"Yes, of course," said Sal. "I was just momentarily speechless. Am I dressed O.K?"

"Yes," laughed Mrs. Crane. "We don't stand on formality here. Mary knows the way to my home. Hopefully we will see you at 6 p.m. for cocktails. I understand you won't be partaking of those so I've taken the liberty of having my cook prepare a variety of drinks more to your liking—lemonade, tea, iced coffee, juice and soft drinks. So there—no excuses. We'll see you at 6—ciao!"

Sal stumbled out to Mary's desk. "Did you know about this?" he asked.

"Sure," Mary smiled. "It'll be fun."

"O.K." said Sal. "I hope so. I'm just a poor Pennsylvania hillbilly kid; I hope I don't embarrass you."

"You'll be fine," said Mary. "Just relax and be yourself. Everyone who meets you loves you." Mary blushed as she said this, which caused Sal to turn red all over again. "Aren't we a couple of shy school kids?" Mary giggled. "I'll be done here in a few minutes; then we can stop by my place and freshen up before we head over to Sabino Canyon where Mrs. Crane lives."

"Great," said Sal. "I'd like to change my shirt."

On the ride up to Sabino Canyon, Sal and Mary held hands as they passed through some impressive landscaping.

"This is definitely the high-rent district," said Sal.

"You'll fit in just fine," reassured Mary. "There won't be any pretentious neighbors there—its just the four of us."

"Right," said Sal a bit nervously. "And a cook, and a butler ..."

When they pulled into the driveway, Mary made the remark that it wasn't "Tara" but it certainly looked like the Southwest equivalent. There were bell towers, parapets, and wooden vigas sticking out of the walls. There were beautiful flowers and trees along with a pond teeming with orange and white fish that Mary told him were "Koi." When Sal gave her a confused look, she explained it was a type of Japanese carp that were not good to eat. She added that Mrs. Crane was having problems with herons scooping up the fish, just helping themselves to lunch. When they rang the doorbell a rather stiff butler answered the door. He lead them to the back patio where Mrs. Crane and Attorney Mayhew were already seated, awaiting their arrival. They shook hands and hugged lightly all around. They took a seat at a large round table with numerous drinks and an ice bucket. Sal poured a white wine for Mary and an iced tea for himself. The others already had their beverages.

"Tell me about your life growing up in Pennsylvania," said Mrs. Crane. "I'm not being nosy; it's just in my circle we don't get to find out how other people make their way through life. Please forgive me for sounding snobbish, I don't mean to, it's just that I'm very interested in how you came to be such a generous, loving young man. You are most unusual, no matter what status or level in life we speak about. I can't tell you how much I respect your attitude and consideration you have for your fellow man. What a terrific world this would be if all people shared your values and lacked detrimental vices of greed and selfishness that permeates our world today."

"Thanks for your praise, Mrs. Crane," Sal said humbly. "I'm not sure I am deserving of all that. It seems that so much has happened in the last few months, a lot of it just fell into my lap."

Mary gave Sal a wink of encouragement along with a big smile. "When I was a drinker, I was not careful of other people's feelings or concerns," Sal continued. "Looking back, I know I was a selfish, self-centered creep. I give AA all the credit for turning my life around. It not only helped me stop drinking, but it showed me how helping others helps me, too."

Mrs. Crane got up and came around the table to give Sal a big hug and a kiss on the top of his head. With tears in her eyes, she said, "Yes, and you know you have passed that lesson on to me and I just love you for it. I am very grateful you did this service for me. Now I have something to get up for in the morning. I look forward to hearing what ideas you have dreamed up and what part I can play in these adventures. You may say you came from humble beginnings, but you have certainly attained lofty heights in your short life. Do not be ashamed or embarrassed about where you started from, that wasn't your choice, it's what you do once you are responsible for your life that matters, and you are doing everything to the best of your abilities. Everyone that makes your acquaintance from here on is blessed for knowing you, I know I am."

Attorney Mayhew and Mary softly applauded, both echoing the sentiments of Mrs. Crane. Sal was at a loss for words, which caused everyone to laugh joyously. At that point the butler brought in a tray of hors d'oeurves and saved him from further embarrassment. The array ranged from pigs in a blanket with mustard sauce to finger sandwiches without crusts.

"O.K., let's dig in," said Mrs. Crane. "Everything is delicious."

Mary smiled at Sal and gave him a quick nod. He was happy he hadn't made any insurmountable faux paux, yet. After everyone had sampled each appetizer, Mrs. Crane got everyone's attention.

"I'd like to discuss a bit of business if you all don't mind," she began. "I've had preliminary discussions with Marvin—Mr. Mayhew—and I'd like to make a proposal to you, Sal. As our informal arrangement has been successful beyond my expectations, I'd like you to consider heading up an organization for me that is funded by a trust fund. I don't want someone else to come along and recognize your capabilities, then grab you away from me. The organization would be a charitable foundation where you would be the Chief Operating Officer. Mr. Mayhew would be the Chairman of the Board of Directors on which I would also have a seat. You would be paid a salary comparable to a position with a private corporation, which I am sure you would approve of. All expenses would be covered along with a new vehicle for your travels since you will probably be traveling extensively considering the varied projects you already have going. I am sure the future will bring many more. Staffing would be managed from the Mayhew Law Firm, which will be adding a new attorney before the summer is past."

Mrs. Crane smiled at Mary as she continued. "My trust owns a small building off Speedway Boulevard here in Tucson that I would like established as the Foundation's headquarters. Is having it headquartered in Tucson O.K. with you?"

"Of course, Mrs. Crane," said Sal. "I am flabbergasted. I never dreamed I would be in this position. I love what I'm doing, but I need you to know I have zero education along these lines. Do you really think I am ready to handle something as important as this?"

"Sal, I trust myself to be a very good judge of character," answered Mrs. Crane. "I would rather have a 100-percent honest novice at the helm of my Foundation than an experienced executive who was untrustworthy. I understand your trepidation with what I am throwing into your lap, but please trust me as I have trusted you. This is a great opportunity for you. You can grow into it, even if it means taking courses at the University of Arizona to raise your acumen level in operating a corporation. I don't expect you to know of the depth of the funding that will eventually become available for this Foundation. We will leave that for the Law Firm to handle."

Sal shook his head in disbelief as Mrs. Crane went on with her dissertation. "It's becoming apparent to me that you have made some inroads in developing a closer relationship with one of the 'soon-to-be-partners.' Please excuse me if I'm speaking out of turn, but it's quite obvious something great is developing between you two, I, for one, applaud it. You are both exceptional individuals. There's no telling what you two will accomplish if you join forces. Please think this over and let me know as soon as you have arrived at a decision. I pray you will accept my proposal. I'm very excited with it's potential. It's been a long time since I have been this excited about the happenings of the day. Now, let's go into the dining room and see what my wonderful cook has put together for us."

It was a feast unlike any Sal had ever had. The only part of it that caused him a little concern was when Mary passed him a plate with funny little circles filled with something he couldn't identify.

"They're snails," smiled Mary. "You'll love them; be brave and try them."

Sal trusted her, so he picked one up and popped it into his mouth. The savory flavor gushed in his mouth. He nodded. "This is delicious. I never would have dreamed these ugly things called 'escargot' could taste like this."

That made everyone laugh, and they explained to him that most people's first reaction is usually about the same. "Well, my mom always soaks everything in butter," said Sal. "So this is pretty much the same thing except the pound of garlic on each one. Sure hope you're eating some, too, Mary."

Mary smiled at Sal as she popped a snail into her mouth. The rest of the dinner was as wonderful as the beginning with only a few more surprises. A Crème Brule made the top of Sal's list to try again. After dessert, Attorney Mayhew asked the ladies if he could borrow Sal for an hour to smoke a couple of Cuban cigars. He also wanted to discuss a few topics.

Sal wondered if Mary's dad was as open-minded as Mary thought. But he figured his conscience was clear and both he and Mary were adults, so it had to be all right. Besides, the cigars sounded great. They sat in lounge chairs on a stone patio overlooking the lights of Tucson. Puffing away, Martin Mayhew looked at Sal with a question in his eyes.

"The cigar is outstanding," Sal said as if reading his mind. "It's the best I've ever smoked. The dinner was also the best I've ever eaten, but of course, with the company I'm keeping a bologna sandwich would have been wonderful. I'd also like you to know Mary and I are developing a strong connection and it's important to me that you fully understand I will never do anything to upset her or cause her to mistrust me. You have all been wonderful to me and I can only hope to live up to your expectations."

"Well, so far, young man, you have exceeded my expectations," said attorney Mayhew. "I honestly can't think of anyone I've met I would rather have romantically linked to my daughter. I want you to know I truly would be proud to have you in my personal life. Now, as far as Mrs. Crane's offer—I hope you're giving it serious consideration."

"I am as we speak, sir," said Sal. "In fact, if we can put these cigars aside for now I'd like to excuse myself and take a stroll around the yard with Mary and discuss it."

"A very good idea," he nodded. "You are a man who is wise beyond his years."

Within a few minutes, Sal and Mary were walking the lighted path around the property. They talked in depth about what it would mean to accept Mrs. Crane's proposition.

"I have to leave it up to you to decide," Mary told Sal. "I can't see a better opportunity arriving for you. Life is so much about contacts and connections. You, have fallen into a unique thing. You've been offered a chance for a career doing exactly what you love to do. As far as we go, I can only see our relationship improving if you're working and living here in Tuscon. I have to concentrate on completing law school and then passing the bar. After that, we'll have a lot more time to spend together. So as I said, it's up to you but if I get any vote, I say go for it!"

With that said, they hugged one another and Sal whispered in her ear, "I'm very glad you voted that way; it makes it unanimous."

When they got back to the patio, there was coffee and more dessert laid out on the table. Though they both had consumed enough food to last them the weekend, they partook of the goodies, anyway.

"Mrs. Crane, I've made a decision about your proposal," said Sal. "I most heartily accept your very generous offer. I promise to never disappoint you and I will do my very best to achieve your expectations of me."

"Oh, I am so pleased, Sal," smiled Mrs. Crane. "Together we will be able to accomplish great things to help others, just look at what has already occurred in such a short time, now we can be more organized and effective. You've made this old woman very happy, and from the smile on Mary's face, I believe you've made this young woman happy, too."

Though they all laughed good heartedly, both Sal and Mary simultaneously blushed.

"I have one request," added Mrs. Crane. "I want a large sign made up and placed on the wall so everyone who walks into the Foundation office has it hit them in the face. I want it to say, 'Do good—Feel good.' That phrase has stuck in my mind since you spoke it to me and honestly, its part of the reason we've come together in this place."

CHAPTER 79

NEW OFFICE

S al and Mary took their leave after thanking their host for the wonderful evening. Fortunately for the couple, no one asked them where they were going or where Sal was staying that night. As they drove to Mary's apartment, they hardly needed the headlights they were glowing so brightly. All Sal could muster was a continuous rant of "what a wonderful evening" and "I love snails."

"I can't wait to tell my mom," said Sal. "Maybe I could send them some; she'll just have to soak them in butter and garlic. Ha! Can't wait until my brother sees them on his plate. He'll probably cover them in horse radish."

"I'm really happy how things are going for you, Sal," said Mary. "This seems like the perfect opportunity. You'll be able to accomplish so much more now, as a real organization with offices. It sure beats working out of your car. As soon as I'm through with my studies I'll be able to assist you, too. In the meantime, you know I'll do anything to help you; just ask. I was going to say earlier I didn't know where we were going as a couple, but honestly, I have a pretty good idea. It's important we get our feet on solid ground first. Things will go so much better for us once we are settled, don't you agree?"

"Yes, mam," smiled Sal. "I do. Life is amazing. I can't ask for more. I'm very willing to wait and let things progress as they will, as long as you know I love you and want to be with you for my whole life."

"I feel the same way, Sal," said Mary, tears filling her eyes. "We'll have a wonderful life. Things have happened so fast I believe we are wise to take it slow for a while. Thanks for understanding."

On Saturday, after eating brunch in spite of their assertion they wouldn't need to eat until Monday, Mary handed Sal a key.

"This is to your new office," she smiled. "Let's go over and check it out!"

"That'd be great," Sal replied. "I still keep pinching myself because this all seems like a dream. How wonderful my life has become—let me hug you again for an hour or two. I promise to leave right after breakfast tomorrow so you can study. Can't have you flunking out of law school. Your dad is amazingly understanding, but if that happened it may cause him to ban me from Tucson."

"O.K." she grinned. "It's a deal. It's not forever; so don't be signing a long lease on an apartment for yourself. I think we may be sharing our own place before too long."

"Yes, mam," Sal answered with muffled excitement. "If you say so; you're my counselor."

Mary directed Sal to the handsome building Mrs. Crane owned. She unlocked the door as Sal offered to carry her over the threshold.

"I ought to be carrying you," she laughed. "It's your new office, but I know I can't lift you. If you'll lie down I'm willing to drag you in by your feet."

Sal declined as he walked into the new office on his own volition. He stared at the impressive surroundings and found it hard to grasp it was his office.

"This is incredible," said Sal in awe. "I never thought I'd be working in a place like this. I never imagined something like this would happen when I left Pennsylvania."

"We'll have to figure out all the supplies you'll need," said Mary. "Fortunately, all the furniture is already here. You can move things around when you know what will work best."

"I'm glad you're willing to help me with these decisions," said Sal. "I have no idea how to manage an office. I thought I'd be working out of Hotel Pontiac for a while, but this is just perfect. I can't wait to get started. My mind is reeling with ideas."

Mary handed Sal the key with a smile. "You can get settled into here this week," she suggested. "We can look for an efficiency apartment for you that is close by for convenience."

"O.K., I'll plan on coming back Wednesday or Thursday," said Sal. "In the meantime, I'd like to drive you up to Mount Lemon and challenge you to a snowball fight. I've heard there's still some snow in the shady spots at the ski resort."

"Ooooh, I accept your challenge," laughed Mary. "Let's stop at my place and grab a couple of jackets. It could be chilly up there."

On the drive up the mountain Mary practically sat in Sal's lap, laughing about everything they had shared in their short time together. After a hilarious afternoon rolling in snowdrifts, and then treating themselves to good food at the Mount Lemon Inn, they drove off the mountain to Mary's place. Sal agreed to quiz Mary on her schoolwork and was amazed at how difficult the subject matter was. She had to memorize a lot. He developed a new respect for the difficulty of being a law student. He was somewhat mollified with his decision not to attend college, after watching how hard she studied. He knew he wasn't cut out to be an academic.

"Are you O.K. with me being just a high-school graduate?" Sal asked humbly. "You'll have a law degree, but I won't have any degree."

"Sal, you have already proven your capabilities to me," Mary assured him. "In these few, short months you have accomplished more than a lot of highly educated professional people I know could not have done in years. You are the type of person that decides what it is you want to do and then does it. You don't waste your time calculating and over analyzing your thoughts ad nauseum. You just get the work done. There is actually a danger in too much education. Also, the professors teach us to think, think, think and then think some more. If you do it too long you find all the negative possibilities and you become defeated before you get started. You are blessed in ways the more educated are not. Never feel embarrassed or ashamed for a lack of formal education. You have a great store of common sense mixed with ambition and enthusiasm. These attributes get things done, no matter the roadblocks. I would never feel you are inferior to anyone; I'm extremely proud of you and I know I will be even more so in the future. It makes me love you more."

Sal and Mary temporarily ended schoolwork quizzes and spent the next few hours in each other's arms. They awoke, still cuddling, as the sun started shining in the window.

"Let me make us breakfast," said Sal as he got up. "I'll stay true to my promise to leave you alone to study after we eat."

Sal cooked up two big omelets with all sorts of ingredients he found in the fridge. After breakfast they hugged good-bye, and he hit the road back to St. David.

CHAPTER 80

UH OH!

P ulling into the driveway of the monastery, Sal felt a sting of nostalgia knowing this might be his last week here. This place had been a magical experience in so many ways. Looking back on what had happened on these grounds, he was very grateful to have met everyone. Brother Alex, Little John, interacting with the spirit that guided him onto his incredible path, all the great people he ran into—the characters, bikers, doctors, law enforcement—even making amends to his friends. And then he was setting up some AA meetings and feeding poor migrants. He was astounded at the list. If someone had told him all this would happen once he left Pennsylvania he would have laughed in their face. No amount of imagination could have foreseen this adventure.

Sal parked at his cottage and walked over to the office to see if he had any messages. He actually had three. One of the monks who gave them to him also told him there had been two pickups that pulled in and turned around a few times over the weekend. The Brother thought they might be looking for Sal, but they never stopped and asked.

Sal read the messages, the first one being from Jake. Everything was O.K. with him and Rob. They were working their programs, attending meetings, and wanted to know if Sal could join them for dinner next week. The second call came from Jenn asking him to stop by or call, but everything was fine. The third call was from Chaplain Cliff, asking Sal to come by sometime during the week, which Sal had intended to do anyway.

Sal decided he better pick up donations at Bud's and the Hot Muffin café. He thought he would drop them off at the bridge in Charleston since his ladies were putting plenty of supplies at the bridge on Route 90. He changed clothes, unloaded his laundry and headed out. He found Bud bent over an engine that quit on a car full of nice folks on Route 80, south of St. David.

"There's a bunch of stuff for you in the store room," Bud told Sal. "Have at it. The meetings going good at the Fort; good to see you."

Sal promised to attend the next meeting, loaded up the food and headed to Tombstone. He happened to notice two beat-up, old pickup trucks parked on the side of the road, but other than that, the town was quiet for a Sunday. It was a drastic contrast to Saturday nights. Funny how Tombstone had always drawn rowdies, hell raisers and banditos ever since it first became a town, thought Sal.

At the Cafe, Lu was exceptionally busy with what looked like last night's revelers. In a back booth Sal saw Sgt. Washington of Fort Huachuca fame, sitting with his family. Sal quickly looked away and told Lu he would pull around back and load up as quick as he could.

"No problem," said Lu. "I'll holler out to Jose and have him carry things out to you."

Once he packed up the Pontiac to near bursting, he stopped at Jenn's, who stuck her head out the front door and and yelled to him, "I thought we were out of Big Books, but I found more so we're O.K., Thanks for stopping, See ya!!!"

He headed down the hill to Charleston, musing about the "Battle of the Bulls" and how he once had a ringside seat to the spectacle, not too many people would believe him if he told them. Especially since he had a reputation for expanding on the truth when he drank; they would just think he was hitting the sauce again.

As Sal put the last of the goodies under the bridge he looked up to see an old pickup truck pull in front of his and a second one pull behind it. "What is this," he thought to himself as alarms went off in his head. He started walking back to the Pontiac as four scruffy, middle-aged, redneck types got out of their vehicles and started toward him. One of them was carrying a pick handle.

"Uh, oh," Sal mumbled aloud. "This can't be good." He didn't recognize any of them. He hoped he hadn't crossed paths with any of their wives or daughters when he was still boozing, although he didn't even have a car back then, so his causing problems like that was quite limited. He couldn't imagine what he had done to tick these characters off.

The biggest of the bunch growled to Sal with menace. "Looks like we caught you red-handed aiding those illegal scum from across the border."

"Speaking of scum," a thought Sal kept to himself, it looked like this group was the Fraternal Order of Louses. Right about now he was wishing he had his old 30-30 rifle to even things up.

"We've been looking for you, boy!" the man continued on. "Kept missing you, but now we're going to have a good talk about this crap you're pulling, putting out water and food for the parasites taking our jobs."

Sal started to ask him how he was hurting them, when all he was doing was helping some poor folks along their way. but the pick handle came down across his kneecap sending him to the ground. All four men began kicking and punching him before he lost consciousness. The last thought he had was that this just wasn't right; all he did was try to help people.

The next thing Sal knew he was opening one eye and squinting at Mary who was looking down at him with worried concern. "Oh Thank God, he's awake," sighed Mary. A nurse appeared next to her and said she would go immediately to find the doctor. Sal seemed to feel pain in every part of his body. He had no idea where he was. Mary touched his cheek and spoke softly. "Don't try to move, Sal. Your leg is in traction the doctor will be here in a moment."

The next thing Sal knew there was a powerful light shining into his eye. He heard the doctor speak, but Sal's view flowed in and out of focus.

"This is one tough hombre. I predict he will be fine, eventually. Just rest young man, you have been through a terrible beating, but unlike humpty dumpty we'll put you back together again, without the king's horses or men." Sal moaned slightly, he could see Mary crying and wondered what had happened. Did he crash his car? The doctor told Mary to try to get Sal to sip a little water, he told her the IV's had taken care of Sal previously but now he wanted Sal's system to come back slowly to normal.

When Sal awakened again, he still felt totally broken, but could look around the room with his right eye. Mary was still there. So was Sgt. Joe of the Cochise Sheriff's Office. Joe leaned down and asked Sal if he remembered anything. It took all his effort to concentrate. He told the sergeant he left Tombstone with food donations to leave at the bridge in Charleston. Then he suddenly recalled the two trucks parked by his car. He stopped for a bit, breathing heavy. The nurse came over to look at Sal and told the sergeant not to over do it with his questions. Sal moved his right hand up. The movement sent fire through his shoulder.

"I remember four men coming towards me," he said slowly. "They were very angry. One of them hit me in the leg with a club. That's all I remember."

Mary gently held Sal's hand as Sgt. Joe spoke. "O.K., Sal. You just get better. We'll work on what you've told us. You're in good hands here; they'll take good care of you. The University of Arizona Medical Center is one of the best."

Sal grimaced at the pain from Mary squeezing his hand, but he held on tightly since she was his anchor to reality. She kissed him on the cheek and spoke. "Just rest, Sal. We love you and we'll make sure you get all the help you need." Mary leaned in closer and whispered in his ear. "Mrs. Crane is the hospital's biggest benefactor. She has every specialist involved in your care. You're going to be as good as new real soon. I love you. Rest."

When Sal woke again it was barely light in the room, but he could see Mary asleep in a lounge chair next to the bed. He was surrounded by monitors and had tubes and wires connected all over his body. He wondered sleepily how doing good could end up hurting so badly. He must have uttered the words out loud because Mary jolted awake and looked at him.

"Good morning, sunshine," she smiled. "Glad to see you're still with us. You sure scared the life out of everybody."

"How long have I been out?" Sal whispered.

"Five days," Mary replied. "I didn't even know you were hurt until Tuesday. Are you up to hearing all that I know?"

"I think so," Sal replied. "Is there any coffee?"

"Oh, now I know you'll be fine," Mary's smile widened. "Let me ask a nurse if you can have some."

Mary was only gone a few minutes when she came back with a cup of lukewarm coffee, which he had to sip through a straw.

"Oh I never tasted anything so good," Sal half mumbled. "Maybe I should have you feed me through a straw from now on, huh?"

"Good—the smart mouth is still working,"

"I can't believe I blacked out for five days and I was sober,"

"Sal, you've received an awful beating. Sgt. Joe called and said they haven't found those animals yet, but he guaranteed us that they would. He has some idea who they may be. He thinks they fled across the border, which is kind of ironic, isn't it?"

CHAPTER 81

RECUPERATION

S al let out a slow sigh as Mary continued. "Let me tell you what I know," she began again. "But let me know if you get tired." Sal nodded and Mary went on. "The last anyone saw of you was when you went to the Hot Muffin Cafe in Tombstone. Jenn said you stopped by the church and when you left you said you were going to Charleston to drop off supplies. After that, all we know is a soldier from Fort Huachuca saw your car burning at the bridge. He and his family found you lying on the ground near your car. They took you to the Fort Hospital since it was only 10 miles away. A Dr. Johnson stabilized you but felt you needed much more care than he could offer.

He arranged for a helicopter from the Fort to transport you to the U. of A. Medical Center. They put you right into intensive care. The next day, which was Monday, Dr. Johnson realized that he knew who you were. He said he met you when you came to his office with two other doctor friends of his. He called the Apache Reservation and was able to reach Dr. Tanner and tell them about your situation. They had met Johnny, were able to contact him the next morning and they informed him of what had happened. He figured he should call us since we were your contacts in Tucson. I received the call and dropped everything to get over here to the hospital. I haven't left your side, since. My dad and Mrs. Crane have been here every day checking on you. That's pretty much all I can tell you."

"Oh God, they burned my car, too?" Sal moaned. "What the hell did I ever do to them?" Sal thought for a few moments as the memories trickled back to his consciousness.

"Oh yeah," said Mary. "I just remembered—they stuck a piece of cardboard under you that said 'Mex Lover.'"

"Oh Jeez," said Sal. "What a bunch of wackos. I still don't know why they were angry enough to want to kill me. Can I please have some more coffee? I can't tell you how good it tastes. Thank you so much for being here for me."

"You're very welcome," Mary touched him gently. "Sal, I love you. When I heard about this I couldn't breathe freely until I saw you. You don't look much like the handsome man I've come to know, but you're still my guy."

"What about your classes?" Sal suddenly remembered. "Aren't you going to be in trouble with your professors?"

"No," she replied. "They were nice enough to give me a two-week excused absence, considering the circumstances. I have another week to help you mend, but I will need to start bringing in some books to study while I sit by your side."

"God, what a crazy deal," Sal sighed. "I'm sorry I caused all this pain and anxiety for everyone."

"Don't worry about that, Sal," she said. "Everyone is just concerned that you get better. Let me see if I can get you another coffee."

"Thanks," he smiled weakly. "You know, I'm not even angry at those guys. I just hope they're caught before they start taking out their viciousness on the Mexican travelers. They're crazy and they need to be stopped before it gets worse."

"The doctor told me last night you have improved substantially," said Mary. "You've gone from extremely critical to guarded, so you can now have visitors once they move you to a private room, that's courtesy of Mrs. Crane, by the way."

"I can't wait to thank her," said Sal. "I find it hard to believe it's only been a few months since they were taking her away in an ambulance. Now here I am flat in a hospital bed."

Mary left again to fetch another cup of coffee for Sal. When she returned she told Sal the nurse had called Dr. Tanji, who was a friend of Dr. Johnson's from the Fort. Turns out he was the Director of Emergency Services at the U. of A. Medical Center and was Sal's main doctor.

"They say it's good for you to drink as much liquid as possible," said Mary. "But you might not like that your doctor said the coffee needs to be diluted 50-50 with water. So drink up; it may not be high octane but I hope it hits the spot. They also said it would be about an hour then you'll be moved to your private room."

Once Sal was settled into his new room, the visitors started arriving. They came in two at a time—first Bud and Jenn, Brother Alex and Brother Casper , Jake and Rob. Later that afternoon, Chaplin Cliff and Johnny showed up. Then Nahteste, who wanted to know everything he could find out about the perpetrators. Nahteste, in particular, was very upset. Sgt. Joe stopped by again, telling Sal the Sheriff had made his case a priority. He even told his deputies whoever brought in the creeps would get an extra one-week paid vacation with a $300 bonus to boot. The Sheriff was definitely pissed.

Sal was happy to see everyone who stopped by, but it made him extremely weary. He asked Mary to shut down the visitations for the day so he could rest. Mary held Sal's hand until he fell asleep, then she tried to get caught up with some of her studies. She would occasionally glance at Sal and would smile to herself at the visible improvement in his condition.

The next morning Dr. Tanji came to visit Sal and told him he would go over the injuries if Sal was up to hearing about them. Sal readily agreed, he really wanted to know what his prognosis was.

"Well, son, you're kind of a mess," the doctor began in layman's terms. "Your patella—kneecap—is fractured. It'll heal with time. You also have three broken ribs I don't want you to sneeze. You also have a concussion.

You have a myriad of cuts, abrasions, contusions, and your right shoulder was dislocated. Your left wrist is fractured; the swelling in your face, lips and left eye will improve over the next week. All your teeth are still in place and you'll walk fine after a couple of months. All in all, your being a strong, young man will see you through, but I wouldn't advise any bull riding for the next six months. Any questions?"

"Just the one everyone asks," grinned Sal. "When can I get out?"

"First you have to get back on solid foods," the doctor replied. "You're doing fine on the liquids, you're passing plenty of urine. We were concerned about your bruised kidneys, but all seems to be in working order. My best guess would be three days after you can walk to the restroom, you're eating normal meals and having normal bowel movements. Then you can leave the hospital, but we'll want you close by so you can come in daily for physical therapy. We want to keep an eye on you. You're a VIP, you know. The papers are full of your story and Mrs. Crane is overseeing your care with the eye of an eagle."

"Sal will be staying with me," Mary offered. "I'll make sure he does everything he's supposed to in order to heal properly."

"Well then, you'll be in good hands," said Dr. Tanji. "So get to eating and we'll get you out of here in a week or so."

"Thanks, Doc," said Sal. "Sorry to be so much trouble. I sure didn't intend for any of this to happen."

"We all want you to get better A.S.A.P.," said the doctor. "Mrs. Crane has explained what you do for her Foundation, so God-speed, young man. I'm proud to have had a hand in your recovery. Next time I see you I hope you're passing out cigars celebrating the birth of a little Sal with this caring young woman."

Both Sal and Mary blushed as the doctor continued. "There is one thing I was wondering," said the doctor. "Who or what is 'Escabrosa?' You kept mentioning it when you were in and out of consciousness."

"Yes, Sal, who is that?" Mary asked with a frown. "You said our daughter should be 'Escabrosa.' Where did you get that name?"

"That's weird," said Sal. "That's the ridge the Mule Mountain tunnel goes through north of Bisbee."

"O.K., I have to make my rounds," said the doctor. "You keep healing fast; I want to keep up my good record. Adios, Sal."

Dr. Tanji left and Mary looked at Sal and burst out laughing. "Escabrosa?"

Sal smiled along with Mary then got a serious look on his face. "We need to reach Irv and Bonnie at the Mule Mountain tunnel. They've been helping with water and food for the travelers. I don't want them to get hurt by these idiots."

"Give me their last name and I'll contact them," said Mary. "We sure want them to be on the alert."

CHAPTER 82

THE CHASE

A s the days passed, Sal improved swiftly, he progressed to solid foods. Mary found a great Italian restaurant that supplied them with their signature pasta dishes. The lasagne became her favorite also. The visitors continued, Sal could hobble around the room, and was even able to stand on one leg to shower. By the seventh day, Dr. Tanji pronounced him fit to leave.

Mary arranged for a rented hospital bed, which she placed close to the bathroom in her apartment. Every day they made their way to physical therapy at the medical center. Mary proved to be an excellent nurse. Sal was soon well on his way to recovery. In addition, the Italian restaurant they loved so much gave Mary private cooking lessons. She astounded Sal by making an Italian feast at least twice a week.

Mary went into her Dad's office for a few hours each day and was back to school on a regular basis. Sal spent his days visiting with friends at his bedside, doing therapy or watching television. His mind still worked overtime with ideas on how to handle the responsibilities he was about to incur. He was surprised that Nahteste hadn't been back since his first visit. The reason why was answered as soon as Sal got a visit from Sgt. Joe.

Mary buzzed the sergeant in and they sat together in the living room waiting to hear what he had to say. He had arrived without Larry, which both Mary and Sal thought was strange. Sgt. Joe began the conversation on an even stranger note.

"What I have to say is for your ears only," said the sergeant. "If you agree, I can tell you—direct orders from the Sheriff."

"We'll never repeat anything you say," both Sal and Mary agreed.

"O.K.," said Sgt. Joe. "From what we've been able to piece together, your friend Nahteste knows some ex-soldiers who live near Fort Huachuca. It appears that after he left your hospital room he went to these friends and told them about what happened to you. As we understand the story, eight of the retired soldiers started going out to different bars in southern Arizona, figuring the perps would show up at one of them. Sure enough, they were spotted at a dive in Bisbee called 'The Bucket of Blood.' They were laughing about how they showed you how Mexican lovers get treated around here. Your guy bought them a few drinks and got chummy. One of them said he found out about a water tank some cowhands had set out to provide water for the travelers. They planned to go out the next night and shoot it full of holes along with any pachucas (derogatory term) they found near it. Your man called the other soldiers at Sierra Vista and informed them of what he heard. They got Nahteste and his two nephews and decided to set up an ambush near the tank.

"When your four attackers showed up in their ratty old pickups, the vigilantes confronted them. The soldiers told them to drop their weapons, but the lead guy fired his rifle, hitting one of the ex-soldiers in the arm. That started a firestorm. When the smoke cleared one was dead, one was wounded and two were lying on the ground pleading and crying for mercy. One of the ex-soldiers wisely drove away and called us, we responded immediately; took away the body along with the wounded man and arrested the other two. No charges are to be filed against the soldiers since it was an honest citizen's arrest with strictly a self-defense shooting. The attackers have been charged with attempted murder, arson of your car, and attempted murder of the soldiers. They won't see sunshine for at least 20 years. Florence State Prison will be their new home."

Sal sat silent, shocked to hear the details of the shooting.

"You've made some good friends, Sal," added Sgt. Joe. "I would not want that crew out to get me. The Sheriff and District Attorney agreed no charges would be brought against your guys; honestly, we'd like to give them a medal. So, don't ever speak about this. You can go about your way without worries of being interfered with again. The sheriff said to thank you and pass on his best wishes for a quick recovery. Also he added that his offer is still open to you. For myself, I must say, you sure stir things up for us in Cochise County, but I'm proud to know you and also wish you the best. I'll always be available to help you anyway I can. Oh—I almost forgot—Deputy Larry and I want you to know anytime we have a meal with you, we're buying."

Sal shook hands with the sergeant and thanked him for everything he had done. Mary followed it up with a hug and walked him to the door. Once he was gone, Mary looked at Sal and said, "Please don't do anything to put yourself in harm's way from now on. I just couldn't go through all the anxiety I've been through again. I'd like to keep my sanity."

"I promise," said Sal earnestly. "From now on I will do my best to stay safe and sound; I won't give you any cause to worry."

CHAPTER 83

PROPOSAL

A Over the next few weeks Sal was able to get to his new office with Mary's assistance. Mrs. Crane came by often to check on him. Dr. Tanji was impressed with his rapid recovery. He told Sal that with all the effort he's put into his physical therapy his recovery was ahead of schedule. The doctor was planning on letting Sal drive again within another two-three weeks. Sal was delighted to hear that; he was extremely independent and hated being a burden on Mary and others for his transportation.

Mary had insisted Sal not get his own apartment. Her father told him that considering the circumstances it was the logical thing to do, and he gave his blessing. Sal was grateful to them all. Mrs. Crane came to visit and wanted to know if Sal had contacted his parents. He said he had called them the day he was released from the hospital. He had a hard time convincing them the Wild West wasn't that wild all the time. He made it a point to call them every Sunday so they would know he was safe and recovering. Mrs. Crane insisted on buying Sal's parents a pair of tickets to fly out and check on Sal with their own eyes. Sal told Mrs. Crane his parents had never been on a plane before, but he'd do his best to convince them to fly out. When Mary popped up with the suggestion that his parents come out at Christmas for a wedding, he was speechless.

"I'll have to ask your father for your hand in marriage," said Sal after he recovered a little composure. "Will you marry me? I'm sorry I can't get down on my knee right now, but I swear I'll be able to carry you over the threshold by Christmas."

"Yes," smiled Mary. "I'd be proud to be your wife and companion for life."

Mrs. Crane beamed with joy and thanked them both for allowing her to be a part of their proposal and plans.

CHAPTER 84

BACK IN THE SADDLE

O nce Sal was able to drive again he made plans to visit all his friends. He was anxious to see how Chaplain Cliff and his ladies were doing as well as Bud and Jenn with their meetings. He was hoping he could make a trip to the reservation to reconnect with Nahteste, Johnny and the Tanners. Making his rounds also meant touching base with Irv and Bonnie in Bisbee, along with Jake and Rob. He had heard good things about all of them. His first stop, though, was going to be the Brothers at the monastery.

Sal figured while he was out and about he should arrange a meeting with the ranchers. He wanted to solidify the water program with the tanks and the bags. He made a note to himself to contact Crisco and set up the regular purchase of water bags, but he would have to insist "No Hugs!" or they would end up putting him into a bag.

While Sal had been recovering from his injuries in the hospital, he had come up with many ideas he wanted to act upon. In Tucson, Mrs. Crane arranged a meeting for Sal with the director of the Food Bank. Sal wanted to set up a steady supply of foodstuffs so he could develop a delivery schedule that blanketed southern Arizona. It would include the Pima reservations, which had sections with some of the highest death rates of travelers along the border. He was hoping to convince the Food Bank to split the supplies half to the Indians and half for the travelers. That would save many lives, especially those who unwittingly started off through the inhospitable desert. Most Americans or Mexicans for that matter, were not aware the lands just north of the border between Nogales and Yuma were considered the most harsh, unwelcoming and dangerous desert in the country.

Sal also wanted to convince the tribes to assist him in placing water stations on tribal land west of the reservation. He was sure that would save hundreds of lives each year.

Because Sal believed the travelers were ignorant of the dangers involved in crossing the Arizona desert, it physically pained him to think about the children and women who never made it across alive. Now that he felt a powerful love for Mary, he couldn't imagine how helpless they must feel when their spouses or children succumbed to dehydration or starvation. It brought tears to his eyes when he pictured the skeletons found by the border patrol almost daily. Sal decided then and there he would continue to expand the program he started, even if it meant hiring drivers to drop off food and water throughout that barren stretch of land.

Sal thought he better contact the area commander for the Border Patrol to get his blessing. If positive result, then ascertain in what areas water stations would do the most good. He knew he would need Mrs. Crane and Attorney Mayhew's political clout to make that connection, to ensure a much warmer reception. "I can't imagine any human being against something like that," Sal thought to himself. Each person has probably experienced some deprivation of water or food, but out there, it's magnified a hundredfold, and deadly.

Sal knew people were angry about illegal border-crossers taking American jobs. They wished the travelers would stay on their own side of the border. On the other hand, these people were starving and without hope in their own homeland, not through any fault of their own. They were willing to make a perilous journey to find a better life for their families, Sal felt that any honest person would admit they would do the same for their own families, if the situation were reversed. Most of the time, the travelers took jobs other Americans didn't want anyway—picking fruit and vegetables, cleaning houses, mowing lawns etc.—but these were jobs that earned them an honest living. The drug mules and dealers were another story. Until conditions improved in the traveler's homeland, whether it be Mexico, Honduras, Nicaragua, anywhere in Latin America no one could convince Sal it was wrong or immoral to do whatever he could to assist people in surviving the journey.

In spite of being an almost anti-religion sort of person, Sal still asked himself the one question he gleaned from his childhood-Catholic upbringing: "What would Jesus do?" He felt it was a good way to measure his actions. He found it hard to understand why someone would sit on their butt watching a ball game on television if they had an opportunity to help someone less fortunate.

Thinking about the four men that almost took his life, Sal wondered if they had looked in the want ads for jobs. Instead they chose to follow a path of hatred, violence and malevolence—and look where it got them. "Forgiving their ignorance and learning from the whole event seemed to be what Jesus would prefer we follow," Sal said to himself. The axiom of "Do Good, Feel Good" did no harm and made everyone involved feel better. "We are all in this world together," thought Sal, "helping each other is the true meaning of love."

Once again, Sal was filled with gratitude that Mrs. Crane came into his life, which allowed him to use his God-given talents towards the betterment of others. It was a blessing he would be forever thankful for.

CHAPTER 85

ON THE ROAD AGAIN

s the days passed, Sal improved. He only needed a cane when walking on uneven ground. Mary graduated and passed her bar exam. Sal hired an assistant for the Foundation and started to settle into a routine. He secretly hoped there wouldn't be any more traumas to work through. Mary got busy developing the law practice and her father was pleased to pass the baton so he soon could spend more time improving his golf game.

Mrs. Crane expressed how pleased she was with the numerous programs Sal was developing. There was no shortage of need in Southern Arizona and fortunately, the funding was there to fill some of them. The home-schooling program on the reservation had proven to be a roaring success. So much so, they were expanding it to the Fort Apache Reservation, too. The fact it had been such a success brought Federal attention; one of the Arizona Senators offered to provide funding for the Foundation to expand it to all the reservations in the state. But Sal and Mrs. Crane preferred the Foundation continue as it began, without bureaucracy or interference. Hopefully, the government could just use the program as a model for other reservations across the country. When several magazine articles appeared touting the success of the San Carlos Reservation program they held steadfast in their determination to remain strictly private,

doing the Foundation work as they saw fit.

Eventually, Sal was able to convince the Pima tribe to assist with supplying water stations across their reservation. The Foundation paid the salaries and expenses of three men to keep the water tanks full. With provisions from the Food Bank, they were able to keep lockers at each station full of canned goods and tortillas.

In addition, Sal brought Johnny down to Tribal Council meetings. They began a program there with the Pima that reached out to mothers to show them how to home school their kids. The Foundation supplied all the books and writing supplies. After Tribal Council members from different reservations toured the San Carlos Reservation and saw how well the program was working, they wanted it implemented on their reservations.

Sal agreed to provide two traveling teachers, who would be members of the tribe, if the Council would make buildings available. The traveling teachers would come to the school buildings every few weeks with slide shows and guest speakers. This would be for the benefit of the home schooled. The idea was to make the kids aware of the possibilities an education could provide. Before long, those who hadn't taken advantage of the education system began to see the advantages.

Sal found he had to provide generators for the classrooms that were too remote to have electricity so slide shows and movies could be shown two-three times a month. He purchased portable generators on little trailers that one of the teachers vehicles could tow and then return to a safe storage spot. Sadly he had tried leaving them at the remote schools but they quickly disappeared. Then they started a lending library that gave a much-needed boost to the kids who wanted to read. Parents were assisted by the traveling teachers to improve their own reading skills so they could effectively help their kids.

Council members told Sal the gang infestation was being affected positively by teenagers now showing up at the reading rooms asking for lessons. The gang activity was beginning to slow down because of it. Sal decided it would be a good idea to hire a part-time psychologist who specialized in the gang culture. He was assigned to travel to all the reservations that had programs running. He spent three days every month at each reservation. It was proving worthwhile to hold group meetings for the teenagers.

The Council at Pima Reservation also approved the starting of AA and NA meetings, which just about bowled Sal over. He knew this could be a huge breakthrough if they made a dent in the drunkenness and drug use on the reservation. Sal's duties precluded him from personally starting any AA meetings, plus the Native people didn't need another white man telling them how to live their lives. He decided he needed Native people who were in recovery to run the meetings.

Sal had made it to several of the meetings in Tucson and met a few Native Americans who might work into his plans. He usually attended two different meetings during the week so he asked the chairmen at each to allow him to speak for a few minutes. Sal spoke to the crowds explaining what he had in mind. He handed out business cards to anyone interested in discussing it further. (Business promotion is never allowed at AA meetings but all agreed this was different.)

The next day, Sal was pleased to receive four phone calls. He set up a meeting in the Foundation offices to explain it to them further. The four Native Americans who showed up—one woman and three men—were very attentive. Sal explained that although AA was not allowed to pay anyone, the Foundation could offset their expenses. As Sal saw it, he wanted AA meetings started at two or three places on the Pima Reservation. With their track record of sobriety and their experience, these four would initiate the meetings while the Foundation supplied literature, coffee maker, snacks, and miscellaneous drinks.

Chaplain Cliff had told Sal he knew of two Chapels on that reservation that could probably offer their space for the meetings. All four members agreed to assist and participate in the pilot program when the Tribal Council approved the meetings and the chapels were procured.

The first week the meetings were introduced on the reservation, attendance was minimal. Then the Council printed a one-page announcement explaining what the meetings were about, along with offering transportation for those who needed a ride. The next meeting had over 50 people, both drinkers and their families. Though the 'Big Book' was given out, too many people couldn't read. Those who could read didn't identify with the stories, so Sal racked his brain over this dilemma. He recalled seeing some books and tapes at the monastery specifically aimed at Native Americans, so Sal drove over to check it out. He spent a pleasant day there, walking Little John, visiting with Brother Al and generally breathing in the fresh air. He found what he wanted and came away with book titles as well as a movie called "FireWater." He purchased it along with every appropriate tape the monastery had. One of the purchases was a real find—it was about using the medicine wheel to help get sober on the Red Road.

Sal was delighted to discover one of the speakers on the tapes lived in Tucson, who was also a Native American. Sal promised himself he would hunt him down and ask him to attend a meeting or two and speak. Sal also made a note to himself to ask Mary if her office had a dictation tape machine he could borrow. The tapes might be useful to people on the rez.

Sal started to realize he might be biting off more than he could chew, bringing sobriety to the reservation was a strong desire of his, and maybe Nahteste would be willing to head it up for all the Reservations. He scribbled another note to himself to call Nahteste as soon as possible.

On the way back from the monastery, Sal stopped in to see Bud. He informed him the ladies from Fort Huachuca would be picking up all donations from now on. He went on to the Benson Library to tell Nicole the same thing. As he walked in the door, Nicole and a few volunteers quietly applauded.

CHAPTER 86

FRIENDS STILL VISIT

"We are so glad to see you looking better," said Nicole with a big smile. "We followed your progress in the papers. I'm sure glad they got those galoots. It's hard to imagine people being that mean and still be human."

Nicole agreed they would continue to gather donations for the program. With all the publicity donations had doubled. A retired couple had volunteered to put out food and water near Patagonia where they lived.

"That's great!" said Sal. "I'll give their number to Chaplain Cliff and have him coordinate with them."

When Sal headed back to Tucson, he began to feel content with the thought he was going home. Not his parent's home, but a place of his own with Mary. He had come a long way since first moving to Arizona and sleeping in his car, begging for food and water jugs, to heading up a solid Foundation. Now he was getting married in less than a month. Sal had no words to express his amazement.

Sal knew he had accomplished a lot in a short amount of time, but there was so much more to do. He also knew he was living his dream largely because of the wonderful people he had met. He made a quick stop at a Rest Area and decided to sit down under a Mesquite tree and daydream a bit before he returned to the office. It didn't take long as he marveled at his life until he realized he wasn't alone. He looked up and saw his Mentor Spirit, Teralisa, who had always before appeared to him along the San Pedro River.

She smiled warmly at Sal as she spoke. "Though you were hurt by those men there were many compassionate spirits watching over you. They interceded on your behalf so you could return to full health and continue your good works. I am very pleased by what you and your helpers have accomplished, but be warned—grandiosity is not a virtue to be desired. Not all that has happened was by your hand alone. Your good intentions have been aided by many in your world and in mine. Continue on your path; take time for visions to enter. Spiritual guidance will come to you as long as you are a worthy vessel through which love and goodness can pass."

Sal started to say he appreciated her words, but when he looked up, Teralisa was gone. Sal knew he had caught himself congratulating himself a few times, but luckily, he recalled he was an aimless, wandering, lost soul until this Spirit Guide was kind enough to show him a new way. Sal shook his head, thinking he needed to share all this with Mary. He hoped she would believe him and not think his concussion had scrambled his brain.

As Sal arrived in Tucson, he laughed at the sight of huge saguaro cacti decorated with holiday lights. Christmas was approaching fast. He hoped Mary would like the briefcase he bought for her as a gift. He had found it at the same place he had purchased his "way too high, but life-saving boots." It was a beautiful, dark brown leather with brass clasps—nothing too gaudy. He was hoping when she used it she would remember that crazy day with the snakes; because as scary as it was, it was the day they fell in love.

CHAPTER 87

THE WEDDING GIFT

A s Sal pulled into the apartment parking lot he spotted Mary. She came rushing out bubbling with excitement, she charged into Sal's arms and almost knocked him over.

"What is happening?" Sal asked, exasperated.

"Mrs. Crane stopped by the office this afternoon," Mary explained breathlessly. "She offered her home to us for the wedding ceremony and reception! I accepted immediately; isn't that great?"

"Wow, it sure is," agreed Sal. "That's a wonderful place for us to get married. Next to you becoming my bride, that's the next best part of all of this."

"My Dad and Mrs. Crane had a friendly argument over who should foot the bill," Mary smiled. "My Dad won, but listen to this—Mrs. Crane would only give in as long as we accepted her wedding gift. I told her you and I had to discuss it first."

"Well, what is she giving us?" inquired Sal. "I'm sure it's great; what is there to discuss?"

"Mrs. Crane inherited a ranch years ago," explained Mary. "It's out by Old Tucson and the Sonora Desert Museum and Zoo. She has maintained it, but never uses it. That's what she wants to give us as our wedding present."

"Oh my God!" Sal shook his head. "Am I dreaming or what? I meet and marry you; I have an incredible job, and now she's giving us a ranch and home? Please—let me sit. Every day gets more intense. What more can happen to us?"

Sal walked with Mary into their apartment and sat down. "How can a kid from the coal mines of Pennsylvania, born of tavern-operating parents, come to Arizona and have all this happen?" Sal shook his head again in disbelief. "The maxim I try to live by keeps popping up in my face— 'Do Good, Feel Good '– Is this what it means? Even the spirit—whoops! –Uhhh! We need to have a long talk, O.K? Also, we really need to relax, this is becoming overwhelming."

Sal remembered he hadn't stopped by the office, but all things considered, he decided it could wait until the morning. Mary put a pitcher of lemonade on the table; it had now become her drink of choice along with Sal's. He slugged down a large glass and continued,

"Before we discuss the ranch, I really need to tell you something," Sal began. "Something's been happening to me for a while now."

With those words, Mary's face went pale.

"No, no, no! It's nothing terrible," Sal assured her. "In fact, it has completely changed my life. Please let me explain, and like Sgt. Joe's disclosure, this is for your ears only. I'm not sure how this would be received by other people in our lives, will you keep this between us?"

"Of course, Sal," Mary looked at him with impatience building. "But hurry up and tell me; you're scaring me to death."

Sal proceeded to tell Mary about his visions, beginning with the first one at Miller Peak Road up to his most recent. When he had finished, he shut his mouth and waited for her reaction,

"I'm so glad you have told me about this," Mary said. "I thought I was getting a little balmy, when you were in Intensive Care. I was sitting on the chair next to your bed, I was sure I saw a figure standing over you several times, it was a beautiful Indian woman in velvet and turquoise. I was afraid to say something about it because I thought you would laugh and say I was asleep or dreaming, I knew I had seen her, now I am sure she was there to help you recover."

"I'm glad you believe me," Sal said with great relief. "I was worried you'd think I was mentally ill or had some residual brain damage from all the booze I had consumed. I never want to hold anything back from you, our marriage must be based on complete trust, I know that's what will keep it solid for all our lives."

"I agree," Mary nodded. "That's exactly what I want, too. These visions, are they something you can experience whenever you want?"

"Not so far," he replied. "But from reading about similar episodes that other people have experienced and the one time I journeyed with Brother Alex, I believe I could learn to journey to the spirits. I would prefer to have someone knowledgeable teach and guide me through the vision. There is a man—a famous anthropologist named Dr. Michael Harner, who is providing education for people interested in learning more about the phenomenon. Maybe he would be willing to show me some techniques if I tell him about my visions. I was hoping he would visit the University of Arizona someday so we could meet him and possibly take some classes ".

Sal paused a moment as he considered what that would mean to his current situation. He sighed with the thought that life could not get any more intense; he looked longingly at Mary and changed the subject.

"Is it possible for us to go out to see this ranch?" Sal asked.

"Oh, I was so hoping you would ask that," Mary smiled. "I have a map and the key to the front door. But, before we go, I need to call the caretaker and let him know we are coming out. With things going great the way they are I wouldn't want us to get shot for trespassing. We can put the rest of the lemonade in a thermos and take it with us."

Sal and Mary drove out Cates Pass Road to Kinney Road. After a couple of quick turns they arrived at a large metal gate decorated with bronze horses. The gate was unlocked thanks to Enrique, the caretaker, who lived in a casita with his wife near the road.

"I've never seen so many saguaros," exclaimed Sal as he stared at the scenery. "They are magnificent. Look at the size of them!"

The driveway was a quarter mile long, which led to an impressive stucco, "Western-territory" house. The covered veranda extended across the front and sides, vigas protruded out of the walls. There was even a bell tower.

"Mrs. Crane told me it was built in 1870," said Mary. "At least it was started then, but due to the Cochise and Geronimo wars they didn't complete all the structures until late 1885. It was very isolated at that time. Let's go in; I can't wait to see it."

Mary slipped the key into the lock and opened the door. The floors were slabs of red stone, there were massive logs everywhere they looked. Sal figured they had been brought down from Mount Lemon, since you can't build out of saguaro cactus. Another surprise was that the house was fully furnished—ready to move in.

"Oh I just love it, Sal," exclaimed Mary. "What do you think? Can we accept it?"

"Well, let's see," said Sal with a smirk. "Come out on the front porch."

When they went out the carved door, Sal turned quickly and picked Mary up. With the assistance of his cane, he pushed open the door and said, "I, Salvadore Dusi, formally carry my bride, Mary Mayhew Dusi, across the threshold of our new home."

With a grunt, Sal set Mary down and she turned to hug him. "I am so happy," she said. "I AM SO HAPPY!"

They both laughed and plopped down onto the stone floor. They just couldn't believe their good fortune. "I have so many people to thank," said Sal. "Our lives are so wonderful. Thank you God, thank you Spirits, thank you Mrs. Crane, thank you Mr. Mayhew, and most importantly, thank you Mrs. Dusi-to-be for loving a guy like me."

Along that line Sal, I've been thinking maybe I should keep my maiden name, Mayhew. It's so well known in legal circles and all, what do you think? Oh man, how can I start the "Dusi Dynasty" with just one Dusi???? Mary laughed very loudly and said, "O.K., O.K. Sal, I will become Mrs. Mary Mayhew Dusi." Are you happy now?" "Absolutely thrilled." "Everything is turning out phenomenal."

Mary smiled at Sal as he continued. "Now Dear Mary, you are going to have to help me up, after carrying you across the threshold and plopping here on the floor I don't think I can get back up on my own."

Sal and Mary rambled around the house for a while. The master bedroom held a gigantic log bed with a magnificent Indian blanket spread across it. The room had French doors leading onto the veranda where there were solid carved chairs that faced a saguaro-covered hillside.

"Let's sit for a minute," said Sal, hoping they would catch an enchanting sunset. "Then we should go over to meet Enrique and his wife."

"Sure," said Mary, as she took in the scenery. "Isn't this more than we could ever have dreamed of? I know we will be so happy here, loving each other and raising a family. I've never asked you—how many children would you like to have?"

"Oh, a place like this could easily hold ten or twelve kids," said Sal. "You know, riding, hiking, etc.; they'll love it."

"What?" asked Mary incredulously. "I was planning on a girl and a boy. That would be enough for me. You really are kidding, I hope?"

"I am," laughed Sal. "Two healthy, rambunctious kids would be plenty for me. I love you with all my heart, so whatever you want I will gladly agree to. I grew up with one brother and that worked out just fine. More than that and we would have killed each other in the back seat of the car when we took Sunday drives with our Mom and Dad. Besides, it would have driven my parents crazy; they had enough trouble just keeping us separated."

"Let's go meet the caretakers," said Mary. "Then I want to head back to Tucson and stop at Mrs. Crane's. I want to tell her how much we love and appreciate the ranch."

Enrique and his wife, Irma, were warm and friendly people. Enrique made a point to tell them his wife's name was pronounced "Yirma". Mary told the couple she and Sal would be back soon to spend a full day exploring the ranch and getting acclimated. Sal and Mary shook hands with the caretakers and headed to Mrs. Crane's house. When they arrived, Mrs. Crane was on her front porch waiting for them.

"I can see by your smiles you liked that old place," Mrs. Crane called out to them. "Am I correct?"

"Oh my gosh!," said Mary. "It's so beautiful and perfect, we just can't believe we'll get to live there."

"I'm happy there will be new life in the place," said Mrs. Crane. "It has sat forlorn and forgotten for too long. I am delighted you can breathe new life into it. I've always loved the place, but it was just too far away from things for my lifestyle. I hope you fill it with little buckaroos over the years."

"If Sal had his way there would be a dozen," laughed Mary.

"Fine, I'll give up on that idea," said Sal. "Two or three will suit me just fine."

"Splendid," said Mrs. Crane. "You just let me know whatever I can do to help you get settled. I'll call your Dad and have him change over the deed in your names. Never having any real children of my own, I hope I'm not over stepping my boundaries. I intend to unofficially adopt you two adorable people."

"Oh, Mrs. Crane, you have done so much for us, we promise to never let you down in any way," said Sal. "Thank you very much for everything you have done. Speaking for myself, I could never have imagined my life becoming this wonderful, and so much of it I owe to you."

With that, Sal hugged Mrs. Crane with Mary joining in.

"I had my cook put up a little dinner for us," said Mrs. Crane as she broke away. "I thought a celebration might be in order."

After a great dinner, Sal and Mary excused themselves and drove back to their apartment. They began to make plans for setting up house at the ranch.

"What would you think about spending our honeymoon at the ranch instead of going somewhere else?" asked Sal, hopefully.

"Those were my thoughts exactly," said Mary. "I would love to spend time alone so we can get to know each other better. I'll arrange for phone service only after the completion of our honeymoon so we won't be disturbed."

"Yea, we'll lock the gate and have Enrique stand guard duty for us," Sal smiled.

CHAPTER 88

PRE~WEDDDING...STUFF

T he next week was taken up with wedding plans for Mary while Sal worked in the Foundation office. He decided to not travel anywhere, knowing his trips were usually filled with unexpected adventures, they both thought it was most wise to keep calm and make it through the wedding with as little drama as possible.

Sal and Mary worked at getting invitations out, arranging flights and accommodations for Sal's parents and brother, and transportation to Mrs. Crane's house. There were a myriad of things to do to ensure everyone had a great time. Mr. Mayhew told Mary she had no responsibilities at the office until after the honeymoon. After that, she would be overseeing the law practice. Sal brought up the suggestion that Little John attend the wedding.

"I've actually spoken to Mrs. Crane about that," said Mary. "She said she has a sizable kennel behind the house. He is welcome to spend the day here. He would be guaranteed some pretty delectable tidbits from the wedding dinner."

That made Sal love her even more. With that being answered, he relaxed into the role of patient groom, and stayed out of the way. Mary dealt with everything that arose, such as where she was going to get her wedding flowers, especially because the type she wanted weren't available in the winter. Then she set up beauty-parlor appointments for herself, her bridesmaids and Sal's mother.

Sal's family arrived three days prior to the event. This gave him the chance to give them the scenic tour of southern Arizona. His Dad wanted to know about fishing and Sal had to admit it was the one thing they would not be doing during this trip. Sal's brother, Jim, wanted to know if they could go to Mexico, but he had to decline that request, too. Sal tried to tell them they would be plenty busy before and during the wedding. He joked about Jim and his riding in the front of the car and their parents riding in the back. This time, the parents could be the ones who asked, "Are we there, yet?"

When Sal picked them up at the airport, he was surprised to hear his Mom say how much she enjoyed the flight. It had been so much more exciting than she had envisioned. The view from her window seat had dazzled her because she had seen so much open land once they crossed over the Mississippi River. Sal's Mom had never been beyond Michigan and had believed the whole country was as populated as the East Coast. Even his Dad was impressed by the wide-open country, and this from a man who had been to Russia and China while in the Navy.

Sal set his parents up in a two-bedroom suite at the Marriott, which happened to be one of the finest in Tucson. They were very impressed, considering they never left their business for more than two or three days to go on vacation, this trip was most likely the biggest adventure of their lives.

Once Sal's parents were settled in, Sal said his good nights and agreed to meet them for breakfast. Sal was going to take them to the office, where they would meet Mary, then drive to Tombstone and a few other sites in Cochise County.

When Sal got back to his apartment Mary was on the phone handling last-minute arrangements. It turned out the reverend she had wanted to do their ceremony was ill with the flu and she was looking for a replacement. He was glad to see she was handling it all with good humor and wasn't frazzled by any of it.

Mary had insisted Sal invite a lot of his friends he had worked with, as well as his Army buddies. That included Jenn and her husband, Bud, and the monks from St. David. Then she floored him by suggesting he invite his old nemesis, Sgt. Washington.

"He is the only enemy from your former life that still has an affect on you," she explained. "Since he's the one who took you to the hospital, it would be a nice gesture on your part."

"Well, I'm stunned," Sal shook his head. "It's not too often I'm struck totally speechless."

"You're starting a new life, Sal," she smiled. "Don't you think doing this would wipe the slate clean? Then you're starting over without any baggage."

"You never cease to amaze me, Mar," Sal said. "Your insight is right on. I will call him right now. I hope it helps him release any animosity towards me, too."

With that thought in mind, Sal called the Batallion Headquarters to obtain Sgt. Washington's phone number. When he placed the call, the first sergeant's wife answered. Sal took the opportunity to thank her for taking him to the hospital at the Fort. She asked how he was recuperating and he assured Mrs. Washington that he was healing ahead of the Doctors schedule. Then she put her husband on the line and Sal reiterated his gratitude and told him about his recovery. Sal then took a deep breath and asked something that in his wildest dreams he never thought he would say.

"I would be honored if you and your wife would attend our wedding," Sal told him.

The silent period that followed was so long, Sal thought he had lost the connection. Finally, Sgt. Washington spoke in a completely different tone of voice.

"Please hang on a moment," he said. "I'll have to ask my wife."

When the sergeant returned to the phone, he told Sal they would be happy to attend. Sal thanked him then gave him the time and directions to Mrs. Crane's house. Mary gave Sal a kiss after he hung up the phone.

"See, that wasn't so hard, was it?" she teased.

"That was one of the hardest things I've ever done," Sal admitted. "Any other great ideas?"

"No," Mary shook her head. "That's it."

"I can't wait to see Kyle's face when he sees Sgt. Washington at the wedding," Sal got a sly look on his face and laughed. "It's too bad Jake has recently been discharged, he's already left for New York." "His eyes would pop out of his head."

They chuckled a few minutes before Sal had a sudden thought. "In the event that the minister you're after can't do our ceremony, what would you think about Chaplain Cliff performing it?"

"Sure," she said. "Call him now, I'll just cancel the backup one I have. It wasn't finalized, anyway."

Once Sal connected with Chaplain Cliff, he told Sal he would be more than pleased to perform the ceremony. He just needed to arrive early and bring some necessary items. Sal explained the Clergyman Mary had originally asked had baptized her when she was a baby. It was her dream to have the same man perform her wedding. However, he was ill, and might not be able to go through with the ceremony. Chaplain Cliff agreed to be on standby in the event he was needed, Sal thanked him and said he would see him Saturday either way.

Mary canceled the replacement and settled in with the current plan. "See," she said. "We are a good team and we know how to compromise. We are going to do just fine together. Total trust and a willingness to work out all the little stumbling blocks, this will make our marriage strong and lasting."

"I'm a lucky man," smiled Sal. "By the way, I just remembered something. I need to arrange a room for myself the night before the wedding. Can't very well spend the night with you here. I'm not allowed to see you the morning before the wedding, am I?"

"That's right," agreed Mary. "Good thinking. Make the call; I'm sure glad you can spend tonight here. I love you so much."

The following morning, Sal drove over to the hotel where he enjoyed breakfast with his family, then drove them to the office. Mary was already there, so after hugs all around they hit the road to St. David. Sal gave them the royal tour of the monastery where they met Little John. It was nice to see everyone hitting it off so well. Sal hadn't been worried, but first impressions were often pretty important.

When they were done at the monastery, Sal drove them to the town "Too Tough to Die." They visited the O.K. Corral, famous for the shootout between the Earps and the Clanton gang. Sal also made sure they saw the tombstone of Lester Moore, which said, "Two shots from a .44, No Les, No Moore." He then took them past the garbage can where he had been confronted by the town constable, they all had a chuckle over that one. The day would not be complete without a visit to the Muffin Cafe, so Sal introduced his parents and Mary to Lu, where they had a light lunch. After wards, they drove to Bisbee where Sal showed them the Lavender Pit Mine, it is the largest open pit mine in the world, and Sal's Dad marveled at its immensity, he had gotten his working start in a Pennsylvania coal mine, at twelve years old, so he was familiar with what mining did to the environment and the miners.

Sal drove his group to Fort Huachuca next. Along the way, he momentarily stopped at the bridge on Route 90. They walked along the riverbank to see the cable car that ran over his fingers. When he had been drunk some time back.

"You know I'm really glad your crazy days are over, Sal," said his Mom. "I am so glad you are settling down with this wonderful woman."

Sal drove them onto the Fort and passed his old barracks. He was careful not to mention all his adventures that got him into trouble, but he did show them the fence he climbed when he thought a mountain lion had jumped on his back. The "Mountain Lion" which had turned out to just be a giant, rambunctious, very thorny, tumbleweed bush. His brother Jim laughed so hard at that he almost wet himself.

Sal drove back through Sierra Vista to Charleston Road to show everyone the bridge where he was attacked. He was experiencing a little trepidation because he wasn't sure how he'd feel when he got there. When they parked the car alongside the road, Sal was glad he had graduated from using his cane. He decided to down play the event and told them he really didn't remember much about it. Sal pointed to where the four men had burnt his car. His mom turned a little pale, saying she was glad St. Anthony heeded her prayers. He seemed to be recovering just fine. To keep it from getting any heavier, Sal walked them over to the historical marker that explained the story of the "Battle of the Bulls." He knew telling them about the scene he had witnessed in a vision would only upset them more, so he kept to the better-known version listed on the historical marker.

"So, do you believe the story?" asked his brother.

"Oh yeah," smirked Sal. "I got it right from the horse's mouth, or mules in this case."

Sal drove his family back through Tombstone to Route 80, pointing out the Dragoon Mountains and Cochise's hideout. When he stopped for gas, he introduced them to Bud so they would know some people attending the wedding. He had already arranged for Bud to sit at his family's table, thinking they would hit it off well.

"Bud is heading up a new AA meeting at the Fort," Sal told them.

"I wish they had one there when Sal was a soldier," lamented his Mom. "Look how well he's doing now that he's sober?"

"It was Sal who gave me the inspiration to start it," said Bud. "I'll do all I can to help the other young soldiers steer clear of the booze and ruining their lives."

"When I see one of my customer's sliding too far down the path of drunkenness I give them the address of the AA meetings," said Sal's dad. "I know many lives have been ruined with booze—and not only the drinkers, but their families."

After chatting a little longer, they said their good-byes and promised to look each other up on Saturday.

Once they were back in their rooms, and had refreshed themselves Sal did as promised. He took them to dinner at a famous Mexican Restaurant in town. Sal knew his Dad had really liked some of his Mexican records, so he picked a restaurant that had a Mariachi Band.

They had a great dinner, laughing with each other, coughing and gagging from the hot sauces that seemed to be on every particle of food they ate, Sal's mom thought even the salad was spicy hot. All were exhausted from the busy day and evening, so they were glad to get back to the Marriott and relax. Sal promised he'd see them bright and early the next day when they would have more fun exploring. Saying "Good Night", Sal headed for his apartment with Mary and wondered what other ideas she might have hatched for him. But he had to admit, he felt lighter knowing his archenemy of the past three years, Sgt Washington, was finally put to rest. Now they both would be better off, no longer holding destructive feelings towards one another.

CHAPTER 89

WEDDING EVE

T he next morning, "Wedding Eve", Sal was up early, all excited just knowing this was the last day he would spend single. He had always thought this day was so far off in the future he hadn't even contemplated it. Now that the fateful day was here he couldn't believe how happy he was. He admonished himself to never do anything to cause problems for Mary or himself. He honestly did believe he had changed completely but deep inside he knew that the demon that wanted to drink was still there just waiting in case there was ever an opportunity to ruin Sal's life. Sal knew if he continued to attend meetings, do good work and never, Never, NEVER pick up that first drink, his life would continue to be incredible beyond his wildest dreams, just as it was today.

Driving over to the hotel he smiled more and more. WOW! "Who would ever believe this fairytale, but I know it's real, cause I'm living it."

His folks decided to have breakfast in the hotel; Jim was waiting in the lobby and guided him into the dining room to greet them. After hugs and good mornings all around, Sal told them he was taking them to see the Saguaro National Park West, so he made sure they were wearing comfortable shoes. After going there and amazing them with the beauty of the giant cactus he continued the tour, Sonora Desert Museum, where Sal's mom was enchanted by all the hummingbirds, Jim likewise by the river otters.

Next they drove the short way to Old Tucson, where they had a western-style lunch, Jim warned Sal not to eat the beans as it could cause too much fun at the ceremony tomorrow. Sal's dad recognized some of the buildings from western movies he had seen.

All in all they had a fun day, "Making Memories!" Sal's mom said. Sal drove them past the driveway of the ranch where he and Mary would start their life together, maybe live out their lives there. Sal's mom said she was just too tired to go look at anything else. Could they please go back to the hotel so she could take a little nap before the rehearsal dinner? To the hotel they went, no problem.

Jim suggested Sal stay in his room that night. It had two double beds, after all. Great idea, as Sal had forgotten to arrange a room for himself. They all lay down for a half hour's rest then changed for the rehearsal dinner at Mrs. Cranes home.

As they drove up Sabino canyon his folks were in awe at the beauty of the area, especially of the homes they could see on the hills. Sal explained that the wedding will be alcohol free. But when he realized how much Mrs. Crane was bothered by that fact, because, she owns a winery near Wilcox, Arizona and had wanted the guests to sample some of her prize squeezings. "She has been so wonderful how could I deny her that pleasure?"

"So I gave in and allowed her wines to be served at the rehearsal dinner," interjected Sal. "Those who want to sample them can. It's a small gathering anyway, so there shouldn't be any problems."

Sal's mom was one of the people who enjoyed her vino and was pleased to sample Mrs. Crane's favorite vintage. They ended up sitting next to one another at the dinner and shared stories about Sal all evening. They got on so well that the guest seating for the wedding reception was changed to accommodate them, rearranged so they sat side by side at the wedding.

After a few glasses of wine, Mrs. Crane hugged Sal and told him she was ready to adopt his family, too. She enjoyed talking with folks from a whole different social level with entirely different life experiences. Besides, she liked to tell off-color jokes and had no inhibitions doing so, in spite of what her stuffier friends might think. She got so comfortable with Sal's family, she invited them to spend a few days at her home while the new couple honeymooned. She even had her travel agent rearrange their flight schedules, and unbeknownst to them, upgraded them to first class for their return trip.

Sal hugged her again and thanked Mrs. Crane for all her generosity. "I feel so much more alive and energized since you and Mary came into my life," she told him. "There's no question that your anthem 'Do Good –Feel Good' has become mine too.

CHAPTER 90

THE WEDDDING

T he fateful morning of the wedding arrived. Sal gathered up his family at the hotel and headed downstairs for an early breakfast. Sal was a little nervous, but he was way beyond excited about the day to come.

Sal's brother Jim was especially concerned about being best man in the wedding ceremony. "Jim's light was on past 2 a.m." Sal's Mom laughed. "He probably kept Sal awake too."

"Yes," Jim admitted. "I was working on the "Best Man's Toast."

"I never even noticed the light was on, don't worry about the toast," smiled Sal. "This is a celebration of love. No one is judging anyone. Just have a great time. As Mom always says, we're making good memories that will last a lifetime. Besides, it ought to be easily remembered just because we aren't serving alcohol."

Sal's mom admitted to a small headache and queasy stomach after sampling so much wine with Mrs. Crane, but the breakfast improved all that. Everyone parted after eating to get dressed for the ceremony. Sal told his parents he would be at their door in two hours to gather them up. They were going to ride together to Mrs. Crane's house for the ceremony.

As Sal put on his tuxedo, he was pleased to see how well it fit. He was especially impressed with the mirror finish of the patent leather shoes on his size 13 feet. "Wish I had had boots like this in the army, it would have saved a lot of spit-shining." Within the hour, he was dressed, chuckling with his brother who was now fully dressed in a tuxedo for the first time in his life. Jim laughing about how he once thought he would make it through this life without ever getting caught in a monkey suit.

"I feel like Humphrey Bogart," Jim told Sal. "Like in the movie, "Casablanca.""

Making small talk seemed to dispel a small amount of the nervousness they both felt about the coming ceremony. They sat and talked for a while, reminiscing about growing up together. They told fishing stories and talked about their old dog, Tippy, until some of the butterflies dissolved. They hugged each other for what was probably the third or fourth time in their lives, and thanked one another for being such a good brother to each other.

Sal looked at his watch and knew it was time to collect his parents. There was a limousine waiting downstairs to transport them all to Mrs. Crane's estate. As Sal looked at his mother she absolutely glowed in her pink pastel gown with a matching corsage of beautiful roses. His father looked dashing in his dark suit, but he told Sal he felt uncomfortable with his equally pink boutonniere.

"Well, this is one good-looking family," smiled Mr. Dusi. "I must say. Sal, you sure gave us plenty to worry about over the years, but as they say, 'All's Well that Ends Well.' In your case, 'All' is just the beginning. Please keep on this path you are on now and your life should be just fine. We're all very proud of you." "Thanks, Dad," blushed Sal. "I'm eternally grateful for all the patience you showed me. I promise to make you proud of me going forward."

As they pulled up to the house, Sal was relieved to see there weren't any problems with the parking. Mr. Mayhew had arranged for a shuttle to bring guests up from a large parking lot at the beginning of Sabino Canyon. He could see most of Mary's guests were already seated on the large lawn in front of the gazebo where his new life would start.

As Sal walked into the estate, Mrs. Crane's butler separated him from his group. He was ushered to another room with Jim and Kyle, who looked as handsome in his tuxedo as the rest of them. Mr. and Mrs. Dusi were escorted to their place of honor in the front row.

Mrs. Crane greeted the men in the parlor, looking regal in her pastel gown. "I know it's not fashionably correct to wear pastels at Christmas," she laughed. "But I've wanted to wear this gown for ages and this is the perfect occasion. So, I don't care a bit." "Your Mom and I laughed last night about the both of us being 'Coutere Incorrect' today in our pastel gowns. We decided we just didn't give a hoot what anyone else thought, as long as we were happy."

Mrs. Crane sat down in a parlor chair and smiled at Sal. "Your Mom has been convincing me to do as I want—it's my life," she said haughtily. "What a wonderful woman she is. She writes different sayings on the blackboard in her tavern every day to cheer people up. No wonder you came up with that saying 'Do Good—Feel Good.' It's in your blood; in another life you might have been a family of poets."

Sal and the guys laughed politely as Mrs. Crane went on. "Well, young man; I think it's time we all head out to the festivities so you can begin the life you've chosen."

As they made their way down the aisle, Sal stopped and greeted nearly everyone sitting on his side. There were considerably more on Mary's side, but that was to be expected. After all, the ceremony was being held in her hometown. Sergeant Washington stood up half a head taller than Sal and held his hand out.

"Well, Sal," he said with a grin. "You've proven this man wrong. I never thought you'd become the fine gentleman you have. Best of luck in all you do. Thank you for having us here to bear witness to you and your bride's special day"

"Thanks for accepting the invitation and sharing this day," Sal said shaking the sergeant's hand. "I appreciate all you have done on my behalf. I'm really glad I proved you wrong about me. Now I better get up there and hope I don't forget the vows I wrote last night."

When Sal got up to the gazebo, Jim said, "Sal, did you remember to bring grandma's ring?"

Sal's heart skipped a few beats. "What?" he asked incredulously.

"Don't worry," Jim grinned. "I have it right here in my pocket, safe and sound." Jim patted his breast pocket and laughed at the look of relief on Sal's face.

Sal looked out at the guests and took it all in. A lot of them had shared certain experiences with him, some during his inebriation, but most during sobriety. They all seemed glad that he made it to this glorious day.

Sal smiled at his mom who smiled back radiantly. He silently mouthed words to her. "Please don't sneeze" and she couldn't hold back a laugh. Sal's mom was well known for emitting sneezes that could blow windows out of a house.

Just then, the organist started to play "Here Comes the Bride." Sal was breathless as Mary and her father appeared at the end of the aisle. They slowly made their way to the gazebo, crushing the flower petals placed by two flower girls. He smiled so wide his cheeks hurt.

"Thank you, God, for bringing me to this moment," Sal murmured a prayer to himself. "I promise to do all I can to deserve the blessing you have bestowed on me."

He chuckled to think that was the most he had prayed in years. It wasn't like saying the Lord's Prayer by rote; he totally meant it, so he added, "God, together we've beaten the devils that have plagued me for most of my youth. Thank you."

With Mary beside him, Mr. Mayhew shook Sal's hand as he said; "I'm placing my little girl in your care. Please do all you can to keep her safe."

"I promise, Sir," Sal nodded. "I intend to be the best husband I can."

As it turned out the minister Mary originally wanted to perform the ceremony was still incapacitated by the flu. It was a very good thing they had arranged for Chaplin Cliff to be here as back up.

"Well, let us begin, shall we?" said Chaplin Cliff, " Mary, I must say you look beautiful".

The chaplain spoke of the sanctity of marriage, of two becoming one and many other heartfelt concepts. He had Mary say her vows first, which brought tears to Sal's eyes. Then Sal said the words he had written the night before. Jim handed Sal the ring, and he placed it on Mary's finger. Before he knew it, Chaplain Cliff uttered the words Sal rejoiced in, "I now pronounce you husband and wife. You may now kiss your bride."

Sal enthusiastically held and kissed Mary while everyone cheered and applauded. They began the long walk down the aisle, this time as Mr. and Mrs. Dusi. Amid tears, smiles and laughter, Sal shook hands, hugged and kissed, and worked his way through the crowd with his wife. Once they reached the flower-covered arbor, they were greeted by handfuls of bird-seed.

"Wow! I was expecting rice," said Mary. "Never saw this before."

"Yea, I hope we're still officially married," laughed Sal.

Instead of hopping into a limo, Sal and Mary scooted around the side of the house to a guest room Mrs. Crane had shown Mary earlier. Mary intended on changing into a smaller, trainless gown and freshening up before the reception commenced. They held each other for a few moments before they headed back out.

"Mary I am happier than I ever could imagine," Sal began. "Thank you for giving me a chance. I will do all I can to keep you happy, always." Mary smiled at Sal just as his rowdy friends started pounding on the door and walls. They were yelling at them to come out and join the party. They embarrassed them both as they yelled out that consummation had to wait until the honeymoon.

Sal quickly helped Mary out of her gown and into her reception clothes. In the time it took them to change clothes, the caterers were already setting up tables on the lawn. When Sal and Mary reappeared the crowd greeted them with cheers. Both of them made sure they talked with every guest, Mary introduced Sal to her family and friends, including important business acquaintances. Sal did the same for her. It took an hour, but eventually they made their way to the head table.

Once everyone was seated, the toasting began. Some were poignant speeches, some were hilarious stories and some were heartfelt wishes. Kyle told stories that were extremely funny, but at least not as incriminating as they could have been. Even Jim's Best-man's speech was heartwarming and entertaining. Everyone raised their glasses with the fake champagne and drank down heartily. Sal smiled at his mom as he saw her eyes filled with tears.

The band started up after the toasts, which gave Mary and Sal a much-needed rest. It was time for the bride-and-groom dance, the dance that finally gave them a moment to look into each other's eyes. Then the people starting lining up—the father of the bride, the mother of the groom, etc. Pretty soon, most of the guests were on the dance floor, singing along and changing partners with good humor. After an hour of music, the bandleader announced that dinner was ready to be served.

The serving of dinner took an extra long time. Various people clinked their glasses for Mary and Sal to kiss. The guests told and retold experiences they had shared with either the bride or groom. Whenever there was a break between serving, Mary moved among the guests enjoying their company. They embraced with Nahteste, who was dressed in a ceremonial cloak, and Johnny, who was laughing at Sal for warning him away from Mary, that she was already spoken for. He never dreamed that it was Sal himself that did the speaking.

"You know, I almost scalped your husband when I first met him," grinned Nahteste.

Mary looked at Sal questioningly. "I'll explain later," he nodded with a smile. Sal then promised he and Mary would drive up to the rez for a few days soon. He wanted Mary to see for herself the programs the Foundation was funding.

The Tanners were also present. They told Mary and Sal they were very fortunate to have found such remarkable partners to share their lives with. "Sal is the one who convinced us to stop our journey and go to the reservation to do some serious work," Dr. Tanner explained, "We couldn't be happier doing what we're doing."

Jenn and her husband spent some time with them, too. Jenn told Mary if she ever wanted to know what Sal was like before she walked into his life, she was available to share. She smiled at Sal's frown and added his wise council had lead her on the current, satisfying path she was traveling. Mary's head was spinning by the time they had spoken with most of the guests on Sal's side.

Chaplain Cliff held both of their hands and thanked them for allowing him the honor of performing their marriage ceremony. He was equally grateful that Sal had come along again into his life, to share some of his radical ideas. It had certainly brought new vigor to his ministry.

Just as Sal thought he and Mary could slip back to their table, Sergeant Washington walked up and introduced his family. "Who would ever believe this guy could have become this man," beamed the sergeant. "I must say, this is the biggest surprise I've experienced in my life. Keep an eye on him, Mary. He has it in him to be a real terror, believe me, I've seen him in action."

The sergeant turned slightly and looked Sal straight in the eyes. "I'll have to hunt down Captain Winslow and tell him about you," he said. "He and I had some serious arguments about you. He wanted to get you into Officer Candidate School and then the Special Forces, so he must have seen something in you that I never did. I wanted you in the stockade. I'm sure glad he was right and I was wrong, Sal." The sergeant shook Sal's hand vigorously as the sarge's wife spoke to Mary. "You'll have to come to the Fort and have dinner with us soon," she smiled, "We would love to have you visit."

Circulating among Mary's people, Sal learned how she used to be a tomboy part of the time, and a lady the rest. She was the subject of as many embarrassing stories as Sal had endured, so she was glad when they hit the dance floor once again. It was a marvelous party and a truly beautiful Tucson day—cloudless and warm. Sal and Mary felt blessed once again for the perfect weather adding to the perfect occasion.

Sal danced some more with his Mom, while his Dad took Mary onto the floor for a fast two-step. When they finished, Mary nudged Sal and told him he hadn't inherited his father's dancing acumen, but she still loved him.

Mary's father found the time to pull Sal aside and share a couple of little Cuban cigars with him and Mary's uncles. When he returned to the dance floor, Sal made sure he danced a few times with Mrs. Crane, even though his confidence in his dancing had been sorely shaken.

As the afternoon wore on, the guests began to thin out. Mary grabbed Sal's hand and tugged him towards the house. "Come on Sal," she grinned. "It's time to start our honeymoon."

"O.K.," he agreed. "Your chariot is awaiting."

They said their good-byes to everyone still milling about and exited the party to find their ride. It wasn't hard to locate—it had trains of shoes and cans dangling from the trunk. They got inside and their driver headed for the ranch.

Enrique and his wife were standing at the gate when they arrived. "Mucho congratulations, senor and Mrs. Dusi," Enrique said with his thick accent. "The refrigerator is full and we don't expect to see you for a week or so. We will guard the gate so you won't be disturbed. "Vaya con Dios."

The limo dropped them at the ranch house and Sal reached out to his wife. "O.K., Mrs. Dusi," he said. "This time I'm carrying you over the threshold for real. No turning back now."

"I never intend to turn back," Mary answered. "You are stuck with me forever. Imagine trying to divorce a lawyer who doesn't want to go."

CHAPTER 91

THE HONEYMOONERS

S al carried Mary through the doorway, but collapsed on the floor once they were inside.

"Give me a minute and I'll get you to that giant log bed," Sal faked a wheeze.

"Hang on there, partner," Mary said as she looked around the room. "Look at all these flowers—the place is full of them. It smells like a florist shop in here."

They got up and wandered around the house in awe. Everywhere they looked there were flowers decorating the room. By the time they found the bed in the master suite, they were surprised to see it was covered in rose petals.

"Wow," mumbled Sal. "I hope the thorns were removed."

Sal and Mary didn't arise again until near noon the next day. Sal could smell coffee percolating. When he stumbled into the kitchen Mary had laid out a breakfast feast—fruits, sweet buns, and more.

"Enrique wasn't kidding," she told Sal. "The fridge is crammed with all sorts of goodies. We really don't have to leave here for a week."

"Good thing," said Sal. "I'll need the time to recuperate. I'm a healing invalid, you know."

"Ha," scoffed Mary. "We'll see about that after breakfast."

"Chaplain Cliff said you have to love, honor and obey me," grinned Sal. "From now on."

"You didn't read the fine print, did you?" argued Mary. "You're dealing with a slick lawyer; it's you who has to obey me."

"O.K., O.K.," Sal said raising his hands in surrender. "I'll force myself—all the way back to the bedroom."

After a few days of marital bliss, Sal and Mary decided they needed to get outside and absorb some sunshine to replenish their vitamin D. They walked along the trails that surrounded the house and marveled at the views. Large and small saguaros sprouted up everywhere. They began to realize that there wasn't going to be any room for cattle or horses on this ranch. If they tried to leave the trail, they could barely fit between the giant cacti.

"If we raised any cattle here they'd have to be skinny ones," laughed Sal. "Then what's the point? We couldn't take them to market."

"I like it just the way it is," said Mary. "I don't want cowboys and cattle wandering around the land. Just you, me, Enrique and Irma. Let's keep it that way forever."

"I'm with you all the way," agreed Sal. "It's so peaceful and quiet. Do you mind if we rename it 'Serenity Ranch'?"

"That's a great idea, Sal! It fits in so many ways."

As they continued to walk they realized they had gone in a big circle and were coming up on the caretaker's house. Irma saw them approach and waved.

"Hola," she smiled. "Please come over and have some lemonade with us."

"Love, to," Sal and Mary nodded. "We appreciate the invitation."

Sitting down at a table in the shade, Irma poured some glasses full of liquid. Within a few minutes, Enrique came out of the house to join them.

"I've never seen so many magnificent saguaros," said Mary. "They are wonderful to look at, but not to lean on."

"Oh yes," smiled Enrique. "Sometimes I think they have a mind of their own. Please allow me to tell you a story of what happened just down the road. Sometime we get young people wandering out here who have no respect for the desert. I do my best to keep them off the ranch, so very seldom do we have trespassers. Maybe two years ago we heard gunfire off the ranch towards the main road. We stayed in the house to be safe, but the next morning when I drove out to go to town I saw a jeep parked in the sand. I thought maybe someone had a problem so I got out to look. I saw a tent with a large saguaro lying on top of it. When I got close I saw a boot sticking out of the tent. I pulled one of the flaps loose and Madre de Dios!, there were two bodies inside. I went back to the house and called the Sheriff for help. The people inside were dead. It took six men to roll the saguaro enough to pull out the bodies.

"They did an investigation and told us the saguaro that fell had been shot up badly. That was the shooting we heard. The two people had used the cactus for target practice, the bullets had weakened it so much that when the wind came up it knocked it over. Whenever we drive out we bless ourselves and say "Saguaro Revenge" as we pass. That is why I say they have their own mind; it could have fallen anywhere, anytime, but it chose to fall right on the tent."

"Oh Enrique, what a story," said Mary. "I feel bad you had to find them like that."

"Yep" agreed Sal. "I have read where certain plants put out a sap that attracts wasps that eat the bugs that attack the plant. Maybe they can think, or at least have survival skills inherent in them. Well, you don't ever have to worry about us ever destroying one of these beauties. We love them and intend to protect them."

"About a year ago, a man came to the gate," said Enrique. "He blew his horn and told me he would pay a thousand dollars for each saguaro we let him dig up and take. I told him no way! I wrote down his license plate and called Mr. Mayhew. I've never seen him since. By the way, now that you own the ranch, we will move away if you tell us to."

"Oh no!" jumped in Mary. "It's wonderful having you here."

"Well, if for money reasons you need me to get a job, I can get one at the Sonoran Desert Museum," said Enrique. "I could still be a caretaker here in return for use of the house."

"We'll have to discuss that," said Sal. "Mary and I are just starting out so that may be a good arrangement for us all."

"I'm just starting my law practice and Sal is just starting at the Foundation," said Mary. "So that might be the best thing to do. But we'll discuss it further and talk again."

"Thank you," said Enrique. "Would you like to see the old silver mine on the hill? I could show it to you; no one has worked it for many years, but silver is selling for more now, and you might want to dig some out."

"We'd love for you to show us all the trails around here, but not today," said Mary. "Just the walk back to the house will be enough for Sal for now. He's still recovering from an accident. Maybe we could do it tomorrow or the next day."

"O.K., whenever you want," he said. "Just let me know, I know every foot of this place and this time of the year is a good, safe time to explore. The snakes are sleeping."

"Uh oh; we forgot about those guys," said Sal. "Now we have a story for you. Mary, please tell them about our snake adventure."

Both Enrique and Irma were impressed with the story, especially about the boots. They all laughed and agreed Sal had a very good guardian angel watching over him.

"Is it possible to put up a snake-proof fence on a couple of acres around the house if I bought the wire?" asked Sal. "We plan on having a dozen ninos as soon as possible."

Mary punched Sal in the arm and said, "No, we aren't. But having a snake-proof fence is a good idea. We want to have a dog and he would be safe inside a fence."

"Sure," nodded Enrique. "Whenever you want; that's a good idea. We have had to be very careful when it warms up, for there are plenty of snakes around here."

"We can do the same around your house," suggested Sal. "Better to be safe than sorry."

Mary stood up and gestured to Sal. "We need to get back to the house," she said. "Thank you for the hospitality. It's wonderful to have such good neighbors."

The couples shook hands and the Dusi's headed home. As they walked at a leisurely pace, Mary shook her head in disbelief. "I can't believe we forgot about the snakes," she said. "Guess we've been a little busy. Thanks for thinking of a way to keep us safe."

"One episode like that is enough," said Sal. "I'll need to get you a pair of those boots for hiking around during the warmer months. I'm only half kidding but really, maybe we should get you some good, snakeproof hiking boots."

"Let's not think about that now," shrugged Mary. "I have other things on my mind."

The rest of the week flew by, as Sal and Mary were totally absorbed in one another. Before they knew it, it was time to return to reality. They spent most of the last day moving Mary's things out to the ranch. Enrique and Irma helped them move the furniture.

The following Monday, Mary went to her office and Sal went to his. Life in the real world had now begun for the newlyweds.

CHAPTER 92

BACK TO WORK

S al was glad to see his associates had handled all the little details that came up during his absence. He only had one big problem he needed to focus on: Sal was notified the Tribal Council on the Pima Reservation had decided against the water tanks on their land. They had also told the two tribal members that worked for the Foundation they had to either quit or move off the reservation. If they were caught placing water anywhere on tribal lands for the travelers, they would be arrested.

Sal drove out to the reservation to meet with the powers that be, but they were immovable on their decision. Nothing Sal said or offered to do changed their minds. "Oh well, thought Sal as he drove away, we tried, at least they agreed that it wouldn't bother them if water was placed just outside their lands."

Sal's next step was to get permission to place water on the lands surrounding the Organ Pipe Cactus National Monument. Upon meeting with Sal, the supervisor readily agreed.

"It's very disheartening to go out into this beautiful park and find bodies," the man said. "I'll agree to allow water stations as long as you agree to have your guys pick up any discarded trash they come upon."

The Monument land and the Cabeza Wildlife Refuge were two places that were as harsh as the Sahara Desert. Both sections accounted for many of the deaths.

The amount of money it would take to fulfill the water-station commitments increased the cost substantially. The men delivering the water would need a very good four-wheel drive to navigate the terrain, and still have enough room to remove trash. That happened to be one of the issues that also irritated the ranchers the most. Sal considered organizing a volunteer corps to go out and perform clean-up duty. He needed all the good will he could generate so he could keep the water and food available to the travelers. He knew he'd never obtain permission to place water stations on the Air-Force shooting range, which happened to be one of the areas the travelers crossed. Many times they lost their way and perished. They would just have to rely on some of the mountain springs and water holes that were interspersed in the range. Possibly Sal could find someone that knew where these springs were and would be willing to get out there to mark trails to them. Sal felt he wisely had averted a total crisis in dealing with the Pima Reservation tribal members by making new arrangements where he could.

Next he decided to check in with Chaplain Cliff's volunteer brigade in Cochise County to see how they were doing. He figured if he left early in the morning he could connect with a few of his people and still return in time for dinner with Mary.

Sal and Mary settled into a routine that worked fine for them; the nights Mary had client meetings, he attended AA meetings. He knew it was critical the meetings develop solidly. They had a phone installed at the ranch so they could keep in contact nearly all the time.

Sal wanted to make sure he had the water tanks in place before summer so he made it a priority to have the program implemented and working as soon as possible. He thought his best chance of doing that was to have a general meeting with all the ranchers. Sal had his office arrange a luncheon at the Copper Queen Hotel and invited as many landowners as would come.

The ranchers who attended made an agreement with Sal to have their ranch hands keep the water tanks full if Sal provided the containers and the canvas bags. There were enough in attendance that a huge area of desert would have water for the travelers to carry as they passed through.

Sal was delighted with the cooperation he got and got busy locating a source for the water tanks. He mentioned his dilemma to Mr. Mayhew who had a client that manufactured tanks. He drove Sal over to meet him and Sal explained what he needed them for. The man offered to provide the tanks at his cost, which allowed Sal to order nearly double what he originally intended.

On their way back to the office, Mr. Mayhew told Sal his desire to play more golf was not coming to fruition. Turned out Mary was developing so many new clients on her own that she couldn't cover his load too.

"Oh well," he sighed. "Maybe when the next law class graduates I'll be able to find a bright, hard working attorney to take on some of my clients."

"I think golf is a silly past time anyway," laughed Sal.

"I expect my son-in-law to join me on the Links in the future," replied Mr. Mayhew with a stern scowl on his face. "Maybe you better learn to play."

Sal gave his father-in-law a lopsided grin, and thought maybe that was the last he'd seen of free Cuban cigars.

"You know, Sal," Mr. Mayhew continued, "It's a real pleasure to see Mary blossoming as an attorney."

"I agree," he answered. "It's such a shame how many cultures in the world discourage women from having successful careers, as if they were lesser citizens. They represent half of the world's population. European countries are different. They encourage women to get an education to become professionals like doctors, lawyers, accountants, and businesswomen. As a result these countries have done better economically than most other countries. You'd think they'd learn from the examples they have around them, even the U.S.A. has a ways to go in this regards."

"You are wise beyond your years, Sal," smiled Mr. Mayhew. "Sometimes I wish you were a lawyer."

"Ha! You just want someone to pick up your load," laughed Sal.

"You see right through me, don't you?" Mr. Mayhew grinned.

And the Cubans are secure once again. Sal smiled to himself.

The next day, Sal was sitting at his desk when a light went off in his head. Now that he could afford twice the number of water tanks, maybe he could have some of them filled from the water faucet at the Ajo gas station, which was a great water resource. Or instead of buying a four-wheel pickup for his guys, he could purchase a used water tanker and have his drivers deliver the water to the tanks. He could probably keep the tanker parked at the gas station as long as he purchased his gas there.

Sal had his assistant call the station and then he spoke to the owner. The owner agreed to assist Sal as much as needed. Sal felt a sigh of relief run through him as he thought about averting the most recent crisis. He felt it was a good solution to get water out into the dry desert lands. Sal even got the gas station owner to allow them the use of his dumpster for the trash they picked up. He figured he could find a trailer to tow behind the tanker to keep the trash separate. It would also serve as a way to tote canned goods that could be left at the water sites.

Sal planned on getting lengths of 20-foot PVC pipe to place blue flags on so the travelers could see the water stations from far away. Things were coming together as best and as fast as they could

CHAPTER 93

THE FAMILY GROWS

Sal scheduled a monthly meeting with all involved so he could keep a handle on all the varied activities. He asked Mrs. Crane, Attorney Mayhew, Mary and all the leaders of his various groups to attend so they could discuss any issues. The last Friday of the month seemed to work the best for everyone involved. He decided lunch should be served so no one lost valuable time hunting down somewhere to eat.

Sal moved into the office conference room one of his plaques that read, "Think what could be accomplished if no one cared who got the credit." Everyone knew they could offer their thoughts and ideas without fear of ridicule, Sal hoped their combined brainpower could be put to good use.

The next item on Sal's list was getting the water tanks to the rancher's properties. One of the more outspoken but supportive ranchers told Sal if he could bring all the tanks to his ranch his men would deliver them to the other ranchers properties. Sal arranged for the manufacturer to deliver all the water tanks to Gil Watras's ranch in Cochise County, which to his delight could happen ten at a time. All the manufacturer requested was to be paid for gas and a day's wages for his driver. Considering the man was selling the water tanks at cost, Sal thought he was getting a great deal.

The next few weeks flew by with incredible speed. Things were working out well at the Foundation offices, so Sal and Mary agreed the weekends were theirs. The newlyweds had not had one argument, which was a surprise to Mary since her friends told her the opposite was true in their unions. Her friends were all going though some rough waters getting settled into their marriages. Sal remembered that his parents never had a heated argument their whole married life, they had said whenever a disagreement arose they set a time to sit down and discuss the problem until they came to a mutual agreement. Sal intended to live his marriage the same way.

One Saturday in the late spring, Mary invited Sal to a nice lunch on their veranda. She told him she had something important to discuss with him. Sal gulped, wondering what he might have done to displease her.

"It looks like the family we spoke about is about to begin," Mary smiled. "I went to the doctor's yesterday and he confirmed what I was feeling—I'm pregnant!"

Sal nearly fell off his chair. "Oh wow!" he said. "That's wonderful! I am so happy. Is everything all right? What did the doctor say? How do you feel? Are you sick in the morning?"

"Whoa, slow down cowboy," Mary grinned. "Everything is fine. I haven't been sick yet, and he said I am about six weeks along. But he gave me some pills for when the nausea starts. I actually feel great right now, but whatever comes will be worth it."

"What will we name the baby?" asked Sal.

"We can decide that later," she said. "Just as long as you don't insist on Escabrosa."

"No, I couldn't do that to our kid," Sal said.

"Is it alright with you if I ask Mrs. Crane and my dad over for lunch tomorrow?" Mary asked. "I'd like to tell them our news."

"Of course," said Sal. "This is very exciting stuff. I guess we're really a married couple now. Does this mean the honey-moon is officially over?"

"With you, I don't plan on it ever being over," Mary smiled.

Sal and Mary spent an intimate afternoon together and marveled how wonderful their life was. Sal felt so grateful for Mary that he couldn't quit telling her.

"Thank you, thank you," he said as he showered her with kisses. "I plan on loving you more every day."

A very happy Sunday brunch with Mrs. Crane and Mary's dad, the meal was wonderful and the news made all four of them cry with joy. Mr. Mayhew told them his tears were for the wonderful news and the realization he was never going to find free time to golf.

"Don't worry about that, Dad," Mary assured him. "I intend to keep working as much as possible. Maybe we can turn the extra room next to my office into a nursery. I want to nurse and be a full-time mommy as much as possible."

"What an amazing couple of years," Sal exclaimed as his head spun. "I could never have imagined all that has happened. Thank you, all of you, for making my life so wonderful. I promise to completely live up to your expectations and be all you could ever want me to be."

"The thank you's ought to go to you, Sal," said Mrs. Crane. "Your generous ways have taught me that if a person is blessed with an abundance of material possessions, they must learn to share if they want to be truly happy. Since you have come into my life I have been rejuvenated and I am happy to support your wonderful ideas to make the lives of less fortunate people a little easier. I've never thought about the hardships people traveling through the desert must endure. Now, I really have no idea how many lives we have saved, but if it's only one, it was well worth every cent spent, I think it's been many, though. Well, whatever has guided us all to do this, I know it's been the right thing to do. I think I understand what people mean when they use the phrase 'Born Again' because I feel I surely have been."

"Even though it's cut back on my golf time, I'm proud to be part of an endeavor that has done so much good," said Mr. Mayhew. "I realize you have just started on this path, but speaking for myself, I intend to do whatever I can to aid and assist the Foundation in its work. As far as becoming a grandfather, well, I thank you both with all my heart. It makes me a very happy man."

"Well, I have often heard that great things come from bad happenings," said Mrs. Crane. "My driving over that bridge has brought us all together. Who would ever have expected that? It's changed all our lives for the better—even if you don't get to play more golf."

After their extended family meeting broke up, Mary and Sal were alone once again. They just looked at each other in wonder; everything was going so perfect.

CHAPTER 94

BUSY~BUSY

L ife became a continuous mix of ideas, crisis, follow-up and management for Sal. He spent a few days on the reservation with Nahteste and Johnny, who took him to see the school they had built. They also toured the clinic where the Tanners were serving the Apache. They had initiated first-aid classes for the parents, immunizations for the kids, and referrals for patients that needed specialists at the Indian hospital in Phoenix. The surprising development was that the Tanners had arranged for their Alma Mater to send nursing and medical students to the reservation for four-eight week internships. They traveled to the far reaches of the rez conducting examinations, teaching hygiene and giving immunizations. Nahteste set up camping spots for the interns as they traveled, making sure they had a full view of the most scenic spots.

The Tanners were even successful in getting four surplus M.A.S.H. Field Trauma Packages from the Army Depot in Sacramento by contacting one of their friends who was still on active duty. Sal tried to reimburse them for their expenses but they gave him an adamant No! This was something they wanted to do with their own money.

All in all, Sal felt it was a very good trip. He began to realize that by gathering exceptional people into his fold great things were bound to occur with or without his involvement. But it still fit in with his mottos "Do

Good—Feel Good" and "Don't worry about who gets the credit".

As Sal drove away from the San Carlos Reservation he decided he would travel back to Tucson via Route 77. He wanted to find the spot where he had parked back when he and Little John made a pit stop. Sal grabbed a cheeseburger at the same little cafe and pulled off at the spot where he had first met the warrior. Sal got out of the car and walked to the river where he took off his boots. It wasn't long before he heard that same deep voice again.

"Ah, it's my do-good friend," said the warrior. "You have stayed on the right path. We who see much know of your good deeds and are proud of what you are doing. So many white men came to our land to take what they could, saying one thing but doing much harm to the Indian. Stay on the good path, my friend, and you will assure yourself a glorious eternity. You are saving many from hunger and thirst, educating our children to make better lives for themselves and this is good. You are watched over by many spirits; they do what is possible to aid you. Go in peace."

Sal suddenly realized the warrior was gone. He was relieved he still had the gift to communicate with the spirits. He didn't want any of them displeased with him. Back on the road, Sal found himself smiling. Going home never felt so good or so right.

When Sal arrived home, he hugged Mary a little more than usual. He was happy to see her growing a little bigger each day.

"What we are accomplishing is so important," said Sal. "We have so many wonderful people helping fulfill our dreams; even the spirits are doing what they can."

"What you are doing is wonderful," Mary replied. "Keep up the momentum; there are so many that need help and for some reason you have been chosen to be the vehicle to help them. What do you have in mind next?"

"I want to solidify everything we have begun," said Sal. "Then I want to put into action some new ideas."

"By the way, Mrs. Washington called and invited us to dinner tomorrow evening."

"Great; I'd like to speak to the Sarge about something I have in mind."

The next evening it felt strange for Sal to drive onto the Fort as a married civilian with his wife at his side. This was really a change for him. Mary had taken the day off so they could also lunch with Chaplin Cliff and his ladies. Fortunately, it was evident that Chaplain's ladies were still very enthusiastic about what they were doing. He was happy to hear they had added four hard-working ladies to their group. They had also extended their water and food distribution all the way to Sonoita. Sal told them he was planning on visiting Tubac soon to see if he could entice a group there to put out water and food on the eastern edge of the Pima Reservation.

Sal gave the Chaplain an update on how things were going on the San Carlos rez and how Johnny was fending. Everyone agreed the programs were a big success. They also agreed to attend monthly meetings at Sal's office so they could report their progress and have occasional brainstorm sessions.

"We've started a visitation program," said one of the ladies. "We visit the wives who have husbands deployed overseas. We make sure they're doing O.K., you know, see that they don't go off base to bars where grief will eventually follow. There are thousands of single soldiers hanging around doing nothing, trouble can easily develop."

"The AA meetings are a huge success, too," chimed in Chaplain Cliff. "Everything has been on track with Bud's help. We're going to start a weekend-long series of meetings and tailgate picnics in two weeks."

"Can I do anything to assist anybody?" asked Sal. "It actually looks like your programs are pretty much self sustaining?"

"They are," agreed the chaplain. "They couldn't be running more smoothly."

"Well in that case, I'd like to drive Mary around to show her some of my history," smiled Sal. "Then we have a dinner engagement to go to. Please come up to the meeting; I would like you all to tell your stories about what you've been doing."

Sal and Mary said their good-byes and left. He drove her around the

Fort telling her more tales of his exploits, where she marveled at the fact he survived his time there considering the crazy things he did.

"Sal, I am so glad you turned into the man I now know and love," said Mary. "Instead of the wild man you used to be. I would never have even spoken to you before."

"I know," Sal laughed. "I would not have deserved you even speaking to me. That's what AA is all about—turning good men's and women's lives around. It's an incredible program. It saved me and millions of others. I wish they had a program in high school before the kids get too far into trouble. I wonder how we could start that?"

"You just never stop thinking, do you?" said Mary.

"Nope, I can't" Sal shook his head. "Even the spirits are rooting for me to accomplish many things. How can I not do all I can? It appears our short life sets the stage for all eternity. I intend to pile up all the good-deeds I can. I figure I have about evened out the bad stuff I did, so from here on out, I am banking a bunch of goodwill to carry me through forever. Now that I have you in my life I think it's important to be at least as good as you are so we can spend eternity together."

"Wow, you sure can go from goofy to profound pretty fast," smiled Mary. "If you're right, pardner, you better do nothing but good deeds from now on. I want you by my side all the way, forever in the afterlife."

"Well, the Catholic nuns told me I would cook awhile in Purgatory," confessed Sal. "The Mormon missionaries I spoke with said if I lead a good life I could get my own planet to spend eternity with my family. I do know for certain that there is an afterlife, and we are definitely judged by what we do here in this life. I'd be some kind of fool not to listen and be the best I can, Now that I sure can't claim ignorance after the visits from Teralisa and her fellow spirits." "I'm with you, hon," nodded Mary. "Let's just do our best and I'm sure we'll stay together forever."

After a visit to the Post Museum, it was time to head over to the Washington' home. When they arrived, Sarge met them at the door.

"Aha!" the Sarge laughed as he saw Mary's condition. "I see Sal's been up to his old tricks, but I witnessed him making it legal, so congratulations! Come on in; let's go see the Mrs., She's been fussing in the kitchen all day."

As they walked into the kitchen, Mrs. Washington greeted them with a smile. "Hello to you both," she said, reaching out her hand to shake theirs. "I know you don't drink, Sal, so what can I get you for a beverage?"

"I've become a lemonade addict," answered Sal. "But anything non-alcoholic will do me fine."

"Well take a seat at the table," she gestured toward the dining room. "I have a pitcher of lemonade chilling in the fridge."

The evening went smoothly and quickly; Mrs. Washington served a great, Southern-style dinner that Sal and Mary couldn't stop talking about. When they were finished, Sarge asked Sal to leave the ladies to talk amongst themselves and come out to the porch to have a cigar.

"Great! I'd love that," said Sal.

As the men got settled into the patio chairs, Sarge asked Sal to tell him what he and Mary had been up to. "Tell me all of it," he said with a big grin. "I can't court martial you for it anymore."

"I haven't been doing anything to get into trouble," Sal raised his hand in honesty. "I have been involved in a lot of programs, from putting food and water out in the desert for the travelers from the south, to helping organize educational opportunities for the kids on some reservations, to starting AA meetings.. I've even talked some army wives into putting out the water and gathering food donations."

"Well, I'm impressed," said the Sarge, "Especially about the AA meetings. I heard about them. They're helping out a lot with my boys, there's not much to do here at night but drink and that causes a lot of problems for everyone."

"Yes sir," agreed Sal. "The 3-2-1 Club and the N.C.O. Club got me into lots of trouble. Heck, even the fifty-cent pitchers of beer at the PX had me staggering back to the barracks many a night. Since I found AA well over a year ago, I've found a whole new life, don't know where I would be now—

maybe not even alive—if I hadn't stopped drinking."

"You're certainly a different guy then when you were a soldier," the Sergeant admitted. "Is there anything I can do to help you with your work?"

"I have one thought," Sal mused. "Don't know if you can do it, though. As I said, I have over 30 ranchers putting water out for the travelers coming across the border. They're pretty fed up with finding dead bodies on their land. The biggest gripe they have is all the trash left out there that they have to clean up. I wonder if there is any way for you to get a bunch of volunteers to go to the ranches and have a 'clean up' weekend?"

"You sure know how to put me on the spot after I asked if there was anything I could do." said the Sarge. "Let me think about that. I can't order my soldiers to do anything off post. We would need transportation. I wonder if I were to speak to the officer-in-charge of Civilian Liaison to offer my boys an "out" from participating in the monthly parades on post, if they would come voluntarily, they could help clean up the ranches. The man has the clout to provide trucks and buses we would need." The Sarge mulled it over for a few minutes before he continued. "I'm sure I could have the kitchen at battalion headquarters bring us lunch," he added. "We could make it a party, then we'd get all the help we'd need. Let me work on that and I'll call you. I know you guys hate those parades. That would be great, Sarge," said Sal. "I hope you can do it, and a big emphatic YES!, we do hate those parades

"Tell me one thing, Sal," the Sgt. looked at him sideways. "Was it you who called me those names over the intercom way back?"

"No, it honestly wasn't," Sal shook his head. "I was in Naco, Mexico when that happened. One of the Southern Hillbilly guys did that and somehow I was blamed."

"I'm glad to hear that," the Sarge smiled. "I carried a grudge for you since that incident, I just couldn't let it go; probably why I was so hard on you, sorry son, that wasn't right."

"It's O.K., Sarge," Sal reached out and touched his arm. "You saved my tail—bringing me to the hospital made up for any grief you ever caused me, truth be known, I caused most of the problems." Glad we're over that," the Sarge nodded. "Let's go see about coffee and the big cake the Mrs. Baked today. After a lovely dessert the Dusi's decided to take their leave, as they drove through Sonoita Sal told Mary about "The Lion under the office shack" story. As Sal told the story it seemed as if it happened many years ago. Actually it hadn't even been two years yet since that crazy day and night.

CHAPTER 95

EXPANDING
WORKLOADS

B ack in Tucson working in their respective offices, Sal and Mary
were kept busy with all the details of their work. Mary got bigger and Sal continued to come up with different ideas. One of his
ideas paid off after he attended a few AA meetings in south Tucson. Sal picked out a couple of possible candidates for his plan. Luckily,
they turned out to be Apache from the San Carlos Reservation. Jobs in
construction in Tucson had lately dried up for these guys.

Sal took the time to explain to them what he had been doing with
Nahteste's help. It turned out both men knew Nahteste and had already
heard of Sal and what he had accomplished in their homeland. They also
had attended meetings on the Pima Reservation and were impressed with
the fact that Sal had a hand in starting them up.

Once Sal explained he needed a few experienced guys getting two
meetings started in San Carlos, they readily agreed. Especially after he
told them the Foundation would pay for all the materials. Sal got them
to come to his office three days later where he had a big coffee maker, 50
Big Books, 50 Step Books and a variety of tapes with tape players. He attempted to give them some money to cover gas, but they refused.

"We did O.K. working here," said one of the men. "It will be a good thing to give back to our people. They know how we were when we drank, and now we can show them we have learned to be sober. We appreciate all you have done for us; please let us give back, too."

"O.K., thank you, contact Nahteste and Johnny when you get there," said Sal. "They have already begun to hunt down places for the meetings."

As Sal watched them go, he thought about when he was a teenager. He remembered pondering his future many times and hoping he could become what he called the "Head of the Octopus." He would come up with many big ideas, hopefully with many others available to be his tentacles. He figured if he could accomplish that, he would be very successful in life. He laughed to himself, realizing that that is exactly what has happened.

Looking back now, Sal thought it was the egotistical ideal of youth to think that way, but he had to admit it was what he was doing now. So he said to himself, "Mr. Octopus head, watch out for that 'grandiosity', it'll get you if you're not careful."

CHAPTER 96

MR. JERSEY RETURNS

S al's assistant came into his office to tell him he had a call from a Mr.
Jersey. "Do you want to take it?" he asked.

"Oh yeah!" Sal eagerly grabbed for the phone. "I sure do."

Sal picked up the line and spoke with enthusiasm. "Hey Jersey,
how are you doing?"

"Great Sal," he heard the voice on the line. "Any chance you could come
down to the monastery and visit with me and the boys this afternoon?"

"Sure," Sal mentally ran down his schedule for the day as he spoke. "I
think I can be there around 1 p.m. Will that work?"

"Yep," said Jersey. "We're just passing through but would like to see
you and catch up."

"O.K., see you then."

As soon as Sal hung up, his assistant came into his office. "I have to
say, Sal, if I didn't need the pay I would work for you for free," his assistant
muttered. "You have the funniest cohorts anyone could ever imagine. Mr.
Jersey's Wild Ride, indeed!"

"Ha!" Thought Sal to himself, "if you only knew the half of it."

On the way to the monastery, Sal stopped at the Benson library to say
hello to Nicole and the other great ladies. He also picked up the donations
they had gathered as well as what was at Bud's. Bud had made it a habit

to haul his donations and what was gained at the library over to Chaplain Cliff's office. The chaplain's ladies took it and distributed it from there.

As Sal pulled into the monastery lot he thought about how much this place meant to him. It was sort of a mini-homecoming. Many a great thing happened for him within these boundaries. Not the least of which was his incredible visitation by the Spirit Woman. It had been a life-changing event. No one could have foreseen it. He knew how true the saying was, "Close your mouth and open your heart; great things will follow." That would never get an argument from Sal. He was living proof of it.

As soon as Sal parked and got out of his car, he got swept up in a group hug by the three big bikers. They growled their hellos and greetings. "Hey man, What's up?" they said in unison.

A warm feeling enveloped Sal; he was so glad to see these guys. They were still in one piece, and they laughed as they pushed each other through the parking lot.

"C'mon, man." said Jersey. "Let's sit by the river and hear about what you've been doing and we'll tell you how our lives have been going."

Once settled, Sal proceeded to bring the bikers up to speed on how much had changed for him. All the developments, like his marriage, Mary's pregnancy, new AA start-ups on the reservations, etc. They were impressed by how much he had accomplished. They shared their adventures on the Mescalero Reservation; Jersey was still single, but the other two were now married. Big John was going to have a child soon, too. The bikers were still doing whatever they could to keep drugs off their rez, including harassing the drug runners as much as they could. They began to tell him a funny story to that effect.

Jersey explained that once the "Bureau of Indian Affairs Police" heard what they were up to; they approached him and his Warriors unofficially. They had been working with the Tribal Council who had also brought in some "Drug Enforcement Agency" people to advise and assist. The Warriors had caused plenty of problems for the cartel bosses attempting to run their drugs from Juarez to Albuquerque. The D.E.A. Guys told them the drug runners had stolen four three-quarter ton trucks from the El Paso National Guard Armory to cross the White Sands Missile Range.

"Here's where it gets good," said Jersey. "Going across the Missile Range on a moonless night they happened to pick the time when there was a substantial missile and drone live-fire test being conducted. It so happened the Army had placed a few groups of derelict trucks out on the range for targets."

The three bikers started laughing as Jersey continued his story. "The Army Missile Guidance guys mistook the four trucks for targets," Jersey could barely contain himself. "They blew the drug smugglers all to hell."

It was days before the Army got around to checking the targets, which was when they found all four trucks—at least what was left of them. Nine bodies and a ton of heroin and marijuana were spread about the desert floor. The commanding officer called in the D.E.A. to check it out. They estimated there must have been three million dollars worth of drugs blowing around the White Sands range, along with pieces of the bad guys, which the coyotes were busy taking care of.

"When the D.E.A. cops informed the B.I.A. Officials about it, they agreed it was a fitting end to that wagon train," grinned Jersey. "A whole lot of misery never made it to the rez or into people's lives."

"Whoa!" said Sal. "That is an amazing story. Makes you believe in Divine intervention, that's for sure."

"The National Guard wasn't too happy about losing their trucks," concluded Jersey. "But they agreed it was a fitting end to the banditos."

As it turned out, the destruction gave the D.E.A. a better idea of how much was coming across the border, so they outfitted the B.I.A. cops with better equipment. They came up with radios, jeeps, weapons, and such to level the playing field. The B.I.A. deputized Jersey and his buddies, along with six others in their Warrior group, so they could legally combat the smugglers. Big John growled, "Yeah, we now have, legal, paying jobs, man."

The Tribal Council began an intense DOPE program , a program geared to school kids showing them the evils of drug use, on the rez in an attempt to reach all the young people. They also initiated an anonymous reporting process so anyone who got wind of drugs coming onto the reservation could "drop a dime" and it would be followed up immediately. There wouldn't be any more looking the other way; the tribal members were going to become the eyes and ears of the B.I.A. & the D.E.A..

Unfortunately, no one said a word about the alcohol being brought onto the rez. There was an unspoken opinion that it was the lesser of the evils. Although there were statistically about 20 heroin addicts, there were probably 200 alcoholics. As long as alcohol was readily available and legal off the reservation, that problem could only be addressed by altering the desire for it. The Tribal Police admitted that more than 60-percent of the calls they responded to were alcohol related: auto accidents, domestic violence, homicides and fights were rooted in booze.

"Well, Sal," said Jersey. "Any ideas for us on that problem?"

"Yeah, sure," said Sal. "Even though it seems like a simple fix, it's not. How about my Foundation funding as many AA meetings as you guys can arrange? We'll provide the seed money."

"Saturday night seems to be when the trouble happens," said Minx.

"What if you set up a 'Pow Wow' every Saturday night?" suggested Sal. "We'll pay for a steer to be roasted every weekend for the first month. After that, you guys will have to arrange for a potluck—if it goes well. The thing is, everyone who wants to eat has to attend a meeting beforehand. It should be open to all the family members; the drinker and all those affected by the drinking. Word will get out—maybe add some music to it. It'll be a big Saturday night party, but no booze."

Jersey and his men nodded in agreement as Sal continued to formulate a plan. "Maybe have the meeting around a big bonfire," said Sal. "Try to hold the meetings at the same spot. Do you think you could hold meetings every Saturday night?"

"Sure, it would do us all good," said Jersey. "We could alternate leaders if we had commitments that interfered with attending the meetings. This just might work. Can the Foundation afford the first four weeks to see what happens?"

"Yep," said Sal. "We can, but you guys will have to do the hard work of getting the drinkers to attend."

"O.K., we'll get right to work on it," said Jersey. "This sounds great. I never heard of such a thing but let's give it a try."

Sal gave Jersey his office address so he could send him the bills they incurred. Sal also told them about the weekend-tailgate picnics Chaplain Cliff and Bud had organized. Seems they were getting a lot of soldiers to hang out all weekend instead of heading to Mexico. There were a lot fewer accidents on the roads from Nogales and Naco.

"Yea, that might work," said Jersey. "There's no electric at most the homes on the rez. There's not much to do except drink, so let's give them something to do. Well, we've got to take off. We've got a long ride home. Thanks for everything, Sal. We'll be in touch."

"It's been great to see you guys alive and well again," said Sal as he shook their hands and they hugged. "Be careful, and thanks for that story. It's a great one."

The men parted ways, looking forward to the next time their paths would cross. Sal headed home to a completely different life with Mary.

CHAPTER 97

CIRCLE OF HELP

When the last Friday of the month came along, Sal felt a little trepidation about the costs of starting untested meetings on the Mescalero Reservation. But that morning, he had received a call from Jersey who told him he had gone to the Tribal Council to get permission to start the Pow Wow's. He said after a semi-heated discussion, they had agreed. They were willing to try it for a month or two. The Council had not been happy about some white guy in Tucson paying for it, though. One of the Council members volunteered to supply four steers to cover the first month, saying he lost that many to the pumas anyway.

The Council also agreed to cover the costs of the fry bread, corn and sodas, so Sal only had to provide funds for the coffee urn and literature.

"It's a great idea," said Jersey. "We got no argument on that. We're going to get it going in three weeks so as soon as you can get the supplies would be great."

"No problem," said Sal. "I'll have them sent down next week. Good luck and thank you, my friend. Adios!" Sal was relieved that that program was getting its first push. He had been afraid he had engaged his mouth before his brain on that one

The monthly meeting started with Chaplin Cliff's "Wives Troop."

Chaplain Cliff and his ladies spoke about how they had expanded their duties. They were now 18 wives strong. They were able to cover a much bigger area with four vehicles between them. Two of them were four-wheel drive so they could go nearly anywhere. Together, they sourced out more places for food donations and now had plenty of food to place with the water. One of the husbands had installed a Citizens Band radio in each vehicle so they could keep in touch with one another and out of trouble.

Sergeant Washington sent word with Chaplain Cliff that all was a go for the clean up of ranch property in the south. In the middle of next month, they were going to have a picnic/clean-up on three of the most trashed ranches.

Nahteste and Johnny both came to the meeting to report progress with the teaching program. They were also able to attest to the fact that the first AA meetings were successfully attended. They intended to start four more across the great expanse of the twin reservations.

Water was still running on the Organ Pipe Monument and even along the borders of the Air Force range. The Cochise County ranchers' representative said they were very satisfied with the program and hadn't found any bodies on their lands in a while, in fact, a few of the largest ranchers requested additional water tanks.

Jenn and Bud were in attendance and were happy to report the meetings were a great success. They were both thinking of scheduling additional evening meetings as soon as conceivable. There didn't seem to be any big problems to deal with and all agreed that Sal and his office staff were quick to handle anything the "tentacles" couldn't.

Sal told the group what had happened at White Sands Missile Range and the desire to create new meetings on the Mescalero Reservation. "If anyone else has a good story to tell, I'd really appreciate it," added Sal.

At this, Nahteste stood and began a story he had a burning desire to tell. He was a good storyteller, and the ladies from Huachuca were particularly taken by his large frame, and Native American dress.

"I was camped alone at the lake I fish at," began Nahteste. "I was sitting by my campfire about to enjoy some fish I caught, when I heard a stick snap. I looked up as this very old man walked up to my fire. I recognized him as "the man who spoke to animals." He asked if he could share my fire, so I said, of course. He looked longingly at the fish laid on the rocks cooking by the fire so I asked if he would like one. He said "yes." We ate our meal together. When we finished, he said, 'Now I would like to tell you what I heard.' I told him to go ahead and tell me his story. So he began slowly. He said, "As you may know, we have had many problems with mountain lions lately. They've been killing our sheep and calves. Some hunters came to the high ground with their dogs to hunt them down. He said he was sleeping by the lake under the spruce trees when an old hound came up and licked his face. It made him jump as fast as an old man could who still remembered seeing Geronimo." He said, "you know I can talk with animals; it's a gift I've had since I was a small child."Then he said "the hound looked him in the eye and conveyed that he had been lost for days since he was brought up here to chase mountain lions. He was starving and had come across a very old pile of deer bones. As he sat down to chew on them, he felt the presence of a mountain lion creeping up behind him. So the dog said aloud, 'Ummm that was good; I wish I had more lion to eat.' Hearing this, the mountain lion ran away, frightened by the hound, believing he had misjudged him, and had almost gotten eaten himself." "A crow in the tree looked down on this and snickered, hoping to get some leftovers, so he flew over to the mountain lion and told him the dog had been lying. The crow perched on the mountain lion's back as he snuck back to kill the hound. When the dog saw them coming, he said loudly, 'Where is that crow? I sent him to bring me another lion hours ago. I guess the mountain lion only 'ate crow' that night."

Everyone laughed and clapped at Nahteste's story. It turned out to be a great lead into a nice buffet that was served shortly after. When everyone was finished eating, they agreed to meet the following month. In the meantime, they all would do what they could to help those in need.

Mrs. Crane saw the troops off as Mary gave Sal a big hug. "You've started a wonderful thing," she said. "You're helping so many people, including these people who are doing the helping." "Sometimes it's the people doing the helping that are helped the most, said Sal."

CHAPTER 98

OOOOHH!

They held hands, smiled and Mary said, "I really need to go to the office for a few hours but tonight let's just go home and just have a quiet dinner. I have something I want to tell you."

Sal agreed, saying he needed to finish a little paperwork and then they could head out. Sal spent the rest of the afternoon going over what the Foundation had accomplished up to now. He took notes, scribbled new ideas, and tried to prioritize. He had an idea about assisting laid-off miners at the Bisbee, Clifton and Morenci Copper Mines.

He also wanted to focus on the elderly travelers who straggled into border towns alone, unable to keep up with their families coming into America. He was thinking of a program for all the wives who were sitting around bored because their husbands were serving in Viet Nam. He was hoping he could connect them to the old people in the border towns. Maybe they could help care for them. Start collecting warm clothing for them. Maybe a lunch program two or three days a week could be developed then all the leftovers could be packed up for the old folks to take with them. Some love shared between them so all would benefit.

He had thoughts about turning Bisbee into a tourist town, enticing artists to move into the abandoned homes left empty by the out of work miners that had chosen to pack up and move on. There were so many empty buildings that could offer low rent and maybe be turned into art galleries.

Sal also wanted to see food banks created on the reservations. He could visualize graduates from the Master Gardener Programs showing people how to raise their own vegetables and fruit. Especially in the poorer sections of Cochise County. The Foundation would provide the seed, fertilizer, supplies and tools.

They also needed after-school programs so mothers could work full time wherever they could find work. It was ambitious, but Sal thought maybe he could lure industries to relocate to Southern Arizona if there was a trained work force available. The Foundation would fund the retraining programs on-the-job.

Sal thought about developing hiking groups so retired military, spouses and bored wives could socially interact without resorting to going to bars to meet other adults with like interests.

Sal set his pencil down for a moment to mentally admonish himself. He needed to be vigilant about falling into grandiosity. "One step at a time," he told himself. "One day at a time."

Sal knew he had a lot of great people working with him. He was very aware that that was why things were going so well. He also knew he had to let things gel a little before he bit off more than he could chew. He had to keep in mind he had a wife now, and a child on the way, which meant life would become very different quite shortly. He told himself once again to remember the most important lesson he had learned from that possum—"I have met the enemy, and he is me". Important that he avoid grandiosity, keep "Mr. Octopus Head" under control allowing the "tentacles" to evolve.

Sal told his assistant he was going home early and checked out of his office. He stopped at the super-market and a florist, picked up fixins' for a meal and a large assortment of cut flowers. His plan was to get home at least an hour before Mary, cook a nice meal and surprise her when she arrived home. He was sensitive to the fact that every day her work at the office took more out of her. The least he could do was try to make it easier at home. After all, a marriage was a partnership; both of them had to do their share. Mary was the greatest thing to ever come into his life; why wouldn't he do everything in his power to assist her?

Once at home, Sal found two vases to place the cut flowers. One large one went on the dining table and the other went on her side of the bed on the nightstand. When Mary pulled up to the house, Sal was ready for her arrival.

"Wow, something smells good!" Mary exclaimed as she came in the door. "Did you pick up take-out?"

"Nope," Sal answered. "I slaved over a hot stove just for my lady."

"Ha, I bet," Mary laughed. She walked into the kitchen and noticed the floor had been mopped, everything was put away, and there was a big bouquet of flowers on the table. She could also smell the lasagne baking away in the oven.

"Sal you are Mr. Wonderful," Mary clasped her hands together. "Thank you so much. I am really tired tonight."

Mary gave Sal a big hug and waited for the meal to be served. When Sal brought the food to the table, he lit the candles and they began their feast. When they were finished, they took their lemonade out to the veranda to watch the magnificent sunset.

"Well now, I believe you wanted to talk to me about something," Sal began.

"Oh yeah, I do," Mary smiled. "Thank you for the memorable evening."

No, no, no," objected Sal. "That's not it. You told me earlier today you had something to tell me. That was long before I slaved away for you."

"Oh, O.K.," grinned Mary. "This morning, before your meeting I had my monthly visit with Dr. Tyler. He checked me over and said everything was fine. Then he told me some exciting news. We are having twins!"

The End...
of the beginning...

Made in the USA
San Bernardino, CA
28 March 2014